All-American Waves of Grain

Other Cookbooks by Barbara Grunes and Virginia Van Vynckt

All-American Vegetarian: A Regional Harvest of Low-Fat Recipes
The Great Big Cookie Book

Other Cookbooks by Barbara Grunes

Kabobs on the Grill
The Heartland Food Society Cookbook
Classic Chocolate Cookbook
Skinny Chocolate
Skinny Potatoes
Skinny Seafood
Skinny Pizza
Roots
Appetizers on the Grill
Home and Grill Cookbook
Grill It In
Puddings and Pies
The Complete Fish Book
The Right Stuff (Meat on the Grill)
Poultry on the Grill
Gourmet Fish on the Grill
Shellfish on the Grill

Southwest Sampler
Chicago Epicure
Fish on the Grill
Joy of Baking
Soups and Stews
Chef's Kitchen Companion
Lunch and Brunch
Fish and Seafood
Cookie Cookbook
All-Holiday Cookbook
Food Processor Cookbook
Mexican Cookbook
Dining in Chicago, Volume II
Dining in Chicago, Volume III
Ultimate Food Processor Cookbook
Inside the Convection Oven
Oriental Express

All-American Waves of Grain

How to buy, store, and

cook every imaginable grain

Barbara Grunes and
Virginia Van Vynckt

HENRY HOLT AND COMPANY

NEW YORK

Henry Holt and Company, Inc.
Publishers since 1866
115 West 18th Street
New York, New York 10011

Henry Holt ® is a registered
trademark of Henry Holt and Company, Inc.

Published in Canada by Fitzhenry & Whiteside Ltd.,
195 Allstate Parkway, Markham, Ontario L3R 4T8.

Library of Congress Cataloging-in-Publication Data

Grunes, Barbara.
    All-American waves of grain/ Barbara Grunes
and Virginia Van Vynckt.—1st ed.
        p.   cm.
    Includes bibliographical references and index.
    1. Cookery (Cereals)   2. Grain.   3. Cookery,
American.   I. Van Vynckt, Virginia.   II. Title.
TX808.G78   1997   96-26589
641.6'31—dc20   CIP

ISBN 0-8050-4131-1

Henry Holt books are available for special
promotions and premiums. For details contact:
Director, Special Markets.

First Edition—1997

Designed by Paula R. Szafranski
Illustrations by Lauren Jarrett

Printed in the United States of America
All first editions are printed on acid-free paper. ∞

1   3   5   7   9   10   8   6   4   2

To my darling granddaughter, Suzanne,
who lives in Thessaloníki, Greece,

and

to Frances and John Van Vynckt,
for encouraging those early kitchen experiments
and gamely eating the failures

Contents

Acknowledgments

Thanks to Grace Kupiec, for long hours in the kitchen testing recipes. And much gratitude to our other testers—Alan Magiera, Jenny Edidin, and Vicki Cave. We couldn't have done it without you.

Many people and organizations were generous with time and information, including Kristen O'Brien of the USA Rice Council, Bart Carter of Arrowhead Mills, Gilbert Stallknecht of Montana State University, Judi Adams of the Wheat Foods Council, Cindy Bishop and Ann Kunze of Quaker Oats, Ann and Robert Quinn and the Kamut Association of North America, Deborah Locke of RiceTec, Ernie Neu of White Mountain Farms, Lundberg Family Farms, the Minnesota Cultivated Wild Rice Council, Dave Reinke of Manitok Wild Rice, Wayne Carlson of the Teff Company, Don Stinchcomb of Purity Foods, Peggy Wagoner of Rodale Institute Research Center, and Nell Bennett of friendly St. George, South Carolina. And we would like to applaud all those who have helped make the Internet a researcher's best friend—especially Jules Janick and Jim Simon of Purdue University's Center for New Crops and Plant Products.

We offer big thank-yous to our agent, Martha Casselman, for prodding and inspiring us, and to our editor, Beth Crossman, for her thoroughness and care.

And to Jerry, Marvin, and Lian for their patience, encouragement, and good appetites.

Introduction

When Katharine Lee Bates penned those immortal lines "O beautiful for spacious skies, for amber waves of grain," she meant them. Fields of grain roll on as endlessly as an ocean in her native land of Colorado—not to mention Kansas, Wyoming, Montana, Nebraska, Oklahoma, North Dakota, South Dakota, Arkansas, Texas, Washington, and several other states. Our teeming cities might not impress a visitor from Tokyo or London, but those forever fields of waving wheat surely inspire awe in anyone from a more compact nation.

The yield from those vast stretches inspires awe as well. The United States is the world's leading exporter of wheat and corn, and routinely ranks second or third in exports of rice. American rice is cooked into Middle Eastern pilafs. American wheat is strung into Chinese noodles. American corn is pressed into Mexican tortillas. Just about every grain you'd ever want to eat—wheat, corn, rice, buckwheat, rye, even the once-exotic quinoa—grows somewhere in this vast nation. Even arborio and jasmine rices, which only a few years ago had to be imported, now grow in the States.

That means there's no excuse for not eating the six to eleven daily servings of grain that form the foundation of the U.S. Agriculture Department's Food Guide

Pyramid. True, most of our grain still goes to feed the livestock that winds up as breakfast sausages and burgers to go, but there's plenty left for people to eat.

We Americans do eat a lot of grain. But most of it is in the form of bread and pasta—not to mention doughnuts and cakes—with rice and cornmeal thrown in for variety. And most of the grains we eat are refined and robbed of nutrients. Fortification with iron and B vitamins does not replace fiber or trace minerals. (One trace mineral lost in refining is chromium, found in whole grains and other foods naturally high in carbohydrates; it works with insulin to help the body digest and use sugars.)

We wrote this book to help cooks expand their knowledge of grains, especially whole grains, and of how to use them. The variety of grains on the market can confound even savvy cooks. Take rice. In addition to those standard bland supermarket rices, you can now buy a rainbow of rices in short, medium, and long grains: basmati, Texmati (a cross between basmati and long-grain), Popcorn, Wild Pecan, jasmine, Valencia, arborio, wehani, japonica.

Even the grains our grandmothers may have favored—millet, whole-grain rye, buckwheat—fell more or less out of favor, only to revive. One can forgive a puzzled shopper for thinking millet is birdseed and not realizing that it's the basis for delicious breads, puddings, crackers, and stuffings. We, too, were ignorant until we began cooking with it. Now we wonder, "What *can't* you do with millet?"

Chefs enjoy playing with grains, and it's not unusual for diners to discover quinoa timbales or wheat berry salads on their plates. We encourage home cooks to experiment as well. For that reason, we included plenty of recipes that call for two or more grains.

All-American Waves of Grain deals with grains that have long been used in American cooking as well as "new" grains that are being discovered, or rediscovered, in this country. Tradition, intuition, and personal preference guided our recipe choices. That's why the oats recipes include so many desserts—nothing's more American, and heavenly, than the marriage of oats and brown sugar. Not surprisingly, barley shows up in a lot of soups, which benefit greatly from its chewiness and mild flavor. Small, chewy kernels, or berries, of nutty-flavored wheat were born for salads and pilafs. Millet, which cooks into a compact, fluffy mass, makes a great stuffing.

We've used a lot of grains in flour form because they're so versatile that way. And in some cases, we found the flour the most appealing form of the grain. We didn't care for the texture of cooked whole grain Kamut, for example, which we found overly large and chewy. So we devised Kamut recipes using the flour and have listed whole grain Kamut as an alternative in other whole grain recipes, for the many people who enjoy both its buttery flavor and its texture.

You'll find plenty of grain-heavy main courses here, but many of the recipes are for baked goods and breakfast dishes, which supply much of the grain allowance in Americans' diets. Plus we confess that we both really like to bake.

We rely heavily on whole grains and stone-ground, usually organically produced flours and meals not only because they're generally more nutritious, but because they have a depth of flavor that's lacking in many of their refined cousins. However, we're not fanatical on the subject and again have bowed at least somewhat to tradition, preference, and availability. For example, we've used brown rice in fried rice, which is as American as it is Chinese these days (besides, the rural Chinese do eat brown rice). But we've used white rice noodles because they're much more readily available than brown rice noodles. We also use white flour to lighten breads and other baked goods.

In addition to the whole grains, we've described some of the products made from them. Rice, for example, is the basis for flour, rice cakes, rice noodles, and rice syrup—not to mention sake and beer.

We've stuck fairly close to a traditional definition of grains as the seeds of food plants, especially cereal plants such as rye, wheat, and corn. We concentrate on foods that most Americans would readily recognize as grains—meaning that they're used in baked goods or starchy side dishes or main courses. You won't find sorghum in this book, for example, because it's used mostly for animal feed and syrup in this country.

We also tried to include only grains that are readily available in health food stores and, increasingly, larger supermarkets. But note that the availability of offbeat grains such as triticale or Job's tears can vary from time to time and place to place. In fact, we could not find Job's tears (*hato mugi* barley) outside of a few Asian markets. Teff's availability is spotty at times; some health food stores have it, some don't.

We couldn't resist tossing in a few high-fat classics because they're so American, but the bulk of the recipes are relatively low in fat and saturated fat.

Each recipe includes a nutritional analysis per serving (or per piece, in the case of such items as cookies and rolls). The nutritional breakdown does not include optional ingredients, the salt in water used to boil pasta, nonstick cooking spray for greasing pans, or suggested garnishes. When a recipe lists a range of amounts, it's analyzed for the larger amount. That is, a recipe that calls for 1 to 2 tablespoons of oil has been analyzed for 2 tablespoons. We figure "salt to taste" as ¼ teaspoon. The amount of fat listed includes saturated fat, which is also listed separately.

We rounded gram numbers up or down to the nearest half, and milligrams up to the nearest whole.

Foods were analyzed using ESHA Research's Food Processor software.

Grain Basics

Grains' basic flavors and muted colors make them the ideal canvas, waiting for you to layer on the flavors and colors to produce a culinary masterpiece. It's easy to "mix and match" them. You're fresh out of amaranth but have quinoa in the house? It will substitute nicely in that stuffing for squash. Coming up short on rice for the fried rice? Toss in that cupful of leftover cooked barley.

The chart on page 3 can help you choose which grains to use where.

We tested various cooking methods for each of the grains. Under "Best Ways to Cook," you'll find the methods that we feel gave the best results for the effort and energy expended. "Yield" refers to the cooked amount you'll get from 1 cup raw grain. The number is just an average; yields will vary according to cooking method. "Flavor" is our opinionated impression of what the grain tastes like. "Consistency" helps determine how best to use the grain. Firm grains make good pilafs and salads and hold up well in soups. Soft grains make good porridges or extenders (added to meat loaves and such). They often cling together nicely in a polenta or mush, meaning the cooked grain can be pressed into a loaf pan, chilled, then sliced and pan-fried. A "yes" under "Soak" or "Toast" means that grain benefits greatly from being

soaked or toasted before cooking. Finally, a "yes" in the "Freeze" column means
that the cooked grain freezes well.

Nutrition

The United States Department of Agriculture honored a millennia-old tradition
when it built the Food Guide Pyramid on a foundation of grains. Grains provide the
building blocks of any nutritious diet. Our meat-centered society tends to forget
that for many people around the world, the rice, or bread, or noodle is the meal's
main event. The meat is a flavoring.

All grains supply abundant amounts of complex carbohydrates, or starches. The
body burns both complex and simple carbohydrates (sugars) for fuel. Whole grains
provide fiber and a wider range of nutrients, including thiamin (vitamin B_1), riboflavin (vitamin B_2), vitamin B_6, folate, chromium, magnesium, manganese,
molybdenum, phosphorus, and potassium. Some also are rich in iron, calcium, or
zinc.

Fiber is another treasure found in whole grains. The body cannot digest fiber,
but it plays an important role in health. The National Cancer Institute and other organizations recommend we eat 20 to 30 grams of dietary fiber daily. The average
American eats more like 10 grams, which explains why laxatives and hemorrhoid
preparations take up so much space on drugstore shelves.

Fiber does more than keep you "regular." It helps prevent or alleviate many intestinal disorders, sweep toxins out of the body, and lower blood cholesterol.

All whole grains supply two kinds of fiber, soluble and insoluble. Insoluble
fiber—or, as Grandma called it "roughage"—helps foods move more quickly
through the bowel, in the process helping to prevent or treat hemorrhoids and irri-
table bowel syndrome and, possibly, colon cancer. Wheat bran is especially loaded
with insoluble fiber, although all whole grains have plenty of it.

People who are watching their weight, their cholesterol, or their blood sugar
should eat plenty of oats, beans, and other foods rich in soluble fiber. Soluble fiber
absorbs water, slowing down the speed at which food empties from the stomach.
Foods rich in soluble fiber help you feel fuller longer, decrease your blood cholesterol levels, and can help stabilize your blood sugar. All whole grains contain soluble fiber, but oats, barley, and brown rice are especially rich sources.

One note of caution: If you're not used to eating a lot of fiber, add it gradually
to your diet and drink plenty of water. A sudden overdose of fiber can make you
uncomfortable and possibly even lead to intestinal blockage.

Preparation, Cooking, and Flavor Chart

	Best Ways to Cook	Yield (cups)	Flavor	Consistency	Soak	Toast	Freeze
Amaranth	Simmer	2½–3	Hay, nuts, pepper	Sticky, slightly gritty	No	Yes	No
Barley (grits)	Simmer, microwave	2¼–2½	Sweet, nutty	Soft, chewy	No	No	No
Barley (pearled)	Simmer, microwave, pressure-cook	3½–4	Sweet, nutty	Chewy, sticky	No	No	Yes
Buckwheat (kasha)	Simmer	2	Toasted cocoa, walnuts	Medium-firm, chewy	No	Yes	Yes
Bulgur	Steep in boiling water	2–2½	Mild, nutty	Gritty, flaky	Yes	No	No
Corn (grits)	Simmer	4	Bland, sweet	Soft, chewy	No	No	No
Corn (meal)	Steam, microwave	4	Bland, sweet	Velvety, faintly gritty	No	No	No
Couscous	Steep in boiling water	3½–4	Bland, sweet	Soft, fluffy	No	No	No
Farina	Simmer, microwave	3½–4	Nutty, sweet	Velvety, faintly gritty	No	No	No
Flaked (rolled) grains (all)	Simmer, microwave	1½–2	Depends on grain	Soft, slightly chewy	No	Yes	No
Kamut (kernels)	Simmer, pressure-cook	2½–2¾	Buttery wheat	Firm, very chewy	Yes	Yes	Yes
Millet	Simmer	3–3½	Corn, almonds	Soft, fluffy	No	Yes	No
Oats (groats)	Simmer, microwave, pressure-cook	2¾	Pecans, sweet	Chewy, sticky	Yes	Yes	Yes
Oats (steel-cut)	Simmer, microwave	2–2½	Pecans, sweet	Chewy, sticky	Yes	Yes	No
Quinoa	Simmer, steam	2	Hay, peanuts	Soft-crunchy	No	Yes	No
Rice (brown)	Simmer, steam, pressure-cook	3	Nutty, sweet	Soft, slightly chewy	No	No	Briefly
Rice (white)	Simmer, steam	3	Bland, sweet	Soft, slightly chewy	No	No	Briefly
Rye (kernels)	Simmer, microwave, pressure-cook	2	Walnuts, hay	Firm, very chewy	Yes	No	Yes
Semolina	Simmer, microwave	4	Bland, sweet	Soft, smooth	No	No	No
Spelt (kernels)	Simmer, microwave, pressure-cook	2–2½	Wheat, pecans	Firm, chewy	Yes	Yes	Yes
Teff	Simmer	3	Wheat, tea, hay	Sticky, slightly gritty	No	No	No
Triticale (kernels)	Simmer, microwave, pressure-cook	2	Nuts, grass	Firm, very chewy	Yes	Yes	Yes
Wheat (cracked)	Simmer	2–2½	Walnuts, toast	Soft, chewy	Yes	Yes	No
Wheat (kernels)	Simmer, microwave, pressure-cook	2–2½	Walnuts, toast	Firm, very chewy	Yes	Yes	Yes
Wild rice	Simmer, pressure-cook	3	Black tea, hazelnuts	Medium-firm, chewy	Yes	Yes	Yes

Often people rate grains in terms of protein. Quinoa, for example, is highly touted because it's nearly a "complete protein." All this means is that it contains significant amounts of all eight essential amino acids. (The body needs about twenty amino acids, the building blocks of protein. It manufactures all but eight of them, which must come from the diet.) In real life, grain proteins matter most to the developing world, where grains make up a huge portion of the diet. In this country, only vegans—vegetarians who eat no animal foods at all—need to pay attention to grain proteins. And since nearly all vegans eat foods such as beans, which make up for any amino acids that grains lack, there's little cause for worry.

If you wish to avoid pesticide and fungicide residues, buy organically grown grains. We also like them because they tend to be less heavily processed and often more flavorful. Mass-market brands of cornmeal, for example, are usually processed

Grain Nutrition Chart

	Nutritional Highlights	Other Nutrients, Minerals
Amaranth	Protein; higher than most grains in amino acid lysine	Copper, magnesium, phosphorus
Barley (hulled)	Rich in soluble fiber, especially beta glucan, shown to lower cholesterol	Niacin, thiamin, copper, iron, magnesium, phosphorus, zinc
Barley (pearled)	Rich in soluble fiber shown to lower cholesterol	Niacin, vitamin B_6, iron
Buckwheat (groats)	Richer than most other cereal grains in amino acid lysine	Niacin, copper, magnesium, phosphorus, zinc
Bulgur	Lower in B vitamins than other whole wheat products, because of precooking	Niacin, iron, magnesium
Cornmeal, grits (degerminated)	Enriched to replace lost nutrients	Niacin, thiamin, riboflavin, iron
Cornmeal, grits (whole)	Low in amino acid lysine, except for high-lysine cornmeal	Fiber, thiamin, vitamin B_6, magnesium, phosphorus
Farina (Cream of Wheat)	Enriched to replace lost nutrients	Thiamin
Farina (Bear Mush)	Rich in calcium	Niacin, thiamin
Kamut	Higher in protein and lower in fiber than standard wheat	Niacin, thiamin, copper, iron, magnesium, phosphorus, zinc
Masa, corn tortillas	Good source of calcium	Fiber, niacin, vitamin B_6, iron, magnesium, phosphorus
Millet	Rich in magnesium	Fiber, folate, niacin, riboflavin, thiamin, vitamin B_6, phosphorus, zinc

Grain Nutrition Chart (*continued*)

	Nutritional Highlights	Other Nutrients, Minerals
Multigrain flours	High in protein (mixes of grain and legume flours)	Varies according to blend, but all rich in fiber
Oats	Rich in soluble fiber shown to lower blood cholesterol	Thiamin, copper, iron, magnesium, phosphorus, zinc
Popcorn	Higher in fiber and lower in fat than most snack foods	Magnesium, phosphorus, copper, zinc
Quinoa	Nearly a complete protein; rich in amino acid lysine	Folate, niacin, riboflavin, thiamin, vitamin B_6, iron, magnesium, phosphorus, potassium, zinc
Rice (brown)	Good source of magnesium, fairly high in fiber	Niacin, thiamin, vitamin B_6, copper, phosphorus, zinc
Rice (white)	Enriched to replace lost nutrients	Niacin, thiamin, iron
Rye	Lower in protein than most grains	Fiber, thiamin, magnesium, phosphorus
Seitan (wheat gluten)	Exceptionally high in protein and iron (when made with both wheat and legumes)	Sodium (when marinated in soy sauce)
Semolina (durum), pasta and couscous	Enriched to replace lost nutrients	Niacin, riboflavin, thiamin, iron, phosphorus
Spelt	High in protein and fiber	Niacin, thiamin, iron, magnesium, phosphorus
Teff	Rich in minerals, especially calcium, iron, magnesium, zinc	Fiber (especially soluble), thiamin
Triticale	Closer in protein content to wheat than to rye	Fiber, folate, niacin, thiamin, vitamin B_6, copper, magnesium, phosphorus, zinc
Wheat berries, cracked wheat	High in fiber	Protein, folate, niacin, thiamin, copper, iron, magnesium, phosphorus, potassium, zinc
Wheat bran	Excellent source of insoluble fiber	Niacin, vitamin B_6, magnesium, phosphorus
Wheat flour and products (refined into white flour)	Rich in gluten for bread making. Allergenic for some people. Enriched to replace lost nutrients.	Niacin, riboflavin, thiamin, iron
Wheat germ	Excellent source of vitamin E	Protein, folate, riboflavin, thiamin, vitamin B_6, iron, magnesium, phosphorus, zinc
Whole wheat flour and products	Rich in gluten for bread making. Allergenic for some people.	Protein, fiber, niacin, vitamin B_6, thiamin, iron, magnesium, phosphorus, zinc
Wild rice	Very low in fat	Folate, niacin, vitamin B_6, copper, magnesium, phosphorus, zinc

to remove the bran and germ, while organically grown cornmeal is more likely to be stone-ground whole to retain the nutrients, along with a more "corny" flavor.

Forms of Grain

Health food stores and supermarkets offer a choice of grains processed in different ways, ranging from the whole seeds to finely ground flours. Here, in a nutshell, are some basic terms you'll find on labels.

Whole grain: This is the least-processed form. It will be hulled (the outer husk removed), cleaned, and sometimes roasted. Whole, hulled kernels of oats and buckwheat are often labeled groats.

Pearled or polished: Barley is pearled; rice is polished. The words refer to the same process: The brown bran—the outer coatings of the kernel—has been wholly or partially removed.

Steel-cut, cracked, grits: These terms refer to grains such as oats, wheat, and corn that have been cut into smaller bits so they cook faster. They're available in various consistencies, from fine to very coarse. They may be lightly or heavily refined, depending on the grain.

Flakes or rolled: Most people know oats in this form, but just about any kernel-type grain, including wheat, rye, spelt, and Kamut, can be rolled and flaked. In this process, the kernels of grain are sliced, then flattened between rollers. (We're referring to flakes of uncooked grain, not ready-to-eat cereal.)

Meal: The grain is coarsely ground to a gritty consistency. Cornmeal, farina, and semolina are meals. Stone-ground means just that: The grain is ground between two stones. Stone-ground meals and flours are coarser and tend to have more bran in them.

Bran or polishings: Bran is the coarsely ground or finely shredded outer husk of wheat, oats, or other grains. Some health food stores sell rice polishings, which come from the bran layers removed from brown rice when it's made into white rice.

Germ: A coarse meal made from the embryo, or sprout, found inside the kernel. Wheat germ is very popular, but you can also find corn germ in some health food stores. The germ is a very concentrated source of vitamins and oils.

Flour: The grain is ground into a powder. Any grain can be processed this way. This is the most versatile form of most grains, since flours can be used in a wide range of breads and baked goods.

Storing Grains

As long as they stay cool and dry, oats and white rice keep practically forever. Brown rice or millet, on the other hand, starts smelling "off" if not used up within a couple of months. How well grains keep depends largely on how much oil, and what kind, they contain. Most of the oil is contained in the bran and germ, which is why whole grains never keep as long as refined grains. (Oats store well because they're rich in antioxidants, which keep fats from turning rancid.) Whole grain flours are especially perishable because grinding a grain distributes its oils throughout.

The best way to keep grains fresh is to eat and bake with them so often that they never get the chance to spoil.

If that's not realistic, freeze whole grain flours and grains for longest storage. Or keep them in the refrigerator in an airtight container. (It's important that the container be airtight so the grains do not absorb humidity from the refrigerator compartment.) At the very least, keep grains in airtight containers in a cool cupboard. Discard grains that smell or taste rancid, and *never* eat grains or grain products that smell or look even slightly moldy.

If you buy a lot of grains, especially organically grown ones, sooner or later you'll probably meet meal moths, those fluttery little beige creatures that love grains. You know they're around when you open up the flour bag to find ropes of cobwebby egg deposits.

Although meal moths and their wormy offspring pose no health threat, few people consider them a delicacy. Freezing grains cuts down drastically on infestations. If that's not possible, store all grains in tightly closed canisters or jars, and clean the pantry or cupboard occasionally to rid it of flour and crumbs. If you find a mild infestation, sift out the moth eggs and stick the grain in the freezer for a couple of days. If the moths have established a major colony, toss out the grain or flour and wash the container.

Soaking or Toasting Grains

Toasting brings out a rich, warm, nutty flavor in some grains and also cuts the cooking time. (See the chart on page 3 for grains that benefit from toasting.) We prefer it to soaking because some nutrients escape when you drain soaked grains. Soaking also does not improve the flavor. It is, however, easier than toasting. Rinse the grain, cover with cold water, and let stand several hours. To preserve nutrients, cook grains in the soaking water, adding fresh water if necessary.

To toast grains, heat a heavy pan or skillet. Add enough grain to cover the bottom of the pan and cook over medium heat, shaking the pan constantly, until the grain smells nutty and turns golden. Or toast grains in the oven: Spread them on a large baking sheet and toast at 350° for 10 to 15 minutes.

General Cooking Notes

Whole grain kernels are often rinsed before cooking. Do not rinse really small seeds such as amaranth and teff; they'll clump together or vanish down the drain. It's also best not to rinse enriched grains such as white rice or grits. They're usually coated with B vitamins, which will drain off with the rinsing water.

To rinse grain, place it in a bowl. Fill the bowl with cold water, swish the grain around, and carefully pour off the water, along with bits of chaff or dust. Rinse again, then drain. If you plan to toast the grain, dry it off after rinsing.

Simmering grains on the stove top is easy, generally requires little attention on the part of the cook, and yields good results. In experimenting with different grains, we did discover the importance of using water conservatively. We often call for smaller amounts of water than you might see on packages and in other printed material. Mushy grains lack appeal. And it's far easier to add boiling water during cooking than it is to subtract it.

The microwave or pressure cooker comes in handy for many grains. And the steamer produces light, fluffy rice and millet. For detailed directions, check the appropriate chapter for each grain, but here is some general guidance:

The microwave works best with grain flakes or meal (such as oatmeal and cornmeal), which absorb water well, or with longer-cooking grains that will be drained. It's a poor way to cook grains such as quinoa and rice; microwaves cook unevenly, so that the grain does not absorb water the way it should.

Microwaving times depend on the make and wattage of your oven and the ebb and flow of power coming into the oven. Liquids boil over easily in the microwave, so choose a container with room to spare. Start out cooking on high (100 percent), then reduce the heat to medium (50 to 60 percent). If you have a low-wattage microwave, add boiling, rather than cold, water to the grain.

The pressure cooker makes quick work of preparing large, hard grains such as wheat, rye, brown rice, or oat groats. Modern pressure cookers have safety-locked lids so you needn't worry about winding up with oatmeal on your ceiling. Bring the water and grain to a boil, then secure the lid. If you have one of the old-time cookers, add 2 to 3 teaspoons of canola or olive oil as well. Bring the cooker up to pressure—the lid will lock and the nozzle will begin to let off small amounts of steam. Lower the heat so that the cooker continues to let off a little steam now and then. Start timing the cooking when the cooker has reached pressure. To release the pressure, either remove the pan from the heat and let the pressure come down naturally, or put the pan in the sink and run cold water over the lid until the pressure is released. Don't release pressure by turning the top knob to let steam escape through the nozzle; grains such as rice or oatmeal release a starchy liquid that will make a mess of your stove top.

The best utensil for steaming grains is a double boiler. Pour enough water into the bottom of the boiler to come just below, but not touch, the top pan when the two pieces are fitted together. Put the grain and hot water (or other liquid) in the top of the double boiler. (Either boil the water before adding it to the grain, or bring the grain and cold water to a simmer over direct heat.) Fit the top over the bottom of the double boiler, cover tightly, and steam as directed. Steaming is a hands-off method; do not peek too often, or you'll increase the cooking time.

You can also use a bamboo steamer set over boiling water in a wok. Combine the grain and boiling water in a shallow pan or baking dish that will fit in the steamer. Place the pan in the steamer, set the steamer in the wok over boiling water, cover, and steam away.

You can save time and effort by cooking firm grains such as wheat or rye berries, oat groats, barley, and wild rice in large batches. Refrigerate or freeze them to use later in pilafs, stews, and breads. Drain the cooked grain and rinse under cold water. Toss with a teaspoon of vegetable oil and place in a container with a tight lid or a self-sealing plastic freezer bag. Refrigerate for up to 3 days or freeze for up to 6 months.

Starchy grains with some shape—brown or white rice, or pasta—can be cooked ahead of time in the same way and refrigerated (although pasta purists might beg to differ). We don't recommend freezing these grains. One exception is rice, which may be frozen briefly (up to a week) to be used in fried rice.

Serve soft, sticky grains such as oatmeal, millet, and amaranth right after cooking. If you do have leftovers, pack them into a nonstick or oiled loaf pan and chill for up to three days. You can slice this mush and pan-fry it to serve plain or with any topping of your choice.

Baking with Whole Grains

Many of the recipes in this book are for breads and other baked goods, so we'd like to share some baking tips:

When buying whole wheat flours, choose the one that's best suited for the purpose. For bread making, use regular whole wheat flour or one labeled for bread. Use whole wheat pastry flour for cakes, biscuits, crackers, and other baked goods that depend on a more melt-in-the-mouth texture.

Bring flour that's stored in the refrigerator or freezer to room temperature before baking with it.

Whole grain breads can be made from a variety of flours, from rye to millet. However, they nearly always contain wheat flour as well. Wheat flour contains two proteins, gliadin and glutenin, which "grab" water and each other to form elastic sheets called gluten. These layered sheets trap the gases produced by the yeast and the steam produced by the water, resulting in a bread that's light and chewy instead of heavy and cakelike.

Whole grain doughs tend to be wet and sticky. The extra water helps create more steam to compensate for the heavier weight of the flours and for the bran, the bits of which cut the gluten like knives. Whole grain breads also rise more slowly than white breads for that reason.

Wet doughs can be messy. In fact, you can't really knead them in the classic sense, since they'll stick to your fingers. Instead, you should repeatedly fold the dough over itself. The easiest way to do this is to lay the dough on a large, lightly floured pastry cloth. Use the cloth to pick up the dough and fold it over itself. Repeat this process until the dough is smooth and elastic. Sprinkle small amounts of flour over the dough or cloth if the dough begins to stick.

If you're kneading a wet dough in a mixer, don't expect it to form a neat ball. Add just enough flour, a teaspoon or so at a time, so the dough forms a rough mass and does not stick all over the sides of the bowl. (If you have an old KitchenAid machine and have not replaced the original dough hook, we recommend doing so. The newer dough hook kneads much better.)

To add a little more fiber and depth of flavor to white bread recipes, try replacing up to 1 cup of the white flour with a whole grain flour. You may have to adjust the amount of flour or liquid in the recipe.

In general, the longer the rise, the lighter and more flavorful the bread. If you have the time, let dough rise slowly at room temperature. This can take anywhere from an hour to several hours.

If you prefer, you can let it rise more quickly in a warm place, about 80°. Professionals use a proofing box, which supplies the kind of warm, humid climate yeasts love. You can turn your microwave oven into a proofing box: Put a cup of water in a microwaveproof measure and microwave it on high for 2 to 3 minutes, until the water boils and releases steam. Remove the cup of water and place the bread dough in the microwave, which should be warm and moist. Close the door and let the dough rise.

Although recipes often call for oiling or spraying the bowl that the dough will rise in, that step is optional for all but the stickiest doughs.

What about making the breads in this book in a bread machine? We recommend that you use recipes specifically formulated for the machine. Heavy doughs may need longer rising times than the machines are set for. You can use the machine to knead the dough, however.

Milk, buttermilk, yogurt, and sugars help tenderize doughs and brown the crust. Despite its name, most buttermilk is low-fat. You'll find 1 percent, 1½ percent or skim buttermilk in most supermarkets. We like to keep nonfat dried milk on hand for baking. To make 1 cup of skim milk, spoon 5 tablespoons of nonfat dry milk into a measuring cup and stir in enough cold water to make a cup.

For a more decorative bread, brush the top of the loaf lightly with an egg white, a little egg substitute, or a whole egg beaten with 1 teaspoon cold water. Then sprinkle the top with sesame, poppy, flax, or sunflower seeds, or uncooked spelt, oats, rye, wheat, barley, or Kamut flakes. An egg wash made with whole egg gives the bread a rich, brown color. A wash made with just egg white or egg substitute will make the top of the loaf shiny but not brown, because it contains virtually no fat. For a browner crust, add just a pinch of sugar to the egg white.

High-Altitude Adjustments

Cooking at altitude didn't mean much to us until Virginia, a lifelong Midwesterner, moved to Colorado. She now lives at an elevation of 5,000 feet, surrounded by air as dry as week-old crackers.

It's easy to compensate for altitude in stove-top cooking: Just add a little more liquid and cook longer. Water boils at a lower temperature the higher you live, so plan to cook hard grains such as wheat berries or to steam polenta longer than the recipe calls for—as much as 50 percent longer at 5,000 feet. Add more liquid if the grains seem to be drying out. A pressure cooker helps speed up cooking time. If you live above 7,000 feet, you'd better use a pressure cooker if you want wheat berries to get tender during your lifetime.

Baking is something else at high altitudes. Because the atmospheric pressure is lower than it is at sea level, leavening agents—baking powder and soda, yeast, the air beaten into eggs—expand quickly. Baked goods can rise like a balloon, only to deflate into tough, flat versions of their former selves.

Also, breads, cakes, and cookies dry out faster. As soon as baked goods are cool, put them in plastic bags or airtight tins. Baked goods made with whole grain flours will keep longer, because they naturally contain a little more fat, a moisturizer, than those made with white flour.

Most recipes in this book will need little, if any, adjusting at altitudes of 3,500 to 6,000 feet. If you live at higher altitudes, or if you experience problems with any of the recipes, give the following methods a try.

Yeast breads: Doughs may need slightly more liquid and/or less flour. Go by feel; the dough should be soft, not stiff.

In breads where you want a longer, slower rise to deepen the flavor (this pertains especially to ryes and sourdoughs), let the dough rise at cool room temperature, and/or reduce the amount of yeast by ¼ to ½ teaspoon.

For larger loaves, boost the oven temperature by 25° for the first 10 minutes of baking time. For rolls or small loaves, no adjustment is needed.

Quick breads and muffins: Set the oven temperature 10° to 25° higher than the recipe calls for. Decrease the baking powder by ¼ to ½ teaspoon.

Cookies and crackers: Unless you live at very high altitude, you shouldn't need to adjust cookie and cracker recipes. If you do have problems, boost the baking temperature by 15° to 25°, and add 2 tablespoons water and 1 tablespoon additional flour to the dough.

Sprouting Grains

Because sprouts are alive, some people insist they have the power to "energize" the body. We're not sure we feel any more energetic after eating them, but there's no argument that sprouts are nutritious (sprouting grains release vitamin C and chlorophyll) and more digestible than the whole grains. They're also delicious in salads and sandwiches.

Most grains can be sprouted; after all, they are seeds. Use food-quality, not garden, seeds; the latter may be treated with fungicides. Wheat berries, oats, amaranth,

The Hollow Loaf

You become a good bread baker the same way you get to Carnegie Hall: practice, practice, practice.

An experienced baker confidently hauls a loaf out of the oven and checks for doneness by giving the bottom of the bread a couple raps with the knuckles. A novice bread baker reads the phrase "Bake until the bread sounds hollow" and grimaces in bewilderment.

To learn to recognize the sound of hollowness, remove the bread from the oven when it has firmed up but definitely is not yet done, turn it out of the pan, and tap the bottom with your fingers or rap lightly with your knuckles. You'll hear a dull thud. Return it to the oven, with or without its pan. (Placing it directly on the shelf results in a more evenly browned, crunchier crust.)

After the baking time is up and the crust looks firm and golden, try again. Tapping on the bread should produce a sharper, more hollow sound, as though you were knocking on a door.

When in doubt, it's better to slightly overbake whole grain breads than to underbake them. Gummy bread really lacks appeal.

An alternative to tapping the bread is to insert an instant-read thermometer through the bottom of the loaf, into the center. Even this method is not foolproof. A regular white loaf is usually cooked enough at 190°, but a heavier whole grain loaf may need to bake to a temperature of almost 200°.

quinoa, and millet are possibilities. To sprout a small amount of seeds, place them in a widemouth glass jar. Fill the jar halfway with water, then cover the top with cheesecloth or plastic screening held firmly in place with a rubber band. Let soak for 4 to 6 hours for small seeds and 10 to 12 hours for large seeds such as wheat. Drain the water, then turn the jar and set it, neck side down, at a 45° angle where it can drain (a dish rack is a good place to set it). Let stand until the seeds sprout, anywhere from a day to several days, depending on the variety. Pat the sprouts dry, check them carefully for mold (and discard if you find any), then refrigerate.

Grinding Grains

If you bake a lot with whole grain flours, you may want to buy a mill or grinder. Hand-operated flour or grain mills, either stand-alone or as accessories to stand mixers, are inexpensive and work fine for small amounts. If you plan to grind only grains, get a mill with buhrstones, which will grind a finer flour. If you'll use it for other purposes (such as grinding peanuts), get one with steel blades, and run the grain through more than once to get a fine flour. Grinding your own grains saves shelf space, since you don't have to buy both the whole and ground forms of a given grain. And by grinding only as much flour as you need at a given time, you don't have to worry about flours turning rancid.

Softer grains such as millet, rice, or rolled oats can be ground in a food processor or a clean coffee or spice grinder. The resulting flour will be gritty, more like meal than true flour.

Miscellaneous Notes on Techniques and Ingredients

Dark sesame oil: Also called toasted sesame seed oil, this refers to the dark, red-brown oil sold for Asian cooking. It's available in Asian groceries, many supermarkets, and health food stores. It has a much more intense flavor than regular, light sesame oil.

Grating citrus zest: The zest is the outermost, colored part of the peel. You can strip it off with a citrus zester or grate the skin of the fruit lightly over the small holes of a grater. Or use a vegetable peeler to remove a very thin outer layer from the peel, then sprinkle with a little sugar or salt and mince finely.

Proofing yeast: If you're using yeast in foil envelopes and it's well within the expiration date listed on the package, you need not proof it. Just dissolve it in the liquid and add to the other ingredients. If you buy your yeast in a jar or in bulk, it's a good idea to proof it—that is, make sure it's still alive. Sprinkle it on warm liquid (usually water with a little sugar added) and let stand for 5 to 10 minutes or until the yeast blooms (foams up).

Reconstituting dried mushrooms and tomatoes: Soak mushrooms in warm water to cover for 20 to 30 minutes, until softened. Soak tomatoes in boiling water for 30 seconds, until softened.

Roasting peppers: Roast peppers over an open flame on a gas stove, on a grill, in the oven, or under the broiler. The easiest way is to cut the peppers in half lengthwise (don't remove the cores or seeds), put them on a broiler pan, cut side down, and stick them under the broiler (you can even use a toaster oven). Roast for 5 to 7 minutes, switching them from front to back once, until the skin is blistered all over. Stick them in a heavy plastic bag and let them steam for 10 to 15 minutes. If they're still hot, run them under cold water. Pull off the skin or scrape it off with a paring knife, and cut out the cores and seeds. You can cover the roasted peppers tightly with plastic wrap and refrigerate for up to 2 days.

Salting and draining eggplant: Dice or slice the eggplant as directed in the recipe. Salt lightly, place in a colander over a bowl or plate, and let drain for 30 minutes. Rinse and pat dry.

Seeding chile peppers: It's a good idea to wear latex or rubber gloves to keep volatile chile oils off your hands. Cut out the seeds and discard them. Don't touch your eyes with fingers that have chile oil on them— it really burns!

Storing and reheating muffins: Put cooled muffins in a large, self-sealing plastic bag and store for up to 2 days at room temperature or for up to 3 months in the freezer. Room-temperature muffins can be reheated in a toaster oven or in the microwave in 30-second increments at 30 or 40 percent power. If you overheat muffins in the microwave, they will turn rubbery. Frozen muffins can be wrapped loosely in aluminum foil and heated in a 325° oven for 10 to 12 minutes or heated unwrapped in the microwave—very carefully.

Vegetable stock or broth: Make vegetable stock by simmering scraps such as carrot ends and peels, potato peels, parsley stems, onion skins, and mushroom stems in water to cover for at least 2 hours. Let the stock cool, strain well, then freeze. Most people prefer the convenience of canned broth. The vegetable broth sold in supermarkets is extremely salty, so we call for diluting it with water.

Wheat, the Staff of Life

Farmers have been planting wheat almost since the dawn of agriculture. No doubt, they have been cursing it almost as long. When the weather got too wet or too dry or the locusts decided to gorge, wheat often fell as the first victim. Meanwhile, the barley, rye, and other "weeds" thrived. It's no accident that the Bible mentions barley so often for bread, that northern Europeans survived for centuries on rye, that the Africans ate (and still eat) plenty of millet, and that the Scots lived on oats.

Barley, rye, millet, and oats do not have enough gluten, however, to form the light, delicious breads and sturdy noodles you can make from wheat. So for centuries, farmers continued to raise wheat wherever they could, and only rich people routinely bought good bread.

The early American settlers treasured wheat as well. Not long after they stepped off the boat, the English planted their favorite bread grain. It fell prey to a fungus in New England and keeled over in Virginia, where tobacco farming had exhausted the soil. European colonists never stopped trying to grow wheat but, being practical sorts, they adopted "Indian maize" (corn) as their grain staple. By the middle of the eighteenth century, a bushel of wheat that would have been ground into flour cost the average American laborer the equivalent of four days' pay. Not surprisingly, most Americans still ate more corn than wheat.

In the 1840s, the California gold rush spawned a secondary industry in wheat. Almost as hungry for bread as they were for gold, the miners needed tons of good flour, and the newly arrived settlers in Oregon happily obliged them. By the time the gold rush petered out, Portland was an international port, and the Pacific Northwest had established itself worldwide as a source of fine wheat. The region still ranks as a major producer of white wheat.

Late in the nineteenth century wheat finally took root as the massive American empire it is today. In the early 1870s, Mennonite settlers from the Crimea arrived in Kansas, bringing with them the seeds of a hard red winter wheat known as Turkey, after its country of origin. Earlier farmers on the Great Plains had lost winter wheat to drought, disease, and assorted insects. The Mennonites, who settled mainly in Kansas, but also in Nebraska, Minnesota, and the Dakotas, knew how to tame cold, inhospitable prairies like the ones they had farmed back home. To this day, most of the winter wheat grown in the central states is descended, however remotely, from Turkey.

After World War I, high grain prices inspired farmers in Kansas, Colorado, New Mexico, Oklahoma, and Texas to plant millions of acres in wheat and corn. Unfortunately, their stewardship of the soil did not keep pace with their eagerness to make a good livelihood. From 1933 to 1939, drought and high winds ravaged the so-called dust bowl, carrying off tons of topsoil and plunging the United States deeper into the darkness of the Depression. It also inspired a classic American novel: John Steinbeck's heart-wrenching *Grapes of Wrath* chronicled the plight of farmers driven to become migrant workers.

Although a new generation eventually reclaimed the land of the dust bowl, there are those who today look over the miles of amber waves of grain shimmering in the sun and warn that a few years of drought and wind could again wreak devastation. In recent years, drought claimed much of the winter wheat crop in Colorado and Kansas.

To be sure, modern wheat farmers still curse drought, hail, wind, and insects—not to mention the vagaries of the commodities market and the winds of political change. But even allowing for bad years, modern technology and more efficient farming methods allow them to grow enough wheat to feed our citizens' massive appetite for hamburger and hot dog buns, sandwich loaves, muffins, tortillas, American Indian fry bread, pita, crackers, cookies, and pastries—and to store and export tons of it as well. The United States grows about a tenth of the world's wheat but is the world's single biggest exporter of the grain.

When the United States cut off grain shipments to the then Soviet Union in 1980 to protest the invasion of Afghanistan, American wheat and corn farmers panicked as much as the Russians did. Until the crisis passed, government subsidies helped ease the pain for the farmers who depended on exports for a significant chunk of their income.

American farmers grow all of the most commonly eaten wheat varieties. Spring wheat, which grows in the northernmost states such as North Dakota and Montana, is planted in the spring and harvested in the fall. Winter wheat, which grows in the southern plains states such as Kansas and Texas, is planted in the fall, lies dormant over the winter, then is harvested in the summer.

Professional bakers divide wheat flours into two general categories. "Strong" flour, so named for the muscle it puts into bread, is made from hard wheat and has a protein content ranging from 10 to 18 percent. Most hard red wheat comes from Kansas, Texas, Oklahoma, Nebraska, North Dakota, South Dakota, Montana, Idaho, Utah, and California.

"Weak" flour produces more tender baked goods such as pastries, biscuits, and egg noodles. It's made from soft wheat, which has a protein content ranging from 8 to 11 percent. Most soft wheat is grown in the Midwest, Southeast, and Pacific Northwest.

All-purpose flours, whether white or whole wheat, generally are blends of hard and soft wheats and fall in the middle in protein content.

Durum wheat, essential for making good macaroni and spaghetti, grows in North Dakota, Montana, Arizona, and southern California.

Hard white wheat, a fairly new variety, grows mostly in California. It's used for yeast breads, hard rolls, and noodles. Bakers like it because the whole grain flour made from it is almost as pale and mildly flavored as white flour.

Unlike corn, which goes mostly into animal feed, nearly all the wheat grown in America and the rest of the world ends up on somebody's table. And it's showing up on more and more tables. According to at least one study, wheat may soon overtake rice as the most widely eaten grain in the developing world.

A kernel of wheat, *Triticum*, consists of the germs, or embryo, which is surrounded by the starchy endosperm. Wheat germ is made from the embryo. Flours and meals are made from the endosperm, the largest part of the kernel. The endosperm is also the part of the wheat that contains the gluten-forming proteins. The endosperm, in turn, is covered by several layers of bran. Finally, the wheat kernel is enclosed by a thin, inedible husk.

Whole Wheat Flour, Farina, and Gluten

Whole Wheat Flour

Commercial millers were already grinding wheat into flour when the Roman Empire was at its peak. Back then, people favored the lightest flour possible. Only the upper classes could afford to eat pale bread, however. Thanks to the painstaking labor and the waste involved in sifting the bran and germ from coarse stone-ground flour, "pure" light flour remained expensive for centuries.

By the late nineteenth century, efficient roller mills replaced the old stone mills, producing flour that was even whiter (and even more deficient in nutrients). Suddenly, the middle and lower classes could enjoy white flour and bread daily.

We modern folk continue to eat white flour—which now is routinely enriched with vitamins and iron—out of habit. Certainly, there's nothing aristocratic about spongy white bread that kids can squish into gummy balls. A good stone-ground whole wheat flour or a silky whole wheat pastry flour rich with the nutty taste of the germ—now, those are special (and generally more expensive than white flour).

We don't deny the value of white flour. A good white flour makes marvelous breads and lightens loaves made with whole grain flours. And nothing but bleached flour will produce white-as-snow wedding cakes or biscuits.

But many, if not most, of the items you usually make with white flour can be made with whole wheat. Bagels, breads, tortillas, noodles, pizza crusts—all translate beautifully to whole wheat. We've even had wonderful piecrusts, angel food cake, and puff pastry made from whole wheat pastry flour.

White flour cannot match the full-bodied, nutty flavor of whole wheat. The whole grain also has more nutrition. But ironically, white flour has the same amount of niacin as whole wheat flour, and it contains as much or more thiamin (vitamin B_1), riboflavin (B_2), folate, and iron—because most food processors enrich flour with those elements after they've milled them out.

But when it's milled into white flour, a kernel of wheat still loses a goodly percentage of other nutrients that are not added back:

- **Vitamin B_6**, which helps the stomach secrete sufficient acid, plays a role in the breakdown of carbohydrates, fats, and proteins, and is necessary for the production of antibodies and red blood cells

- **Vitamin E**, an important antioxidant that helps prevent the formation of free radicals, molecules that cause damage to the body
- **Calcium**, necessary for building strong bones and regulating heartbeat
- **Copper**, which helps in the formation of hemoglobin and red blood cells
- **Magnesium**, a mineral that helps in the metabolism of carbohydrates and amino acids and helps regulate the body's acid–alkaline balance
- **Phosphorus**, which acts in concert with calcium as a bone builder and is essential to almost every chemical reaction in the body
- **Potassium**, which helps regulate the body's water balance and blood pressure
- **Zinc**, which is essential for the growth and health of the reproductive tissues and is involved in digestion and metabolism
- **Chromium**, an active ingredient in glucose tolerance factor, which helps regulate blood sugar levels
- **Fiber**, vital to good intestinal health

Because of its high gluten content, wheat flour is the most versatile of the whole grain flours. It can be used alone in everything from breads to piecrusts, and in conjunction with other flours such as barley or rye to produce pleasing breads.

Because it contains the oily germ of the wheat, whole wheat flour can become rancid. Use up whole wheat flour soon after buying it and, if possible, store it in the freezer. It also is heavier than white flour, making it less suitable for some baked goods where you want a light, airy texture. There are two ways around this problem. You can use whole wheat pastry flour, which is made from soft wheat. Or you can use a mixture of whole wheat and white flours.

Whole wheat flour contains more fat and is coarser than white flour, so it absorbs liquid differently. Its bits of bran make it more fragile and difficult to roll out for cookies and piecrusts. It's best to use recipes specifically designed for whole wheat flour, but if you are an experienced baker, you can try experimenting with substituting whole wheat flour for white in your favorite recipes.

Whole wheat flour, like white flour, comes in different hardnesses, defined by protein content. Whole wheat pastry flour is made from soft, low-protein wheat. Whole wheat bread flour is made from hard, high-protein wheat. Regular whole wheat flour, the most widely available, lies nearer the bread end of the spectrum but can be used for pastries. We recommend using only whole wheat pastry flour for cakes.

To make whole wheat flour, most commercial millers separate the bran and germ from white flour, then add some or all of them back after milling. They do this to increase shelf life. When the germ is ground along with the starchy endosperm, the oil gets distributed throughout the flour, making it more likely to turn rancid quickly.

Stone-ground whole wheat flour consists of whole wheat kernels ground between stones that are powered electrically or, in some historic mills, by water.

White whole wheat flour, which has become available to consumers in the last five years, is a creamy, mildly flavored flour suited for breads and rolls.

"Graham flour" means whatever someone wants it to. It was named after Sylvester Graham, a nineteenth-century health pioneer—some would say nut—who believed that to refine flour and sift out the bran was "to put asunder what God joined together." Some companies grind their graham flour more finely than their regular whole wheat flour; others grind it coarsely. Take "graham flour" to mean whole wheat flour, no more, no less.

Panocha flour, common in the Southwest, is a coarse, sweet flour ground from sprouted wheat. It is used in *panocha*, a pudding traditionally made by the pueblo dwellers of the Southwest, but also tastes great in muffins and pancakes.

One of the easiest ways to work more whole wheat flour into your diet is to substitute whole wheat bread for white in sandwiches, bread puddings, and turkey stuffings. Remember that "wheat bread" on the label refers to a blend of whole wheat and white flours. "Whole wheat bread" is made with whole wheat flour only.

One of our favorite ways to eat whole wheat bread is flat, in the form of tortillas. Fortunately, food processors seem to realize that whole grains are making a comeback, and it's easier to find whole wheat tortillas in the supermarket. Some brands are made with vegetable oil, and some are even fat free. Check the labels; brands made with vegetable shortening can be high in fat and saturated fat.

In the United States, tortillas have become a convenient cross-cultural bread. We know a Pakistani American who sometimes substitutes tortillas for chapati, a Chinese American who uses tortillas when she doesn't feel like making mu shu pancakes from scratch, and a Filipina American who uses tortillas as a wrapper for spring rolls.

In addition to being a wrapper for nearly any filling you can think of, whole wheat tortillas are good for breakfast, smeared with a little butter or cream cheese and sprinkled lightly with cinnamon sugar, then baked until crisp. We also like to smear them with a little salsa, sprinkle them lightly with cheese, and bake them for a Tex-Mex-style "pizza."

Farina

When whole wheat is ground a little more coarsely than flour, the result is meal, or farina, designed to be cooked as a porridge. It is readily available in supermarkets and health food stores, where most people know it by its brand names: Cream of Wheat, which is enriched wheat with the germ but minus the bran; Malt-O-Meal, farina with malted barley; and Bear Mush, a whole grain farina ground from red winter wheat.

Like whole wheat flour, whole grain farina will grow rancid if it sits on a shelf too long. Use it up within a couple of months, or refrigerate.

Directions for preparing hot farina cereal vary from brand to brand and among types; follow the package directions. The recipes in this section were tested with regular (not quick-cooking) Cream of Wheat. The same technique works for all kinds, however: Bring the water and salt to a boil, and add the farina in a slow, steady trickle, whisking or stirring constantly. Reduce the heat to low, and simmer until thickened, stirring or whisking often. Again, the cooking time varies by brand but will be anywhere from 1½ to 10 minutes.

For a richer-tasting cereal, cook farina in skim milk. Serve with a drizzle of maple syrup, or sprinkle with dried fruit or a little sugar and cinnamon.

Farina also cooks well in the microwave. Place the cereal, salt, and water in a microwaveproof bowl and cook on high, stirring once, for 1 to 3 minutes, until thickened.

To turn farina into mush, pour the cooked cereal into a loaf or cake pan, let cool, then chill. Slice or cut into squares. Pan-fry in a sprayed nonstick pan, or brush lightly with olive oil and grill. Serve with maple syrup or fruit, or with a savory topping, such as stir-fried vegetables or spaghetti sauce, for dinner.

Wheat Gluten

Think of gluten as the stuff that puts the "chew" in a bagel and the snap in a baguette. Made from the protein-rich part of the endosperm, gluten is flour minus the starch. Professional bakers use dried gluten, which contains 75 to 85 percent protein, to give their breads more structure. The food industry uses processed gluten as a meat extender or flavoring for soups and sauces.

Wheat gluten, also known as seitan (SAY-tan), is whole wheat dough that is rinsed repeatedly until the starch is gone and only the chewy gluten remains. Most commercial processors mix the wheat gluten with legume flours such as chickpea or soybean to make a complete, meat-quality protein.

Along with tofu, boiled gluten, or "wheat meat," also has a long history as a meat alternative. Wheat gluten is an ingredient in the popular Chinese-restaurant vegetarian dish Buddha's Delight. In American history, gluten shows up in the cooking of Mormons and Seventh-Day Adventists, whose religious beliefs emphasize healthful lifestyles. Since the 1970s, gluten has won acceptance among vegetarians looking for something to replace the chewiness of meat.

Seitan's mild, wheaty flavor offends few. Its texture is another story. Some people think its chewiness nicely mimics the mouth feel of meat. Others say they'd rather eat erasers. Generally, we've had the best seitan from restaurants or vegetarian delis, when it's made on the premises by an experienced hand. You can also make seitan yourself—make a dough of whole wheat flour and water, then rinse and rinse and rinse—but that's too much bother unless you eat seitan very frequently.

Seitan is sold in Asian groceries, health food stores, and some supermarkets. You'll find it in jars or in packages in the refrigerated or frozen-food section. It should be refrigerated. It's traditionally cooked or marinated in water with soy sauce and other flavorings. It comes in chunks or cutlets.

Seitan is easy to use. Just drain and rinse it, then slice or dice it. Use it in stir-fries, pan-fries, fajitas, stroganoffs, sandwiches, grilled dishes—anyplace you would normally use sliced meat. Because it has no fat, it benefits from being cooked or marinated in a little oil.

Whole Wheat Flour, Farina, and Gluten

Chicken-Vegetable Potpie with Whole Wheat Crust

Southwestern Turkey Club Pinwheels

Summer Breakfast Burritos

Spicy Chinese Cabbage with Seitan (Wheat Gluten)

Warm Focaccia Goat Cheese Sandwich

Whole Wheat Molasses-Raisin Bread

Cracked Wheat in Whole Wheat Bread

Wheat Germ Whole Wheat Bread

Braided Sesame Seed Loaves

Whole Wheat Spaghetti Bread

New England Blueberry Pancakes with Maple Syrup

Banana Bread with Dried Fruits

Small Graham Apple Muffins

Homemade Honey Graham Crackers

Apple Betty

Chocolate-Cherry Farina Pudding

Orange Farina Pudding with Raspberry Sauce and Pistachios

Chicken-Vegetable Potpie with Whole Wheat Crust

This is reminiscent of the frozen chicken potpies so many of us loved as kids. But it has less fat, far less sodium, a delicious whole wheat crust, and much more vegetables and chicken and less gravy. You can vary the filling according to what you have on hand: a parsnip instead of some of the potatoes, turkey instead of chicken. For an even nicer flavor, substitute ¼ cup white wine for ¼ cup of the chicken broth.

This is nice with a crisp green salad. If you're serving the potpie alone and your guests are hungry, figure on 6 servings.

Makes 8 servings

CRUST

1½ cups stone-ground whole
   wheat flour
½ teaspoon salt
5 tablespoons cold unsalted
   butter, cut into bits

¼ cup plain nonfat yogurt
3 to 4 tablespoons ice water

FILLING

1 tablespoon olive or canola oil
1½ cups finely diced onion
1 cup finely diced carrots
¾ cup finely diced celery
¼ cup unbleached all-purpose
   flour
2½ cups hot low-sodium chicken
   stock
1 tablespoon chopped celery leaves
2 tablespoons chopped fresh
   parsley

¼ teaspoon poultry seasoning or
   dried, crumbled sage
¼ teaspoon salt
¼ teaspoon freshly ground black
   pepper
2 cups diced cooked boneless,
   skinless chicken or turkey
2½ cups diced cooked potatoes
   (preferably boiling potatoes)
1 cup frozen peas
Skim milk (optional)

To make the crust: Place the flour and salt in a food processor and process just to mix. Add the butter and pulse the machine on and off until the butter is incorporated. Add the yogurt and pulse until the mixture is crumbly. With the machine running, add enough ice water so that the dough clumps together; process only until the dough rides up on the blade.

Pat the dough into a disk, wrap in plastic wrap, and refrigerate while you prepare the filling.

To make the filling: Heat the oil in a large, heavy saucepan. Add the onion, carrots, and celery and cook over medium heat, stirring occasionally, for 7 to 8 minutes, or until the onion softens. Sprinkle the vegetables with the flour. Cook, stirring, for 1 minute. Gradually stir in the hot stock. Add the celery leaves, parsley, and seasonings. Cook over medium–low heat, stirring frequently, for about 8 minutes, or until the gravy has thickened and the carrots are barely tender. Stir in the chicken, potatoes, and peas.

Preheat the oven to 375°. Lightly oil or spray a 10-inch deep-dish pie pan or ceramic or glass baking dish.

Pour the filling into the prepared pan. Set aside.

On a lightly floured board, roll out the chilled pastry to an 11- to 12-inch circle. Place the pastry atop the filling. Trim the edges of the pastry and press the pastry against the rim of the pie pan so it sticks. Crimp the edges of the dough or press with the tines of a fork. Cut several slits in the top of the pie. Brush with skim milk, if desired (this helps the crust brown).

Bake for 35 to 45 minutes, or until the crust is golden and the filling is bubbly. Let stand 5 minutes before serving.

---

312 calories, 11.5 g fat, 5 g saturated fat,
49 mg cholesterol, 6 g dietary fiber, 281 mg sodium

Southwestern Turkey Club Pinwheels

The turkey club sandwich gets a different treatment when the fixings (leaner than usual, of course) are zipped up with southwestern seasonings and rolled in a tortilla. This makes a good party appetizer; the recipe can be doubled. You can save some time by skipping the cilantro, garlic, and jalapeño and mixing the cream cheese with 1 tablespoon of bottled salsa.

If you'd rather just serve these to 2 to 4 people for lunch, don't cut them into pinwheels.

Makes 24 pieces; 8 appetizer servings

3 tablespoons light cream cheese

¼ cup finely minced red onion

*1 tablespoon minced fresh
  cilantro*

1 clove garlic, minced

*½ small jalapeño pepper, seeded
  and finely minced*

*4 low-fat whole wheat flour
  tortillas (made with oil, not
  vegetable shortening)*

*4 strips lean turkey bacon, fried
  until crisp and finely chopped*

*4 ounces roasted, thinly sliced
  turkey breast*

*1 tomato, sliced as thinly as
  possible and seeded*

1 cup shredded lettuce

In a small bowl, mix the cream cheese, onion, cilantro, garlic, and jalapeño until well blended.

Spread the cream cheese mixture thinly and evenly over the tortillas, covering them to the edges. Sprinkle the chopped bacon evenly over the cream cheese mixture. Layer the sliced turkey, then the tomato, evenly over the tortillas, stopping the fillings about 1 inch short of the top of the tortilla round. Sprinkle with the lettuce, again stopping about 1 inch short of the top. Starting at the bottom of one tortilla, roll up as tightly as possible. Roll the remaining tortillas. Trim the ends of the tortilla rolls, then use a very sharp knife to cut each tortilla roll into 6 pieces. Arrange the pinwheels, cut side up, on a platter. Cover with plastic wrap and refrigerate until serving. Serve within 4 hours of assembling the tortilla pinwheels.

*136 calories, 4.5 g fat, 1 g saturated fat,
22 mg cholesterol, 1.5 g dietary fiber, 223 mg sodium*

Summer Breakfast Burritos

Long favorites in casual eateries in the Southwest, breakfast burritos have spread around the rest of the country as well. Often, these behemoths are stuffed with cheese, sausage, and enough fat to slow you down before you even start the day. This slimmer version is tasty, hearty, and much better for you—the perfect solution for a weekend breakfast for two—or serve it as a light dinner with a salad.

For a winter burrito, omit the tomato and zucchini and use only potatoes.

Makes 2 servings

2 teaspoons olive oil

1 small baking potato, cut into
   ¼-inch dice (about 1 cup)

½ cup seeded, diced fresh tomato

½ cup diced zucchini

1 small serrano pepper, seeded
   and minced

1 teaspoon minced fresh cilantro,
   or a pinch of dried oregano

2 eggs

2 egg whites, or ¼ cup egg
   substitute

Salt

Freshly ground black pepper

2 low-fat whole wheat flour
   tortillas

Nonfat sour cream, as needed

Salsa, as needed

Coat a frying pan with nonstick cooking spray, add the olive oil, and heat. Add the potato and cook over medium heat, stirring occasionally, for 7 to 8 minutes, or until golden and tender.

Add the tomato, zucchini, serrano pepper, and cilantro. Cook for 1 to 2 minutes, until just heated through. With a fork, whisk the eggs with the egg whites, then add to the vegetables. Cook over medium-low heat, stirring, until the eggs are softly set. Remove from the heat. Season with salt and pepper to taste.

In another frying pan or griddle, heat the tortillas until warmed through. Spread each tortilla with about a tablespoon of nonfat sour cream and/or salsa, if desired. Spoon the egg-vegetable mixture down the center of each tortilla, and roll the tortilla. Place the burritos on plates, seam side down. Serve immediately, with additional salsa, if desired.

---

200 calories, 10 g fat, 2 g saturated fat,
212 mg cholesterol, 2 g dietary fiber, 392 mg sodium

Spicy Chinese Cabbage with Seitan
(Wheat Gluten)

Wheat gluten is a traditional ingredient in Buddha's Delight and other Chinese and Japanese vegetarian dishes. Here, it gets a Sichuan accent. Seitan that has been seasoned with soy, garlic, and ginger is available in tubs or jars in health food stores and some supermarkets. Serve hot with rice.

Makes 4 servings

8 ounces soy sauce–seasoned
seitan, drained and patted dry

1 medium head (about 2 pounds)
Chinese cabbage

1 tablespoon plus 1 teaspoon
canola oil

2 tablespoons rice wine, sake, or
sherry

2 tablespoons water or vegetable
stock

1 teaspoon dark sesame oil

1 teaspoon hot red pepper flakes

2 tablespoons minced fresh ginger

1 tablespoon soy sauce

2 teaspoons black Chinese
vinegar or balsamic vinegar

1 tablespoon packed dark brown
sugar

1 tablespoon cornstarch

¼ teaspoon salt (optional)

Cut the seitan into ⅛-inch slices, then into narrow strips. Trim the cabbage and cut crosswise into narrow strips.

Heat a wok. Add the 1 tablespoon canola oil and heat until very hot. Add the seitan and stir-fry until golden. Remove to a large bowl and set aside. Heat the 1 teaspoon canola oil in the wok and add the cabbage. Stir-fry for 30 seconds. Add 1 tablespoon of the wine and all of the water, and stir-fry for 1 to 1½ minutes, just until the cabbage begins to wilt. Remove the cabbage to the bowl with the seitan.

Wipe out the wok, add the sesame oil and heat. Add the hot red pepper flakes and stir-fry a few seconds until it turns dark. Add the ginger and stir-fry for a few seconds. Add the cabbage and seitan and stir-fry to heat through. Whisk together the soy sauce, the remaining 1 tablespoon wine, and the vinegar, brown sugar, cornstarch, and salt, if using. Add to the cabbage and seitan and cook until the sauce thickens and coats the cabbage.

*173 calories, 6 g fat, 0.5 g saturated fat, no cholesterol,
2.5 g dietary fiber, 393 mg sodium*

Warm Focaccia Goat Cheese Sandwich

No one's sure if focaccia is the precursor to pizza or was invented to make use of left-over pizza dough. Whatever its origins, this dimpled Italian flatbread is enjoying a renaissance in the United States.

The filling in this is delicious but fairly high in saturated fat. You could omit the filling and serve the focaccia alone.

Makes one 10- to 12-inch focaccia; 6 servings

1 package (2¼ teaspoons) active
   dry yeast
½ cup warm water (110° to 115°)
1 teaspoon sugar
1¾ cups bread flour, plus more as
   needed

1 cup whole wheat flour
1 tablespoon olive oil
½ teaspoon salt

CHEESE FILLING

5 ounces plain goat cheese,
   crumbled
4 ounces light cream cheese
3 tablespoons nonfat sour cream

¼ cup chopped red onion
¼ cup minced fresh parsley
¼ teaspoon freshly ground black
   pepper

TOPPING

2½ tablespoons olive oil
½ cup chopped red onion
¼ cup chopped fresh basil
¾ cup reconstituted dried
   tomatoes (see page 16),
   chopped

½ teaspoon salt
½ teaspoon freshly ground black
   pepper

Dissolve the yeast in the warm water with the sugar and let stand until bubbly, about 5 minutes.

In the large bowl of an electric mixer fitted with the dough hook, or using a food processor, mix the flours, oil, and salt. Pour in the yeast mixture and mix until a soft, somewhat sticky dough is formed, a few minutes in the mixer or about 10 seconds in a processor. Turn the dough out onto a lightly floured pastry cloth and knead until smooth, a few minutes. Lift the sides of the cloth to help in the kneading process. It might be necessary to add a few tablespoons of bread flour, 1 tablespoon at a time, to form a soft, somewhat sticky dough.

Put the dough into a bowl, cover lightly with plastic wrap or a damp kitchen towel, and let rise until doubled, about 1½ hours.

While the dough is rising, prepare the cheese filling. Mix the goat cheese, cream cheese, sour cream, red onion, parsley, and pepper together until well blended. Cover and refrigerate until ready to use.

Punch down the dough and let stand for 5 minutes. Knead the dough on a lightly floured pastry cloth or board for 1 minute.

Meanwhile, prepare the topping. Heat 1 tablespoon of the olive oil in a sprayed nonstick frying pan. Cook the onion, partially covered, until soft, stirring occasionally, about 5 minutes. Stir in the basil, chopped tomatoes, salt, and pepper. Remove from the heat and set aside.

Preheat the oven to 450°. Shape the dough into a 10- to 12-inch circle in a sprayed ovenproof frying pan or on a sprayed nonstick baking sheet. Press the dough lightly all over with your thumb to make indentations.

Brush the dough with the remaining 1½ tablespoons oil, starting around the edges. Sprinkle with the onion-tomato mixture.

Bake in the center of the oven for 12 to 15 minutes or until the focaccia is golden brown around the edges and cooked through. Unmold onto a wire rack. When the focaccia is cool enough to handle, cut horizontally with a serrated knife. Spread with the cheese filling and replace the top of the focaccia. Slice into wedges and serve warm.

426 calories, 19 g fat, 7.5 g saturated fat,
28 mg cholesterol, 5 g dietary fiber, 659 mg sodium
Without the cheese filling: 292 calories, 9 g fat,
1 g saturated fat, no cholesterol, 5 g dietary fiber, 482 mg sodium

Whole Wheat Molasses-Raisin Bread

This bread uses all whole wheat flour, making it denser and more flavorful than breads made with a combination of whole wheat and white flours. Also, it will take longer to rise. The addition of the raisins makes this bread almost like a cake.

Makes 1 loaf; about 14 servings

1 package (2¼ teaspoons) active
   dry yeast
¾ cup warm water (100° to 115°)
2 teaspoons sugar
1 cup warm skim milk
⅓ cup molasses
2 tablespoons canola oil
¾ teaspoon salt

3½ to 4 cups stone-ground whole
   wheat flour
1 cup dark raisins
1 egg white, lightly beaten
1 teaspoon water
2 tablespoons sesame seeds
   (optional)

In a medium-size bowl, dissolve the yeast in the warm water mixed with the sugar. Let stand until foamy, about 5 minutes.

While the yeast is proofing, mix together the warm milk, molasses, oil, and salt. Add the yeast mixture. Mix in just enough whole wheat flour to make a soft, somewhat sticky dough. The dough will feel damp, tacky, and slightly rough.

Using a heavy-duty electric mixer fitted with the dough hook, knead the dough until smooth and springy. Or knead the dough by hand for a few minutes on a lightly floured pastry cloth or tea towel. Knead this soft dough by lifting the sides of the cloth and folding the dough and rolling it around on the cloth. Put the dough in a bowl, cover with plastic wrap or a damp kitchen towel, and let rise in a draft-free area until doubled in bulk, about 1½ hours.

Spray a 9-by-5-inch loaf pan. Punch down the dough, mix in the raisins, and shape into a loaf. Set the dough in the prepared pan. Lightly cover the dough and let rise until it reaches at least to the top of the pan.

Preheat the oven to 375.°

Brush the top of the loaf with the egg white mixed with the water and sprinkle with the sesame seeds, if desired. Bake for 45 minutes or until the bread makes a hollow sound when tapped. Turn the bread out onto a wire rack to cool.

196 calories, 3 g fat, 0.5 g saturated fat, no cholesterol,
5 g dietary fiber, 133 mg sodium

Cracked Wheat in Whole Wheat Bread

We have tried three styles of preparing whole wheat bread: making it with all whole wheat flour, producing a heavy, dense loaf; preparing it as we do here with almost half bread flour and half stone-ground whole wheat flour to yield a light, high loaf that's good for sandwiches; and using a sponge of 1 cup bread flour mixed with proofed yeast, with the remaining flour added later, producing a somewhat heavy yet delicious bread.

Makes 1 loaf; about 12 servings

1 package (2¼ teaspoons) active
*   dry yeast*
¼ cup warm water (110° to 115°)
1 teaspoon sugar
1 cup warm skim milk
2 tablespoons canola oil
2 tablespoons honey, preferably
*   clover, at room temperature*
1 teaspoon salt

1½ cups bread flour, plus more as
*   needed*
2 cups stone-ground whole wheat
*   flour*
⅓ cup uncooked millet (optional)
⅓ cup cooked, drained cracked
*   wheat, at room temperature*
1 egg white, lightly beaten
1 teaspoon water

In a small bowl, dissolve the yeast in the warm water mixed with the sugar. Let stand until foamy, about 5 minutes.

While the yeast is proofing, in a bowl combine the warm milk, oil, honey, and salt. Stir in the proofed yeast. Mix in the bread flour and whole wheat flour. Add the millet, if using, and the cracked wheat. The dough should be moist but not wet. Knead the dough using a heavy-duty mixer fitted with the dough hook, or turn out onto a lightly floured pastry cloth and knead by hand for a few minutes, until the dough feels smooth.

Put the dough in a bowl, cover with plastic wrap or a damp kitchen towel, and let rise in a draft-free area until doubled in size, about 1 hour.

Spray a 9-by-5-inch loaf pan. Punch down the dough, and shape it into a loaf. Set the dough in the prepared pan. Again cover the dough with plastic wrap or a damp towel and let rise until it reaches at least to the top of the pan, about 1 hour.

Preheat the oven to 375°. Mix the egg white with the water and brush the top of the bread (this makes the top of the bread shinier).

Bake for 45 minutes or until the bread makes a hollow sound when tapped on the bottom. Remove the bread from the pan. Let cool on a wire rack.

---

186 calories, 3.5 g fat, 0.5 g saturated fat,
1 mg cholesterol, 3.5 g dietary fiber, 194 mg sodium

Wheat Germ Whole Wheat Bread

This recipe is prepared with a yeast "sponge," which gives the bread a fuller flavor. Eat one loaf now, and wrap and freeze the other.

Makes 2 loaves; about 20 servings

SPONGE

3 cups warm water (110° to 115°)

2 packages (4½ teaspoons) active
   dry yeast

1 cup bread flour

⅓ packed dark brown sugar

¼ cup canola oil

1½ teaspoons salt

½ cup toasted wheat germ

3 to 4 cups stone-ground whole
   wheat flour

1 egg white, lightly beaten

1 teaspoon water

3 tablespoons poppy seeds

To make the sponge: Put 1 cup of the warm water in a bowl, and mix in the yeast and flour using a wooden spoon. Cover with plastic wrap and let the sponge stand on the counter in a draft-free area for 30 minutes or until it is light and bubbly.

In a large bowl, mix together the remaining 2 cups warm water and the sugar, oil, and salt. Stir in the risen sponge, the wheat germ, and the flour, 1 cup at a time. You want the dough to be damp and slightly sticky. Knead the dough using a heavy-duty mixer fitted with the dough hook, or knead by hand on a lightly floured pastry cloth or tea towel for a few minutes, until smooth yet soft. Put the dough in a bowl, cover with plastic wrap or a damp kitchen towel, and set to rise in a draft-free area until doubled in bulk, about 1½ hours.

Spray two 9-by-5-inch loaf pans or 8-inch cake pans. Punch down the dough, and shape into 2 loaves. Set the dough in the pans, cover lightly, and let rise until doubled in bulk.

Preheat the oven to 375°. Brush the tops of the loaves with the lightly beaten egg white mixed with the water, then sprinkle with the poppy seeds. Bake in the center of the oven for 40 to 50 minutes or until the bread makes a hollow sound when tapped. Remove the loaves from the pans. Let cool on a wire rack.

158 calories, 4 g fat, 0.5 g saturated fat, no cholesterol,
4 g dietary fiber, 166 mg sodium

Braided Sesame Seed Loaves

This recipe is from Elizabeth Clark, who is famous for her cooking classes and is considered the "first lady of Iowa cuisine." She successfully integrates local ingredients, such as Nauvoo flour, with popular trends.

Braiding bread dough is no more difficult than making the pigtails of childhood. Instead of starting at one end, cross the three strips of dough in the center and braid outward. This will assure you of a more even finish at each end.

To toast sesame seeds, spread them out in a single layer in a shallow baking pan and toast in a 350° oven for 8 to 10 minutes, stirring once, until the sesame seeds are a light golden color and smell nutty. Be sure to allow them to cool before using.

Makes 2 loaves; about 20 servings

1 package (2¼ teaspoons) active
    dry yeast
2½ cups warm water (110° to
    115°)
1 tablespoon sugar
1 tablespoon sea salt
2 cups stone-ground whole wheat
    flour

2¼ to 3 cups unbleached all-
    purpose flour
1 cup toasted sesame seeds
2 tablespoons cornmeal
1 egg white, lightly beaten with
    1 teaspoon water

In the large bowl of an electric mixer fitted with the dough hook, dissolve the yeast in ½ cup of the warm water with the sugar. Stir with a wire whisk and allow to foam. Stir in the remaining 2 cups warm water and the sea salt, then add the whole wheat flour and enough of the unbleached flour to make a workable, soft dough. Add ¾ cup of the toasted sesame seeds. Knead the batter with the dough hook until the mixture forms a ball and cleans the sides of the bowl. The dough should be wet and sticky.

Place the dough in an oiled bowl and turn to coat. Cover with a tea towel or plastic wrap. Place in a warm spot and allow to rise until doubled in bulk, about 1 hour.

Turn the dough out onto a floured surface and divide into 6 pieces. Braid 3 of the pieces together, then twist into a circle. Braid the other 3 pieces together, but don't form into a circle. Cover lightly and let rise a second time, about 1 hour.

Preheat the oven to 400°. Spray a large cookie sheet and sprinkle with the cornmeal.

Brush the loaves with the egg white mixture and sprinkle with the remaining ¼ cup toasted sesame seeds. Place on the prepared cookie sheet. Bake for 30 minutes or until the loaves sound hollow when tapped. Let the bread cool on wire racks.

---

157 calories, 4.5 g fat, 0.5 g saturated fat, no cholesterol,
2.5 g dietary fiber, 327 mg sodium

Whole Wheat Spaghetti Bread

The idea for this bread came years ago when Barbara's daughter Dorothy was young. It was a school holiday, and mother and daughter were making bread. To make it more interesting for Dorothy, Barbara tossed some leftover, sauced spaghetti into the dough. The results were delicious and interesting.

Makes 1 loaf; about 12 servings

1½ cups warm water (110° to
   115°)

1 package (2¼ teaspoons) active
   dry yeast

1½ cups bread flour

3 tablespoons packed dark brown
   sugar

2 tablespoons unsalted butter or
   margarine, melted and cooled

1 teaspoon salt

3 cups stone-ground whole wheat
   flour

⅓ cup cold cooked whole wheat
   spaghetti, with a small
   amount of tomato sauce
   clinging to it (see page 53)

Olive oil, as needed

1 teaspoon dried onion flakes

1 teaspoon dried oregano

To make the sponge: Put ½ cup of the warm water in a glass bowl. Mix in the yeast and ½ cup of the bread flour using a wooden spoon. Cover the sponge with plastic wrap and let it stand in a warm, draft-free area for 30 minutes or until it has risen and is bubbling.

Mix together the remaining 1 cup warm water and the brown sugar, melted butter, and salt. Stir in the risen sponge and the flours, 1 cup at a time, to form a very damp, somewhat sticky dough. Turn the dough out onto a lightly floured board, and knead for a few minutes by folding the dough over itself until it is smooth. Put the dough in a bowl, cover with plastic wrap or a damp kitchen towel, and let rise in a warm, draft-free area until doubled in size, about 1½ hours.

Punch down the dough and press it out on a lightly floured board. Spread single strands of the spaghetti over the dough. Roll up the dough and place in a sprayed 9-by-5-inch loaf pan. Lightly cover the dough and let rise until it has doubled in bulk, about 1 hour and 15 minutes.

Preheat the oven to 375°.

Brush the loaf with olive oil and sprinkle with the dried onion flakes and oregano. Bake in the center of the oven for 45 minutes or until the bread makes a hollow sound when tapped. Remove from the pan. Let cool on a wire rack.

200 calories, 3.5 g fat, 1.5 g saturated fat,
5 mg cholesterol, 4.5 g dietary fiber, 188 mg sodium

New England Blueberry Pancakes with Maple Syrup

Try to use small, very ripe blueberries in this recipe. Rinse them well, and drain thoroughly on paper towels. In the winter, you can use dried blueberries, which do not need to be rinsed.

Makes 24 pancakes; 6 to 8 servings

1 cup unbleached all-purpose flour
¾ cup whole wheat flour
3 tablespoons packed light brown sugar
2 teaspoons baking powder
½ teaspoon salt
½ cup egg substitute, or 2 eggs, lightly beaten

1 tablespoon unsalted butter or margarine, melted and cooled
1½ cups skim milk
1 cup fresh blueberries, or ½ cup dried blueberries
1 tablespoon canola oil

In a bowl, combine the all-purpose flour, whole wheat flour, sugar, baking powder, and salt. Add the egg substitute, butter, and milk, and stir until smooth. Mix in the blueberries. Let the batter stand 20 minutes at room temperature. (This allows the flour to "relax" and absorb the liquid, making the pancakes more tender.) Stir before using.

Heat the oil in a nonstick frying pan over medium heat. Pour the pancake batter, about 3 tablespoons at a time, into the frying pan, being careful not to crowd the pancakes. Cook until bubbles form on the top and the edges are firm. Flip the pancakes and cook until the other side is golden.

Serve hot with maple syrup or blueberry syrup.

391 calories, 13 g fat, 6 g saturated fat, 25 mg cholesterol,
4.5 g dietary fiber, 594 mg sodium

Banana Bread with Dried Fruits

You can vary the mixture of dried fruits to taste.

Makes 1 loaf; about 10 servings

3 ripe medium bananas (about
   1 cup)
½ cup packed dark brown sugar
⅓ cup granulated sugar
¼ cup unsalted butter or
   margarine, at room
   temperature
2 egg whites, or 1 egg, lightly
   beaten

½ teaspoon salt
1¾ cups whole wheat pastry flour
1 teaspoon baking powder
1 teaspoon baking soda
1 teaspoon ground cinnamon
¼ cup currants
¼ cup golden raisins
¼ cup chopped dried apricots
¼ cup skim milk

Preheat the oven to 350°.

Mash the bananas until smooth. With an electric mixer beat together the brown sugar, sugar, butter, egg whites, and salt. Mix in the mashed banana.

Stir in the whole wheat pastry flour, baking powder, baking soda, and cinnamon. Add the currants, raisins, apricots, and milk, and stir to combine. The batter will be of medium density.

Pour the batter into a sprayed 8-by-4-inch loaf pan. Bake in the center of the oven for 1 hour or until the bread feels firm and a tester inserted in the center comes out dry.

Let the bread cool for 5 minutes, then remove it from the pan and let cool completely on a wire rack.

192 calories, 4.5 g fat, 2.5 g saturated fat,
10 mg cholesterol, 3.5 g dietary fiber, 202 mg sodium

Small Graham Apple Muffins

These are sized just right for a party.

Makes about 30 small muffins

1 cup stone-ground whole wheat
   flour
½ cup whole wheat pastry flour
1½ teaspoons baking powder
¾ teaspoon baking soda
½ teaspoon salt
¼ cup egg substitute, or 2 egg
   whites, lightly beaten

⅓ cup packed dark brown sugar
⅓ cup canola oil
¾ cup buttermilk
½ teaspoon vanilla
1½ cups peeled, cored, and finely
   chopped cooking or all–
   purpose apples, such as
   Granny Smith

Preheat the oven to 400°. Insert paper liners in miniature muffin pans. Set aside.

In a large bowl, combine the whole wheat flour, pastry flour, baking powder, baking soda, and salt.

Stir in the egg substitute, brown sugar, oil, buttermilk, vanilla, and apples just until mixed. Do not overbeat.

Spoon the mixture into the muffin cups, filling about three-quarters full. Bake in the center of the oven for 15 minutes or until the muffins are firm and a tester inserted in the center of a muffin comes out dry.

Cool the muffins on a wire rack. The muffins are best served warm.

55 calories, 2.5 g fat, no saturated fat, no cholesterol,
1 g dietary fiber, 90 mg sodium

Homemade Honey Graham Crackers

The graham crackers sold in stores bear the name of health pioneer Sylvester Graham but little of his spirit, since they're made mostly with refined white flour. These are whole grain and delicious.

To make these more fun for kids, use special cookie cutters to cut them into shapes such as dinosaurs, hearts, or teddy bears.

Makes about 36 three-inch crackers

⅓ cup unsalted butter or
   margarine, at room
   temperature
2 cups stone-ground whole wheat
   flour
½ teaspoon cream of tartar
1 teaspoon baking soda

¼ cup egg substitute, or 1 egg
¼ cup honey
¼ cup hot water, plus more as
   needed
¼ cup sugar (optional)
2 teaspoons ground cinnamon
   (optional)

Preheat the oven to 350°.

In a food processor or mixing bowl, cut the butter into the flour until crumbly. Add the cream of tartar, baking soda, egg substitute, and honey, and combine. Add enough water to form a soft dough.

On a lightly floured pastry cloth or pastry board, roll out the dough to ⅛-inch thickness. Cut into 3-inch rounds.

Transfer the rounds to a nonstick baking sheet with a spatula. If desired, combine the sugar and cinnamon and sprinkle over the unbaked crackers. Bake for 12 to 15 minutes or until the crackers begin to brown around the edges. Remove to a wire rack and let cool before serving.

46 calories, 2 g fat, 1 g saturated fat, 4 mg cholesterol,
1 g dietary fiber, 26 mg sodium

Apple Betty

An apple betty, a popular New England fall dessert, is applesauce or sliced apples baked in a crumb crust. Sometimes bread crumbs are used, but we like graham cracker crumbs. Barbara's mother would sprinkle an additional layer of graham cracker crumbs over the top of the apple betty and serve it spooned into a shallow dessert dish and topped with sweetened whipped cream.(This is also good with low-fat vanilla yogurt or ice cream.)

If you'd rather not bother with making your own applesauce, you can use a top-quality bottled applesauce.

Makes 6 servings

CRUST

*1½ cups graham cracker crumbs
   (preferably from homemade
   graham crackers; see page 42)*
¼ cup sugar

½ teaspoon cinnamon
*¼ cup unsalted butter or
   margarine, melted and cooled*

APPLESAUCE

*3 pounds cooking apples (such as
   Granny Smith), peeled, cored,
   and chopped*
1 cup sugar

½ cup dry white wine
2 teaspoons grated lemon zest
1 teaspoon ground cinnamon

To make the crust: Reserve ¼ cup of the crumbs for the top of the apple betty, and set aside. In a bowl, toss the remaining 1¼ cups crumbs with the sugar, cinnamon, and butter. Pat the crumb mixture firmly into a 9-inch pie plate.

To make the applesauce: Put the apples, sugar, wine, lemon zest, and cinnamon in a large saucepan. Simmer, partially covered, until the apples are soft. Continue cooking for about 20 to 30 minutes, stirring occasionally with a wooden spoon and adding water as necessary to keep the applesauce moist. Let cool, then puree the applesauce with a potato masher, food mill, or food processor. Taste to adjust the seasonings.

Preheat the oven to 350°.

Spoon the cooled applesauce into the prepared graham cracker crust. Sprinkle the reserved crumbs over the applesauce.

Bake the apple betty in the center of the oven for 25 to 30 minutes. Serve warm.

*492 calories, 11.5 g fat, 5.5 g saturated fat,
21 mg cholesterol, 5 g dietary fiber, 183 mg sodium*

Chocolate-Cherry Farina Pudding

Although many Americans know farina only as a breakfast cereal, the Greeks and others use it in desserts. Here, farina grows irresistible with the addition of chocolate and cherries.

Makes 8 servings

1 can (16 ounces) dark cherries, including juice
3 cups skim milk, as needed
⅓ cup unsweetened cocoa
¾ cup sugar
¾ cup farina, preferably whole grain

1 tablespoon kirsch or cherry liqueur (optional)
Light whipped cream (optional)
Dried cherries for garnish (optional)

Lightly grease an 8-by-4-inch loaf pan.

Drain the cherries, reserving the juice into a measuring cup. Add enough skim milk to measure 4 cups of liquid. Set the cherries aside.

In a saucepan over low heat, combine the cocoa with ½ cup of the liquid, whisking until the mixture is smooth. Stir in the remaining liquid. Add the sugar and bring the mixture to a boil. Lower the heat and whisk in the farina. Simmer, whisking often, until the farina is cooked through and the pudding is very thick, about 4 to 5 minutes. Blend in the reserved cherries and the kirsch, if using. Pour the pudding into the prepared pan and smooth the top of the pudding with the back of a spoon. Loosely cover the pudding with aluminum foil and refrigerate for 2 hours or until firm.

When ready to serve, use a sharp knife to cut the pudding into 8 slices. If desired, garnish with whipped cream and dried cherries, if using.

220 calories, 1 g fat, 0.5 g saturated fat,
1.5 mg cholesterol, 2 g dietary fiber, 50 mg sodium

Orange Farina Pudding with Raspberry
Sauce and Pistachios

This very light pudding takes on the flavors of California, where oranges, raspberries, and pistachios are all major crops.

Makes 4 to 6 servings

2 cups skim milk

½ teaspoon salt

2 tablespoons grated orange or
    lemon zest

¼ cup sugar

⅓ cup plus 1 tablespoon farina

2 tablespoons ground pistachios

SAUCE

2 cups fresh or defrosted
    raspberries

¼ to ½ cup fresh orange juice or
    water

½ cup sugar

1 tablespoon cornstarch, dissolved
    in ¼ cup water

⅛ teaspoon ground ginger

⅛ teaspoon ground nutmeg

Pour the milk into a saucepan with the salt, zest, and sugar. Bring the mixture to a boil over medium heat. Whisk in the farina and return the mixture to a boil, whisking constantly to prevent lumping.

Reduce the heat to low and continue cooking 8 to 10 minutes, whisking occasionally, until the pudding is thick. Remove from the heat.

While the pudding is cooking, prepare the sauce: Put the berries, orange juice (use ¼ cup with frozen berries, ½ cup with fresh), and sugar in a small saucepan. Simmer for a few minutes, until the ingredients are mixed together and hot. Stir in the cornstarch mixture and spices. Cook, stirring occasionally, until the sauce thickens slightly and is clear. If the sauce seems too thick, thin with a little water. Let cool. Sauce can be made ahead of time and refrigerated. Warm up before serving.

To serve, spoon the warm pudding into shallow dessert dishes, drizzle with the sauce, and sprinkle with the ground pistachios. Pass any remaining sauce at the table.

234 calories, 3 g fat, 0.5 g saturated fat, 2 mg cholesterol,
3 g dietary fiber, 221 mg sodium

Durum and Semolina, Pasta and Noodles, and Couscous

Durum and Semolina

Durum, a hard spring wheat, has one characteristic that endears it to cooks—it does not fall apart in water. In other words, it's perfect for pasta.

North Dakota grows virtually all of the country's durum wheat, trailed by Montana, Arizona, and southern California. Although it accounts for only about one twenty-fifth of the nation's total wheat acreage, durum acreage is increasing as pasta and couscous grow ever more popular.

Durum flour is called semolina, and labels on pasta packages use "durum flour" and "semolina" interchangeably. Semolina is granular, like farina, but ground more finely. It has a lovely golden hue and makes attractive breads and pizza crusts. It's too hard and chewy to be used alone in breads and must be mixed with regular flour. Semolina is sold in bulk or in bags and is often labeled as pasta flour, even though recipes for homemade fettuccine or other egg noodles nearly always call for the more tender regular wheat flour.

Pasta and Noodles

Thomas Jefferson brought pasta back with him from Italy, but the "spaghetti" his cooks made was really an egg noodle. America's first pasta factory finally opened in Brooklyn, New York, in 1848, but durum wheat, imported from Russia, was not planted in the United States until after the Civil War. Pasta didn't really take off in the United States until the great wave of immigrants arrived from southern Italy in the late nineteenth and early twentieth centuries.

Today, the average American puts away about twenty pounds of pasta per year.

Traditionally, Italians divide pasta into two categories, dried and fresh. Macaroni in various shapes (bows, corkscrews, elbows, shells, and so on) and spaghetti are factory-extruded pastas made of semolina and water. Tender egg noodles such as fettuccine, tagliarini, lasagna, and ravioli are freshly made—either at home or in a local shop—with regular wheat flour, water, and eggs.

In the real world, of course, cooks crave convenience. So American supermarkets carry dried fettuccine and lasagna noodles, made with semolina and water and sometimes egg. The reliance on semolina, which is sturdier than regular wheat flour and holds up better in shipping and storage, has carried over to fresh pastas, which increasingly are made with durum, rather than regular, wheat flour.

Most types of pasta come in whole wheat varieties as well, although many supermarkets banish whole wheat spaghetti to the "health food" aisle. Health food stores carry a greater variety of whole wheat pastas, as well as alternative, nonwheat pastas.

Origin bears little relationship to quality. When a panel of experts at one cooking magazine put pastas to the taste test, an old American brand won first place hands down. The same holds true for price; we've had one-dollar-a-pound rotini that were better crafted than four-dollar-a-pound "boutique" varieties.

We don't think there's enough difference between "fresh" refrigerated noodles and dried pasta to justify the former's high price. Ravioli and similar filled noodles are an exception; they don't work as dried or, heaven forbid, canned noodles, and must be purchased fresh, refrigerated, or frozen. Refrigerated ravioli are a good-tasting, wonderfully convenient food. If you're after fresh fettuccine or similar egg noodles, we suggest making your own or buying them from a shop that makes them.

Asian-style egg noodles, such as ramen, udon, and mein, are usually made of softer wheat flour, with or without eggs. Like pasta, Asian egg noodles come both dried and fresh. They are not as chewy as Italian pasta and should be cooked until tender.

Dried pasta, even the whole wheat variety, keeps nearly forever. Once the bag is opened, store pasta in airtight containers. Keep it away from moisture.

Fresh pasta should be refrigerated and used as quickly as possible. Except for filled noodles such as ravioli or wontons, we do not recommend freezing, as it will turn the pasta sticky and mushy.

The package directions, especially on American brands, often call for overly long cooking times. Dried pasta made from durum flour (semolina) should be cooked al dente—"to the tooth." It's done when it's no longer hard and starchy in the center but still has plenty of chew. Because it contains the bran, whole wheat pasta has a slightly more fragile texture and definitely should not be overcooked.

The al dente rule applies only to dried pasta. Fresh noodles made from regular flour and eggs should be tender. In fact, if the noodles are really fresh, it's nearly impossible to cook them al dente; they'll be tender within seconds of when the water returns to a boil.

Cook both dried and fresh pasta in plenty of boiling water, at least 5 quarts per pound of pasta, to keep it from sticking. You can salt the water or not, as you wish. Do not add oil to the water; it coats the pasta and makes the sauce slide off. Drain the cooked pasta briefly; it should still be a little wet when you put it in the bowl. The moisture helps thin out the sauce so it coats the pasta evenly. Overdraining pasta makes it gummy.

Couscous

Think of couscous as baby pasta. Like Italian pasta, couscous (KOOS-koos) is made of semolina, but unlike other pastas, couscous cooks into a light, fluffy mass.

Couscous originated in northern Africa, especially Morocco. Patient African cooks would make couscous from scratch, an art that puts ravioli making to shame. The couscous maker would moisten semolina with a little water and salt, then roll it with the palms of her hands, adding flour and more water and salt at intervals, to form progressively smaller grains. She would sort the grains by size. Then she would put the couscous in the top of a steamer and steam it over a stew or water containing vegetables or spices. Finally, she would separate the couscous grains and either sprinkle the couscous with cold water to allow it to swell and get fluffy or spread it on a cloth and dry it in the sun for later use.

It's not difficult to see why most cooks, here and in Morocco, prefer buying couscous to making it. The couscous we buy in boxes—or in bulk—has already been rolled, steamed, and dried. We especially like the nutty flavor of whole wheat couscous, which is made of whole grain durum flour and often rolled with brown rice flour.

Couscous is now produced in large quantities in the United States and shows up nearly everywhere, from restaurant menus to the supermarket shelf, in an assortment of flavors. Unfortunately it's fallen prey to America's love affair with badly seasoned boxed goods and tends to come packaged with indifferent spice mixes in overpriced little boxes.

Health food stores are a good source for couscous in bulk and usually have the whole wheat variety, which tastes great and cooks just as quickly as the regular variety.

Regular couscous, like pasta, will keep virtually forever. The whole wheat kind is more perishable; store it in a cool place and use it within a couple of months.

You don't actually cook couscous, you steep it. Use 1½ cups liquid—water, broth, or juice—to 1 cup couscous. Bring the liquid to a boil. Remove from the heat and stir in the couscous. Cover the pan tightly and let sit, undisturbed, for about 5 to 7 minutes, or until the couscous has absorbed all the liquid. Fluff with a fork.

For a softer consistency, you can use slightly more liquid and cook the couscous, covered, over low heat for 15 minutes after adding it to the boiling liquid. Couscous cooked this way makes a good breakfast porridge.

Generally, there's no reason to cook couscous in a microwave, unless you're making it for breakfast and want to dirty just one bowl. Place ¾ cup water or skim milk in a microwaveproof bowl and cook on high for 1 to 2 minutes, until steaming hot. Stir in ½ cup couscous. Return to the microwave and cook on high, stirring twice, for 2 to 3 minutes, or until the couscous has absorbed most of the liquid. Let stand for 2 to 3 minutes.

Like pasta, couscous is bland and goes with just about anything, from tomato sauce to chicken gravy. Unlike macaroni, it's a good breakfast cereal. Just add brown sugar, maple syrup, cinnamon, raisins, or whatever you like.

Durum and Semolina, Pasta and Noodles, and Couscous

Grilled Vegetables with Whole Wheat Lasagna

Whole Wheat Spaghetti with Quick Tomato-Basil Sauce

Pasta with Broccoli, Raisins, and Walnuts

Chicken Lo Mein with Vegetables

Orzo Salad with Olives, Feta Cheese, Spinach, and Tomatoes

Whole Wheat Couscous, Vegetables, and Mediterranean Spices

Couscous and Tuna Salad with Beans, Tomatoes, and Capers

Clam and Leek Pizza with Semolina Crust

Poppy Seed Noodles

Semolina Bread with Hazelnuts and Dried Tomatoes

Honeyed Couscous with Dried Fruits and Nuts

Grilled Vegetables with Whole Wheat Lasagna

The vegetables can be grilled on an outdoor grill or indoor stove-top grill, or sautéed in a lightly oiled pan. They can be prepared the day before assembling the lasagna, as can the sauce.

Makes 9 to 10 servings

SAUCE

1 tablespoon olive oil, plus more
   as needed
1 cup chopped onion
3 cloves garlic, minced
1 can (28 ounces) crushed
   tomatoes
1 teaspoon dried oregano
1 teaspoon dried basil
½ teaspoon salt, as needed

1 large eggplant, peeled, sliced,
   salted, and drained (see page
   16)
1 large onion, thinly sliced
2 green or red bell peppers, seeded
   and sliced
2 whole tomatoes, sliced
Balsamic vinegar
Salt
Freshly ground black pepper
1 pound dried whole wheat
   lasagna noodles
½ cup grated part-skim
   mozzarella cheese (optional)

To make the sauce: Heat the oil over medium heat in a sprayed nonstick pan. Add the onion and garlic and cook, partially covered, for a few minutes until they are tender, stirring occasionally. Stir in the crushed tomatoes, oregano, basil, and salt. Cook for 20 minutes, stirring occasionally. Remove from the heat and set aside.

Brush the eggplant, onion, peppers, and tomatoes lightly with additional olive oil. Grill on a sprayed grill rack over hot coals. The eggplant will take the longest time to grill, so place it on the grill first. After about 10 minutes, add the remaining vegetables. Grill the vegetables on both sides until tender, basting with additional olive oil as needed. Place the vegetables on a platter and sprinkle with balsamic vinegar, salt, and pepper. Set aside.

Cook noodles according to package directions. Drain the noodles and lay out flat on clean, thin kitchen towels.

Preheat the oven to 375°. To assemble, spread ¾ cup of the prepared sauce on the bottom of a sprayed 9-by-13-inch ovenproof casserole. Top with half of the drained noodles. Layer half the vegetables in overlapping rows over the noodles. Add the rest of the noodles, then top with the remaining vegetables. Spread the remaining sauce over the lasagna and sprinkle with the cheese, if using.

Bake uncovered on the center rack for 40 minutes. Serve hot. The lasagna can be refrigerated overnight and reheated before serving.

285 calories, 8 g fat, 1 g saturated fat, no cholesterol,
9 g dietary fiber, 337 mg sodium

Whole Wheat Spaghetti with Quick Tomato-Basil Sauce

In these days of rushing around, who has time to simmer a tomato sauce for hours? We offer a sauce that tastes as though it has simmered a long time yet takes only about half an hour to prepare and cook. The sauce can be placed in a covered container and refrigerated for up to 5 days.

Makes 4 servings

2 tablespoons olive oil
4 cloves garlic, minced
1 cup chopped onion
1 carrot, peeled and grated
1 can (28 ounces) crushed
*   tomatoes*
2 tablespoons minced fresh basil,
*   or 1 tablespoon dried basil*

2 teaspoons minced fresh oregano,
*   or ½ teaspoon dried oregano*
2 to 4 tablespoons dry red wine
1 teaspoon honey
½ teaspoon salt
¼ teaspoon hot red pepper flakes
1 pound whole wheat spaghetti
Freshly grated Parmesan,
*   Romano, or Asiago cheese*

To make the sauce: In a saucepan, heat the oil over medium heat, and add the garlic, onion, and carrot, cooking partially covered, until the onion is soft. Stir occasionally.

Add the crushed tomatoes, basil, oregano, wine, and honey. Bring the mixture to a simmer and cook for 20 minutes, stirring occasionally. Season with the salt and hot red pepper flakes. Remove the sauce from the heat.

While the sauce is cooking, boil the spaghetti according to package directions, then drain.

Divide the hot spaghetti onto plates. Ladle the sauce over the spaghetti and serve immediately. Pass freshly grated Parmesan, Romano, or Asiago cheese if desired.

552 calories, 11 g fat, 1 g saturated fat, no cholesterol,
13.5 g dietary fiber, 598 mg sodium

Pasta with Broccoli, Raisins, and Walnuts

This dish is for garlic lovers. It's also good with cauliflower or Broccoflower, the lime-green cross between cauliflower and broccoli. You can use spelt, quinoa, or regular pasta instead of whole wheat.

Makes 4 servings

½ pound broccoli florets, cut into
  bite-size pieces
12 ounces whole wheat rotini,
  elbow macaroni, or shells
3 tablespoons olive oil
½ cup coarsely chopped walnuts

¼ cup dark raisins
3 to 4 cloves garlic, minced
Hot red pepper flakes
Salt
Freshly ground black pepper

Bring a large pot of water to a boil. Add the broccoli and cook for 2 minutes; remove with a slotted spoon and set aside. When the water returns to a boil, add the pasta and cook according to package directions.

While the pasta is cooking, heat the oil in a nonstick pan. Add the walnuts and raisins and sauté until the walnuts are golden. Remove from the pan with a slotted spoon and set aside. Add the garlic to the pan and sauté just until it begins to turn tan; remove from the heat immediately. Stir in the hot red pepper flakes to taste.

Drain the hot pasta. Toss with the broccoli, walnuts and raisins, and garlic. Season with salt and pepper to taste. Serve immediately.

*494 calories, 21 g fat, 2.5 g saturated fat, no cholesterol,
10 g dietary fiber, 291 mg sodium*

Chicken Lo Mein with Vegetables

Lo mein, a popular one-dish meal in Chinese eateries, is made with thin, golden egg noodles. They're available at Asian food stores and large supermarkets. You could also use thin whole wheat noodles.

Makes 4 servings

2½ tablespoons oyster sauce

3 teaspoons reduced-sodium soy
  sauce

¼ cup low-sodium chicken stock,
  plus more as needed

½ teaspoon sugar

2½ tablespoons cornstarch

3 tablespoons water or chicken
  stock

¾ pound boneless, skinless
  chicken breast

¼ teaspoon salt

1 egg white, lightly beaten

1½ tablespoons canola oil

2 cloves garlic, minced

2 teaspoons minced fresh ginger

4 green onions, cut lengthwise
  and then into 1½-inch pieces

1 red bell pepper, seeded and
  thinly sliced

1½ cups fresh bean sprouts,
  rinsed in hot water and
  drained

⅓ cup vegetable or chicken stock
  (optional)

½ pound fresh or dried thin
  Chinese egg noodles

In a small bowl, combine the oyster sauce, 2 teaspoons of the soy sauce, ¼ cup chicken stock, and sugar. Dissolve 1½ tablespoons of the cornstarch with the water, and mix into the sauce. Set aside.

In a medium-size bowl, toss the chicken with the salt, remaining 1 teaspoon of soy sauce, egg white, and remaining 1 tablespoon cornstarch. Set aside.

Heat the oil in a sprayed nonstick wok or frying pan. Sauté the garlic, ginger, and green onions only until tender, less than 1 minute. Add the chicken and stir-fry until no longer pink. Add the red pepper and bean sprouts. If the mixture is too dry, add more chicken stock as necessary.

Working quickly, add the sauce mixture, and continue cooking until the sauce thickens slightly.

While the chicken is cooking, heat lightly salted water in a large pan over high heat. Add the noodles, separating them as you add them to the water. Cook, uncovered, over medium heat for 3 to 4 minutes or until the noodles are tender. Drain. If using dried noodles, cook according to package directions.

Add the noodles to the stir-fried chicken and vegetables and toss. Spoon onto a serving platter. Serve hot.

---

*407 calories, 10 g fat, 1.5 g saturated fat,
99 mg cholesterol, 5 g dietary fiber, 762 mg sodium*

Orzo Salad with Olives, Feta Cheese, Spinach, and Tomatoes

Orzo, rice-shaped pasta, is the ideal size for a salad. This dish would also taste fine made with brown rice.

Makes 4 servings

4 cups cooked orzo
⅓ cup crumbled feta cheese
¼ cup sliced black olives
¼ cup chopped fresh parsley

1 cup cherry tomatoes, halved
*2 cups rinsed, trimmed spinach,
   torn into pieces*
1 tablespoon olive oil

¼ cup cider vinegar

Salt

Freshly ground black pepper

⅓ cup chopped fresh cilantro

In a deep serving bowl, combine the orzo with the cheese, olives, parsley, tomatoes, and spinach, and toss. Sprinkle the salad with the olive oil, vinegar, salt and pepper to taste, and cilantro. Toss again.

Serve at room temperature or chilled.

332 calories, 10 g fat, 4 g saturated fat, 18 mg cholesterol,
4 g dietary fiber, 314 mg sodium

Whole Wheat Couscous, Vegetables, and Mediterranean Spices

Sweetened with raisins and surrounded with a fragrant mélange of stewed vegetables, this makes a great dinner or party dish.

Makes 4 servings

2 tablespoons canola oil

1½ cups sliced onion

3 cloves garlic, minced

2 large carrots, peeled and sliced

½ small head cabbage, cut into wedges

1 small eggplant, peeled, sliced, salted, and drained (see page 16)

2 large boiling potatoes, washed and diced

1½ teaspoons ground cumin

1 teaspoon ground turmeric

¾ teaspoon ground allspice

½ teaspoon salt

1 cup vegetable stock, or ½ cup canned vegetable broth diluted with ½ cup water

2 cups water

1 cup whole wheat couscous

¾ cup dark raisins

Heat the oil over medium heat in a heavy 6-quart pan. Add the onion and garlic and sauté for a few minutes, stirring occasionally. Add the carrots, cabbage, eggplant, potatoes, spices, salt, and vegetable stock. Cook, covered, about 45 minutes or until the vegetables are tender, stirring occasionally.

Bring the water to a boil in a small saucepan. Stir in the couscous, cover, and remove from the heat. In 4 to 5 minutes, the couscous should have absorbed all the water. To serve, either fluff the couscous with a fork, and spoon onto a platter, or mold the couscous for a prettier presentation. To mold, pack the couscous into four ¾-cup molds that have been sprayed with nonstick cooking spray. Invert the molds onto a platter.

Surround the couscous with the hot vegetables and sprinkle with the raisins. Serve hot.

477 calories, 8 g fat, 0.5 g saturated fat, no cholesterol,
13.6 g dietary fiber, 447 mg sodium

Couscous and Tuna Salad with Beans, Tomatoes, and Capers

If you're feeling ambitious, grill a fresh tuna steak and use it in place of the canned tuna.

Makes 4 servings

2 tablespoons fresh orange juice
2 tablespoons white wine vinegar
3 tablespoons extra-virgin olive oil
2 cloves garlic, crushed
¼ teaspoon ground red pepper
1¾ cups water
½ teaspoon salt
1¼ cups whole wheat couscous

1 cup cooked white beans (drain and rinse well if canned)
1 can (6 ounces) tuna packed in water, drained and flaked
1 medium tomato, seeded and diced
3 tablespoons chopped fresh parsley
1 tablespoon capers, rinsed and drained

Make the dressing at least 30 minutes before assembling the salad. To make the dressing: Whisk together the orange juice and vinegar, then gradually add the oil, a few drops at a time. Stir in the garlic and red pepper. Set aside.

Bring the water and salt to a boil in a heavy saucepan. Remove from the heat and stir in the couscous. Cover and let stand for 4 to 5 minutes, until the couscous has absorbed the liquid. Fluff the couscous with a fork and let cool.

In a medium bowl, toss the cooled couscous with the beans, tuna, tomato, parsley, and capers. Add dressing and toss again. Serve at room temperature.

426 calories, 11.5 g fat, 1.5 g saturated fat,
12 mg cholesterol, 10 g dietary fiber, 520 mg sodium

Clam and Leek Pizza with Semolina Crust

Along the coast of New England, pizzas are made with regional seafood ranging from lobster to clams. Clam pizza is especially popular in Connecticut. This one benefits from the pungent yet sweet addition of leeks.

Makes one 12-inch pizza; 8 appetizer or 4 main-course servings

CRUST

1 package (2¼ teaspoons) active
   dry yeast
1 cup warm water (110° to 115°)
½ teaspoon sugar

1 cup semolina (pasta flour)
1¾ cups bread flour
½ teaspoon salt
1 tablespoon olive oil

TOPPING

2 cups sliced leeks (about 2
   medium leeks, well washed)
1½ cups peeled, chopped, and
   squeezed tomatoes (fresh or
   canned)
½ teaspoon dried tarragon
½ teaspoon dried, crushed
   rosemary

½ teaspoon salt
½ teaspoon freshly ground black
   pepper
1 cup chopped, drained fresh
   shucked clams (raw)
Freshly grated Parmesan or
   Romano cheese (optional)

To make the crust: Proof the yeast by stirring into the water combined with the sugar. Let stand in a warm place about 5 minutes or until the yeast begins to foam.

While the yeast is proofing, mix the semolina and bread flour with the salt and oil in a food processor or in the bowl of an electric mixer. Add the yeast mixture. Mix the dough about 8 seconds in a food processor or 3 minutes in a mixer, until the dough comes together. Turn the dough out onto a lightly floured pastry cloth and knead until a smooth, soft dough is formed. (You may have to add up to 2 tablespoons of extra water to make a smooth dough.) Place the dough in a bowl and cover with plastic wrap or a damp kitchen towel. Let rise for 1 hour or until the dough has doubled in size.

Punch down the dough and let stand for 10 minutes. Preheat the oven to 425°. If you have a pizza stone, place the stone on the lowest rack of the oven and preheat for at least 20 minutes; also sprinkle a baker's peel or baking sheet (without sides) with cornmeal. If you do not have a baking stone, spray a 12-inch pizza pan with nonstick cooking spray.

Knead the dough for a few seconds on a pastry cloth. Stretch or roll the dough to fit the pan and press into the pan, building up the edges to make a slight rim. Or press or stretch into a 12- to 13-inch circle and place on the baker's peel or baking sheet. Set aside.

To make the topping: Spray a nonstick frying pan with nonstick cooking spray, and over medium heat sauté the leeks, partially covered, until tender, stirring occasionally. Add the tomatoes, tarragon, rosemary, salt, and pepper. Continue cooking about 3 minutes, stirring once or twice. Stir in the clams and remove from the heat.

Spread the sauce over the crust, leaving a ½-inch edge.

Bake on the lowest oven rack for 30 to 40 minutes or until the crust is golden and the sauce is hot. Serve the pizza hot with freshly grated Parmesan or Romano cheese, if desired.

---

457 calories, 5 g fat, 0.5 g saturated fat, 14 mg cholesterol,
5 g dietary fiber,
573 mg sodium

Poppy Seed Noodles

Although you can use any kind of noodles in this recipe, which marries the technique of making Chinese lo mein with the seasonings of Eastern Europe, we like it with extra-thin noodles, such as angel hair, because they get crispier. Use homemade noodles, or buy whole wheat noodles.

This works well as a supper side dish, but it makes a nice lunch, with just a green salad.

Makes 4 servings as a side dish

½ pound fresh whole wheat egg
  noodles
1 teaspoon unsalted butter or
  margarine
1 tablespoon canola oil
½ teaspoon paprika

¼ teaspoon salt
⅓ cup light or nonfat sour cream
2 tablespoons skim milk
2 teaspoons poppy seeds, or as
  needed

Cook the noodles in boiling salted water until tender, 2 to 5 minutes. Drain well.

Heat the butter and oil in a large frying pan or stir-fry pan until the butter sizzles. Add the paprika and cook, stirring, for about 30 seconds. Add the noodles, spreading them out in the pan, and cook over medium heat, stirring and tossing, until the noodles begin to turn golden. Sprinkle with the salt and toss well. Combine the sour cream and milk. Remove from the heat and add the milk mixture. Toss the noodles to coat with the sour cream. Add the poppy seeds and toss again. Serve warm.

---

100 calories, 7 g fat, 2 g saturated fat, 21 mg cholesterol,
1 g dietary fiber, 160 mg sodium

Semolina Bread with Hazelnuts and Dried Tomatoes

Legendary cooking teacher and cookbook author James Beard once called semolina bread "the ice cream of breads," and we couldn't agree more. This fine yellow flour gives bread a creamy color and texture. If you prefer a sweeter bread to a savory one, substitute raisins, currants, or dried cherries for the tomatoes, and add another tablespoon of honey when finishing the dough.

Makes 1 large loaf; about 16 servings

1½ teaspoons active dry yeast
1¼ cups warm water (110° to 115°)
1 tablespoon honey
2 to 2½ cups bread flour
¼ cup warm skim or 1 percent milk (110° to 115°)
1 teaspoon salt

¼ cup extra-virgin olive oil, plus more as needed
1¾ cups semolina (pasta flour)
½ cup toasted hazelnuts (filberts), finely chopped
¼ cup reconstituted (see page 16) dried tomatoes, chopped

To make the sponge: In a large bowl, dissolve the yeast in the warm water. Stir in the honey and 2 cups of the bread flour. Cover loosely with plastic wrap and let stand in a warm place until risen and bubbly, about 30 minutes.

Stir down the risen sponge. Add the milk, salt, and olive oil to the sponge, then stir in the semolina. Add enough of the remaining bread flour to make a soft, fairly sticky dough. Stir in the hazelnuts. Stir the chopped tomatoes into the dough.

Knead the dough with a heavy-duty electric mixer fitted with the dough hook, or by hand on a floured board or cloth, until smooth and elastic; it will be a bit sticky.

Place the dough in an oiled bowl, turn to coat, cover with a damp kitchen towel or plastic wrap, and set aside in a warm place to rise until doubled in bulk, about 1½ to 2 hours.

Punch down the dough. Knead for 1 to 2 minutes, then form the dough into a round loaf. Cover loosely with plastic wrap and let rise in a warm place until light, about 45 minutes.

Preheat the oven to 375°. Brush the loaf lightly with olive oil, then use a single-edge razor blade or serrated knife to slash the top of the loaf in 3 to 4 places. Bake until the bread is golden and sounds hollow when tapped, about 40 to 50 minutes. Let cool before slicing.

---

197 calories, 6 g fat, 1 g saturated fat, no cholesterol,
1.5 g dietary fiber, 154 mg sodium

Honeyed Couscous with Dried Fruits and Nuts

Make a mixture of your favorite nuts and dried fruits for this dessert. We suggest using ⅓ cup chopped walnuts, ⅓ cup slivered almonds, ⅓ cup chopped pecans, ½ cup chopped candied cherries, and ½ cup golden raisins.

Makes 6 servings

3½ cups water
2 cups couscous
⅓ to ½ cup honey, as needed
2 teaspoons unsalted butter or
    margarine
1 teaspoon ground cinnamon,
    plus more as needed
½ teaspoon ground ginger

Dash of ground nutmeg
1 cup chopped mixed nuts (choose
    from walnuts, almonds,
    pecans, or pine nuts)
1 cup chopped dried fruit (choose
    from candied orange peel,
    dates, candied ginger, candied
    cherries, or golden raisins)

In a large pan, bring the water to a boil. Stir in the couscous. Cover the pan tightly and remove from the heat. Let stand for 5 to 10 minutes, until the couscous has absorbed all the water. Fluff the couscous with a fork. You should have about 6 cups of couscous.

Pour the honey into a small saucepan. Add the butter. Mix in the cinnamon, ginger, nutmeg, and nuts. Bring the honey-nut mixture to a boil over medium heat. Reduce the heat and simmer for 5 minutes, stirring occasionally. Remove from the heat.

Toss the dried fruit with the couscous, then stir in the hot honey-nut mixture.

Spoon the couscous into footed glasses or dessert bowls. Serve warm, sprinkled with additional cinnamon, if desired.

---

468 calories, 13.5 g fat, 2 g saturated fat, 3 mg cholesterol,
3 g dietary fiber, 5 mg sodium

Wheat Berries, Cracked Wheat and Bulgur, Wheat Germ and Bran

Wheat Berries

We're not really sure how wheat berries came to be called by that name. They are, of course, not berries at all, but kernels of whole wheat that have been husked. Wonderfully chewy, with the deep flavor of the whole grain, they're not eaten nearly as much as they should be. (Folks in the major wheat-growing regions, however, do know 101 uses for wheat berries.) We're gratified to see that chefs and other cooks are discovering them. Because they hold their shape so well, wheat berries are ideal for pilafs, salads, and stir-fries.

Labels on whole wheat grains can be confusing. Health food stores and some bulk food stores and supermarkets often carry whole wheat berries in two shades: a dark, slightly reddish brown and a golden tan. The dark berries, which are more common, may be labeled simply "wheat berries," "whole wheat," or "hard wheat berries." We've also heard chefs refer to them as "spring wheat berries." Although it's not possible to know exactly what you're getting, generally you should assume the darker wheat berries are hard red spring wheat. They can be used whole or ground into a whole wheat bread flour.

The light berries are often labeled "soft wheat berries" or "pastry berries." In that case, it's safe to assume they're soft wheat, probably soft white winter wheat. They're softer and more starchy than the hard wheat berries. They can be used whole in soups or puddings, or ground to make whole wheat pastry flour. We also like to soak them overnight and bake them in whole wheat breads for more texture. They're a little easier to chew in breads than are the hard wheat berries.

Wheat berries are readily available in health food stores and some supermarkets. Health food stores often carry wheat flakes, which are wheat berries that have been sliced and rolled. They can be cooked as a breakfast cereal, like oatmeal: Bring 1 cup water to a boil, stir in ½ cup flaked wheat, and cook for 8 to 10 minutes, until tender.

Wheat berries, wheat flakes, and cracked wheat have all the nutrition of whole wheat; see the chart on page 5.

Wheat berries will keep for a couple of months in a cool cupboard; for longer storage, freeze or refrigerate them. The flakes are more perishable; use them up or keep in the freezer.

Wheat berries cook faster if they're soaked or toasted first. Soaking is a little easier—just cover with cold water and soak overnight, like beans, then either drain or cook right in the soaking water. Toasting, however, brings out wheat's nutty flavor. To toast, spread the wheat berries in a single layer on a large baking sheet and roast in a 375° oven for about 10 minutes or until they begin to give off a nutty aroma.

To cook, bring 1 cup soaked or toasted wheat berries and 3 to 4 cups water to a boil. Reduce the heat to low, loosely cover the pan, and cook for 45 to 60 minutes for soaked berries, or 75 to 90 minutes for toasted wheat. The wheat berries should be cooked through but still quite chewy. Drain. This will yield about 2½ to 2¾ cups wheat berries.

If you have a pressure cooker, you can cook wheat berries quickly without bothering to soak or toast them first (although toasting will enhance their flavor). Put the wheat berries and the water (plus 2 to 3 teaspoons oil, if you have an old jiggle-top cooker) in the pressure cooker. Cook 35 to 40 minutes after the cooker reaches pressure.

You can also cook wheat berries in the microwave. Cover them loosely and cook for 30 minutes on high (100 percent), then another 10 to 15 minutes on medium (50 percent). You do not have to soak them first.

Cracked Wheat and Bulgur

Cracked wheat is uncooked whole wheat kernels that simply have been cracked. It requires cooking. Although food writers—and food labels—often tend to treat cracked wheat and bulgur as interchangeable, they are not the same thing. Bulgur is wheat kernels that have had some of the bran removed, been precooked (by par-boiling or steaming), then cracked. Bulgur requires only steeping in boiling water (or even cold water, for the fine granulation), although it can be cooked. Cracked wheat *must* be cooked. Cooked cracked wheat and soaked bulgur can be used interchangeably in many recipes.

Finely cracked whole wheat might be labeled grits and sold as a hot cereal. Even more finely crushed whole wheat is marketed as a hot cereal under various brand names, including Wheatena and Ralston 100% Wheat. These cereals are similar to farina (see page 23) but are a bit coarser and darker. To cook them, just follow the directions on the labels.

Supermarkets usually sell bulgur in small boxes, labeled as tabbouleh or tabouli mix, but it's more expensive that way and contains a spice packet that does not re-create real tabbouleh—a salad made of bulgur and plenty of fresh parsley lightly seasoned with lemon juice and olive oil—in the slightest. Middle Eastern grocers offer the greatest variety of bulgurs—which come in fine, medium, and coarse granulations—at the best prices. A health food store is the next best bet, especially if it carries bulgur in bulk. Health food stores and Middle Eastern markets are also good sources for cracked wheat.

Cracked wheat keeps fairly well, although the refrigerator or freezer is the best place to store it if you don't plan to use it within a month or so. Because it's cooked, bulgur keeps longer than raw wheat but should still be used within 2 to 3 months or kept in the freezer.

To cook cracked wheat, bring 2½ cups water to a boil; stir in 1 cup cracked wheat. Turn the heat to low, cover, and simmer for about 15 minutes or until tender. Drain if necessary. Cracked wheat is wonderful in salads and pilafs or as a hearty breakfast cereal. If you plan to use the cracked wheat in a salad, rinse it under cold water after cooking.

To steep fine or medium bulgur, place it in a heatproof bowl, add boiling water to cover, and let stand 30 minutes. Drain and squeeze out any excess water. Finely granulated bulgur can be soaked in cold water for a chewier texture. Coarse bulgur should be steeped for 60 minutes; to save time, you may prefer to cook it. To cook medium or coarse bulgur, bring 3 cups water to a boil. Add 1 cup bulgur. Cover and simmer over low heat for 10 to 15 minutes, then cover tightly and let stand for 15 minutes. Drain well.

Finely granulated bulgur is an excellent "extender"; mix it with meats, vegetables, or other grains to make kebabs, meat loaves, meat or vegetable balls, and burgers. Medium bulgur is ideal for tabbouleh, which can also be made with fine bulgur. Coarse bulgur makes excellent pilafs.

Wheat Germ and Bran

Wheat germ and bran are the parts of the wheat left over when it's refined into white flour. Wheat germ, the oil-rich embryo of the seed, is sold flaked and plain or toasted. The toasted germ has a deeper, nuttier flavor. Wheat bran consists of the outer layers that cover the kernel. It is sold flaked on its own or as the major ingredient in cold breakfast cereals such as 100% Bran and All-Bran, where it is valued for its wealth of insoluble fiber, or "roughage."

Wheat germ and bran are readily available in glass jars in the supermarket. Because it contains so much oil, wheat germ spoils quickly and should be kept refrigerated in a tightly closed jar. Wheat bran is more stable but still benefits from refrigeration.

Wheat germ and bran both work best as ingredients in baked goods or as "condiments." Put a little germ or bran in muffins, breads, cookies, and pancakes, or sprinkle on yogurt, fruit, and cold breakfast cereal, or stir into hot cereals such as oatmeal. We like wheat germ or crushed whole bran cereal (100% Bran or All-Bran) in crumb crusts; substitute it for up to a third of the graham cracker or cookie crumbs.

Wheat Berries, Cracked Wheat and Bulgur, Wheat Germ and Bran

Wheat Berry Confetti Salad with Lime-Chile Vinaigrette

Herbed Wheat Berry Salad

Wheat Berries with Smoked Turkey, Apples, and Sage

Great Plains Buffalo and Wheat Chili

Bulgur and Lamb with Toasted Pine Nuts

Bulgur and Brown Rice Burgers

Savory Wheat Germ Crackers with Sunflower Seeds

Wheat Berry Confetti Salad with Lime-Chile Vinaigrette

The vinaigrette gives this salad an intriguing blend of tartness, sweetness, and heat. The wheat berries should be firm and fairly chewy.

This is also good made with 2 cups cooked cracked wheat, or with bulgur: Soak ⅔ to ¾ cup fine to medium bulgur in 2 cups boiling water for 15 minutes, squeeze out any liquid, drain well, and fluff with a fork.

Makes 4 servings

VINAIGRETTE

3 tablespoons fresh lime juice

1 tablespoon honey

1 tablespoon minced shallot or
   onion

¼ teaspoon ground cumin

¼ to ½ teaspoon hot red pepper
   flakes

3 tablespoons olive oil

SALAD

2¼ to 2½ cups cooked wheat
   berries

1 cup coarsely grated carrot

1 yellow bell pepper, seeded and
   finely diced

1 red bell pepper, seeded and
   finely diced

1 cup cooked corn kernels (fresh,
   frozen, or canned, drained and
   rinsed)

Salt

To make the vinaigrette: Whisk together the lime juice, honey, shallot, cumin, and hot red pepper flakes. Whisk in the oil, a few drops at a time, until incorporated. Set aside.

To make the salad: Toss the wheat berries with the carrot, yellow and red bell pepper, and corn in a large bowl. Add the vinaigrette and toss thoroughly. Add salt to taste. Let stand at least 30 minutes before serving. If keeping longer, refrigerate. Let the salad come to room temperature before serving.

229 calories, 11 g fat, 1.5 g saturated fat, no cholesterol,
6 g dietary fiber, 152 mg sodium

Herbed Wheat Berry Salad

This nutty, refreshing salad recipe is a slight adaptation of one provided by rising young chef Jack Campbell of Lettuce Entertain You Enterprises' Mity Nice Grill, a popular 1940s-style grill in Chicago's Water Tower Place.

Toasting the wheat berries brings out their nutty flavor and cuts the cooking time slightly. Campbell recommends serving this with grilled pork loin roast or broiled seafood; it's also good on its own. Be sure to use flavorful olives such as kalamata.

Makes 6 servings

VINAIGRETTE

⅓ cup olive oil

1½ tablespoons fresh lemon juice

1 shallot, minced

2 tablespoons julienned fresh
  basil

1 tablespoon chopped fresh parsley

1 tablespoon snipped fresh chives

1½ teaspoons chopped fresh
  tarragon

2 cloves garlic, minced

1 teaspoon salt, as needed

SALAD

2 cups wheat berries

8 cups water

3 to 4 Roma tomatoes, seeded
  and diced

⅓ cup pitted and coarsely
  chopped black and/or green
  olives

½ roasted red bell pepper (see
   page 16), peeled, seeded, and
   julienned

To make the vinaigrette: Whisk together the olive oil, lemon juice, shallot, basil, parsley, chives, tarragon, garlic, and salt to taste. Set aside. Preheat the oven to 375°. Lay the wheat berries on a large baking sheet and toast for about 10 minutes, stirring occasionally, until they begin to give off a nutty aroma. Let cool. In a heavy saucepan combine the wheat berries and water and bring to a boil. Lower the heat to a simmer, and cook the berries until tender, about 75 to 90 minutes, depending on how chewy you like them. Drain and let cool.

To assemble the salad: Toss the cooled wheat berries with the vinaigrette. (At this point, they may be refrigerated for up to several hours.) Shortly before serving, add the tomatoes, olives, and roasted pepper, and toss again. Serve at room temperature.

338 calories, 14 g fat, 2 g saturated fat, no cholesterol,
9 g dietary fiber, 587 mg sodium

Wheat Berries with Smoked Turkey, Apples, and Sage

This pilaf celebrates the fiery colors and deep, smoky flavors of autumn. If using cooked, frozen wheat berries, defrost thoroughly and use only 1 teaspoon of canola oil. This pilaf is also excellent made with Kamut, spelt, or rye kernels.

Makes 4 main-dish servings

2 teaspoons canola oil
1 cup diced celery
1 cup diced red onion
1 large or 2 small tart apples,
   peeled, cored, and diced
3 cups cooked, cooled wheat
   berries
2 tablespoons apple cider or juice

2 tablespoons chopped fresh sage,
   or 2 teaspoons dried, crumbled
   sage
4 ounces smoked turkey breast,
   diced
Salt
Freshly ground black pepper

Heat the oil in a large, nonstick skillet. Add the celery and onion; cook over medium heat until the onion softens, about 5 minutes. Add the apples, wheat berries, cider, and sage. Cook over medium heat, stirring, for 2 minutes. Stir in the turkey, and add salt and pepper to taste. Cook until just heated through. Serve warm.

178 calories, 4.5 g fat, 0.5 g saturated fat,
16 mg cholesterol, 5 g dietary fiber, 184 mg sodium

Great Plains Buffalo and Wheat Chili

We've cooked up a potful of the best of the Plains States: buffalo, wheat, Great North-ern beans, and beer (made with barley). Buffalo, which is leaner than beef, lends a cer-tain cachet to this dish, but like all game meats, it tends to be expensive. You could use a really lean ground beef instead. This tastes great with cornbread (see page 98) or mock sourdough (page 245).

Like all chilies—and other spicy stews, for that matter—this tastes best a day after it's made.

You could substitute cooked Kamut or spelt for the wheat berries.

Makes 6 servings

1 tablespoon canola oil
1 large onion, finely diced
3 to 4 cloves garlic, minced
1 pound ground buffalo meat or
   very lean ground beef
3 tablespoons chili powder
1 to 2 teaspoons ground red
   pepper
2 teaspoons ground cumin
¼ teaspoon ground cinnamon

1 can (28 ounces) crushed
   tomatoes
1 bottle (12 ounces) beer
1 cup water
1½ cups cooked wheat berries or
   cracked wheat
2 cups cooked Great Northern or
   other white beans (drain and
   rinse well if canned)
Salt (optional)

In a soup pot, heat the oil over medium heat. Add the onion and garlic and cook until the onion begins to soften, about 5 minutes. Add the buffalo meat and sauté, breaking up chunks with a spoon, until no longer pink. Stir in the chili powder, red pepper, cumin, and cinnamon. Cook, stirring, for 1 minute. Stir in the tomatoes, beer, and water. Bring to a boil, then reduce the heat to low, partially cover, and simmer for 1 hour.

Add the wheat berries and beans. Simmer for another 30 minutes. If desired, add salt to taste. The chili can be served at this point, or allow to cool slightly, then refrigerate overnight and reheat to serve.

With beef: 375 calories, 13 g fat, 4 g saturated fat,
56 mg cholesterol, 10.5 g dietary fiber, 619 mg sodium

Bulgur and Lamb with Toasted Pine Nuts

This dish, known as kibbeh, is found in Lebanese and other Middle Eastern restaurants around the country. The lamb-wheat mixture is often served raw but may be fried, baked, grilled, or steamed. These are good with pita bread and a cucumber-yogurt salad.

Makes 4 servings

1½ cups fine bulgur
½ pound lamb, cut from the leg,
   trimmed of all fat and cut into
   cubes
¾ cup chopped onion
2 tablespoons fresh mint leaves

¼ teaspoon salt
⅛ teaspoon ground cumin
¼ cup pine nuts, or as needed
1 tablespoon olive oil
¼ cup minced fresh parsley

Place the bulgur in a bowl, add about 2 cups boiling water to barely cover, and let stand for 30 minutes. Drain off any remaining water. Let cool.

Grind the lamb cubes in a food processor fitted with the steel blade or in a meat grinder. Add the onion, mint, salt, and cumin. Continue grinding until the lamb mixture is finely ground. Add the bulgur and mix thoroughly. Chill for at least 1 to 2 hours.

In a nonstick frying pan, briefly toast the pine nuts only until they begin to color. Remove from pan and set aside.

When ready to serve, press the lamb-bulgur mixture into 4 thin patties, reserving a little of the mixture to check for seasoning. Heat the oil in a large nonstick frying pan. Fry the reserved lamb-bulgur mixture until cooked through, and taste. Adjust the seasonings if necessary.

Fry the patties about 3 minutes per side or until heated completely through. Serve immediately, sprinkled with the pine nuts and parsley.

349 calories, 12 g fat, 2.5 g saturated fat,
38 mg cholesterol, 11 g dietary fiber, 174 mg sodium

Bulgur and Brown Rice Burgers

These vegetarian patties are especially nice on homemade rolls, but you can use good whole grain hamburger rolls, available at health food stores and some supermarkets.

Makes 6 servings

¾ cup fine bulgur
2 tablespoons olive oil
½ cup chopped onion
3 cloves garlic, minced
½ cup grated zucchini
½ cup chopped brown or white
   mushrooms
1 cup cooked brown or white rice
½ cup egg substitute, or 2 eggs
½ teaspoon salt
½ teaspoon dried basil
¼ teaspoon freshly ground black
   pepper

1 cup whole wheat bread crumbs
6 rye burger rolls (see page 246),
   sliced, or other whole grain
   hamburger rolls
2 tablespoons reduced-fat or
   nonfat mayonnaise
6 lettuce leaves, washed and
   patted dry
6 slices tomato
6 red onion rings

Put the bulgur in a bowl and cover with about 1½ cups boiling water. Let stand for 30 minutes, then drain well.

Heat 1 tablespoon of the oil in a frying pan over medium heat. Add the onion and garlic and cook, partially covered, until the onion softens, about 5 minutes, stirring occasionally. Remove the cover. Add the zucchini and mushrooms, and cook until softened. Add the rice and drained wheat, and stir. Remove from the heat. Add the egg substitute, salt, basil, pepper, and bread crumbs. Mix well.

Heat the remaining 1 tablespoon oil in a second frying pan. Shape the rice-wheat mixture into patties. Fry until golden brown, turn with a spatula, and continue cooking until heated through and golden brown on the other side.

To serve, spread the bottom of each opened roll with 1 teaspoon of mayonnaise. Put a lettuce leaf on the bottom, and set the burger on top. Add a tomato slice and an onion ring. Serve immediately.

With rye rolls: 467 calories, 15 g fat, 1.5 g saturated fat,
1 mg cholesterol, 7.5 g dietary fiber, 439 mg sodium

Savory Wheat Germ Crackers with Sunflower Seeds

Serve these crackers as an appetizer with green onions and carrot and celery sticks. Store in a covered container.

Makes about 2 dozen crackers

¾ *cup wheat germ*
¾ *cup whole wheat flour*
½ *cup old-fashioned oats*
¼ *teaspoon salt*
⅓ *cup unsalted butter or*
   margarine, melted and cooled

¼ *cup water*
1 *egg white, lightly beaten with*
   1 *teaspoon water*
¼ *cup sunflower seed kernels*

In the large bowl of an electric mixer fitted with the dough hook, or using a mixing bowl, combine the wheat germ, flour, oats, and salt. Stir in the melted butter and the water to make a soft, sticky dough. Shape into a ball.

Let the dough stand for 10 minutes. Preheat the oven to 375°.

On a lightly floured pastry cloth or board, roll out the dough about ⅛ inch thick. Brush the dough with the egg white mixture, then sprinkle with the sunflower seeds. Using a 1½-inch round cookie cutter, cut the crackers and set on a sprayed nonstick baking sheet. Reroll the remaining scraps of dough, glaze with egg white, sprinkle with the seeds, and cut. Repeat until all dough has been cut

Bake the crackers for 10 to 15 minutes or until firm. Let cool on a wire rack.

Per cracker: 65 calories, 4 g fat, 2 g saturated fat,
7 mg cholesterol, 1 g dietary fiber, 26 mg sodium

Corn, the All-American Grain

Maize, derived from the Native American word, is the true name for corn. Since ancient times, "corn" has referred to grain of all types, including wheat. Americans took to using it to mean maize, and the name stuck.

Maize is mystical. Other grains feed our bodies, but corn has always fed Americans' souls as well, all the way back ten thousand years ago to when Americans were scattered bands of people gathering corn seeds in the wild. Corn was sacred to the Olmecs and the Aztecs and then to the Mayans, who worshiped corn gods and carved pictures of the grain into everything from utensils to public buildings.

In the Southwest, tradition-minded pueblo people still throw corn pollen into the wind for prayer or special occasions and perform corn dances to invite good fortune and maintain the order of the universe.

Anyone who has stood in downtown Mitchell, South Dakota, gazing awestruck on the Corn Palace, realizes that America erects temples to its most successful grain. Built in 1892 as a successor to similar palaces in Iowa, Mitchell's block-long, minaret-topped tourist attraction features an annually changing facade of geometrical patterns and historical tableaux designed in corn (with other grains tossed in)—about a hundred thousand cobs of corn in various colors.

When the first European settlers arrived, the Native Americans showed them the secrets of maize: how to roast it over coals; how to dry it; how to mix green (fresh) corn and beans into succotash; how to combine charred corn, venison, and fat into nutritious pack food for hunters or fur traders; how to cook it into a pudding sweetened with maple syrup. The white settlers further developed corn bread—named johnnycake in New England and pone in the South—by kneading cornmeal, water, and fat into a dough they baked on hot stones.

Africans who had been wrested from their homelands found familiar comfort in the corn that thrived in the South. West Africans had been cultivating corn since at least the sixteenth century. Today, *Muhindi*, an ear of corn, is one of the seven primary symbols in the African-American holiday of Kwanzaa. It represents the offspring (children) or potential offspring of the stalk (father).

Corn in a rainbow of colors defines American cooking, old and new. Blue corn was the essential ingredient in *piki*, a crepelike flatbread that any Hopi woman worth her salt knew how to make. Now blue corn is an essential ingredient in trendy corn chips and a staple on upscale Southwestern restaurant menus. The colonists served fried cornmeal mush with maple syrup in New England and mixed it with sausage and herbs to make scrapple in Pennsylvania. Mush is again popular—although we prefer to call it by its Italian name, polenta.

Corn as we know it would likely become extinct without its human companions. Unlike other cereals, which can scatter their seeds, corn keeps its kernels wrapped in a green sheaf, waiting for somebody to plant them.

One could argue that modern American society would not exist without corn and its by-products. Much of the meat that, for better or worse, Americans love so well comes from animals fattened on corn. Corn syrup and sugars (dextrose) sweeten the millions of gallons of soft drinks we guzzle each year, not to mention cookies, crackers, breads, cereals, and dozens of other products, including medicines. Corn oil is used in margarines, mayonnaise, salad dressings, paint, and linoleum. Cornstarch goes into paper, packing materials, baby powder, adhesives, aspirin, and surgical gloves. We drink bourbon made from corn mash and put ethanol-containing gas in our cars. Ground corn cobs are used for face powder, abrasives, and compost and yield a liquid used in manufacturing nylon and plastics.

Although food lovers swoon when sweet-corn season arrives, only a tiny portion of the crop gets eaten as corn or cornmeal. About 60 percent of the harvest, which averages 7 million to 10 million bushels annually, goes to feed cattle, hogs, poultry, and other animals (including our dogs and cats). Another 20 percent is exported. Nearly all the rest is used in processed foods or liquor.

One of those processed foods is cornflakes, an American institution. At the end of the nineteenth century, John Harvey Kellogg and his younger brother, Will, rolled toasted corn into thin flakes and sweetened it with malt. The resulting cornflakes were a hit and helped spawn the ready-to-eat-cereal industry.

Corn, Cornmeal, and Popcorn

Corn

The United States is by far the world's largest producer and exporter of corn, with an average annual production of more than 200 million metric tons, or about 40 percent of the world's supply. Some Americans might be surprised to learn that the world's number-two corn supplier is China, which has been growing the grain for centuries. Up until this century, some botanists believed Asia could be the birthplace of corn. But the discovery of 80,000-year-old corn pollen near Mexico City pretty much nixed that theory.

A combination of moderately hot summers, warm nights, just enough rainfall, and black prairie loam have made the central part of the United States—Illinois, Indiana, Iowa, and Nebraska—famous worldwide as the corn belt. Corn, however, grows in every state, and the South, especially, raises a lot of sweet corn.

Corn, *Zea mays*, is a very unusual grain. As noted before, it does not disperse its seed. It's the only grain commonly eaten fresh, as a vegetable. It's even unique in the way it reproduces. The plant's ovaries lie at the bottom of the ear, well out of reach of the male tassel on the same or another plant. In an elegant example of how long-distance relationships can work, the ovaries send out silks to catch pollen from the tassel. The pollinated silks form kernels of corn.

Flint corn, a hardy variety with hard kernels, was probably the type Christopher Columbus and his crew first encountered. The decorative Indian corn you see in markets in the fall is usually flint corn. It is edible when ground into meal. The Native Americans also grew flour corn, a soft, starchy variety that was easy to grind into flour and that is still popular in Central and South America.

Dent corn, which dominates most of those fields in the corn belt, is a starchy variety so named because the seed has a dent in the crown.

Sweet corn differs from dent corn by one gene, which keeps some of the sugar in the kernel from turning into starch. In recent years, sugar-enhanced hybrids, which stay sweeter longer than regular sweet corn, have grown popular.

Hybrid corn dates to the 1930s. Old-fashioned corn must be cross-pollinated by wind or insects. Hybrid corn, created by crossbreeding inbred lines of corn, is self-pollinating, meaning its silks are fertilized by its own tassel. Hybrids are protected from chance pollination and are more productive. Since the introduction of hybrids, corn yields have grown by leaps and bounds. But inbreeding and the resulting lack of genetic diversity does have its price. Because today's corn varieties are so closely related, disease can sweep through them like fire. In 1970 and 1971, blight that started in the southern states quickly worked its way as far north as Canada, wiping out a huge portion of the nation's corn crop.

Scientists know more about the genetics of corn than of any other commercially grown plant, making it a prime candidate for bioengineering. In 1995, the Environmental Protection Agency approved a variety of corn genetically engineered with built-in *Bacillus thuringiensis* (a natural microorganism that's safe to humans but fatal to caterpillars) to resist the European corn borer. Corn was the first plant to be successfully engineered with Bt.

Cornmeal

It is amazing how many of the trendy "new" things we embrace have been kicking around forever.

Take polenta, the Italian "import" that used to be called mush when it was American. Virginia Randolph's *Virginia Housewife* of 1824 gave directions for making "polenta." (She layered cold mush with butter and cheese, then baked it.) And at the turn of the century, food writer Celestine Eusti shared the secrets of the constantly stirred polenta alla Toscana, introducing our nation to "the polenta mystique taught today to rich Americans by expensive Italian cooking teachers," according to corn maven Betty Fussell.

While mush—okay, polenta—is one of the nicer things you can do with cornmeal, it's obviously not the only thing. Cornmeal—or corn flour, which is the same thing only more finely ground—is wonderful in pancakes, muffins, and, of course, corn bread. It also lends sweetness and a golden color to yeast breads but must be mixed with wheat flour because it lacks gluten. Most corn bread recipes call for some wheat flour to temper the cornmeal, but you can make a fine, if coarser, corn bread with cornmeal alone, or a mixture of cornmeal and corn flour.

Cornmeal's nutrition depends on how it has been processed. Whole cornmeal (often stone-ground) contains the bran and germ and is a decent source of vitamins and minerals. Degerminated, enriched cornmeal—the kind most commonly found in the supermarkets—loses most of its fiber and nutrients but is enriched to have higher levels of thiamin, riboflavin, niacin, and iron.

The label will tell you how cornmeal has been processed. Plain "cornmeal" must be whole, meaning it contains the bran and the germ. "Bolted" cornmeal has been sifted to remove the bran but not the germ. "Degerminated" cornmeal has had both the bran and the germ removed.

Whether we're making plain old mush or trendy polenta, we like to buy organically grown, stone-ground cornmeal. It's reasonably priced and carries all the natural sweetness and nutrients of the corn. In a pinch, we'll succumb to the degerminated, enriched cornmeal that dominates the supermarket. We think overpriced boxes of "special" polenta cornmeal, instant or otherwise, pay tribute more to marketing savvy than to need. The packaged loaves of ready-cooked polenta in supermarkets and health food stores are a better deal. You cut off a couple of slices and—*bravissimo*—polenta that is ready for the frying pan or grill. The expense and the slight trade-off in flavor (due to preservatives) are well worth the convenience.

The polenta mystique Fussell referred to involves pouring the cornmeal in a steady stream into plenty of boiling water, then cooking it for up to an hour while stirring it very frequently. The long cooking gives the polenta a lovely, velvety texture, which may or may not be worth the ache in your stirring arm. We prefer to cook it for 10 to 20 minutes, or until it thickens and pulls away from the sides of the pan, and take a little graininess with our polenta. After all, it is just mush—and we doubt any self-respecting colonial mom was standing over the fireplace stirring cornmeal for an hour while her babies crawled on the hearth.

Actually, most colonial moms steamed their "Indian pudding." Steaming is the easiest, if not the fastest, way to make polenta. Whisk 1 part meal with 4 parts cold water in the top of a double boiler, and cook, whisking frequently, until it's steaming hot. Meanwhile, bring water to a boil in the bottom of the double boiler. When the cornmeal mixture has come to a boil, fit the top of the double boiler over the bottom, cover tightly, and steam for 1 to 1½ hours, or until the polenta is smooth and thick. Polenta made this way doesn't need stirring, but we like to whisk it once or twice.

A faster, if less traditional, way to cook polenta or mush is to microwave it. The timing will depend on the wattage of your oven. Whisk the corn and water in a deep, microwaveproof bowl. Cook, uncovered, on high (100 percent) for 8 to 9 minutes, whisking once or twice to make sure it is free of lumps. Cover and continue to microwave on high for 6 to 8 minutes, whisking once. Remove the polenta from the microwave and let it stand for 2 to 3 minutes.

Lumping can be a problem with cornmeal cooked on top of the stove. To prevent it, pour the meal into the boiling water in a thin, steady trickle, whisking constantly. It also helps to moisten the cornmeal with a bit of the (cold) water used in the recipe, then bring the remaining water to a boil, and whisk the cornmeal paste into that. Or, bring all but 1 cup of the water to a boil, then stir the reserved cold water into it before adding the cornmeal.

Popcorn

Some scientists think popcorn may have been the first kind of cultivated corn. Unlike regular corn, which has to be boiled or dried and ground for food, popcorn need only fall accidentally into a fire to yield a snack that's both edible and beautiful. At any rate, by the time the European settlers arrived in the sixteenth and seventeenth centuries, native South and North Americans were eating plenty of "parched corn" and using it for necklaces and other decorations.

America's fascination with this ultimate fun food has never lessened. We eat the equivalent of 70 quarts of popcorn a year per man, woman, and child in the United States. It's strung on old-fashioned Christmas trees, sold at every movie theater, and featured prominently at fairs and festivals.

Midwesterners eat more popcorn than anybody else, and who can blame them? Some of the world's best popcorn lies just down the road. Indiana is far and away the biggest producer of popcorn, followed by Illinois and Nebraska. The most recognizable popcorn grower and promoter in the United States, the late Orville Redenbacher, hailed from outside Valparaiso in northwest Indiana, which also throws an annual popcorn festival just after Labor Day.

Thanks largely in part to microwave ovens, popcorn consumption has exploded in the last few decades. According to the Chicago-based Popcorn Institute, sales of unpopped corn rose from about 400 million pounds in 1974 to more than a billion pounds in 1994. We eat about 70 percent of that at home and about 30 percent in theaters, schools, festivals, and the like.

Popcorn is a hard flint corn. Its tough, elastic endosperm resists the buildup of steam created when the water in the kernel is heated, until it finally reaches explosive force. Popcorn is harvested in late summer and early fall, then stored in cribs until the moisture gets down to around 14 percent, the best level for popping. Popcorn comes in various colors, but white and yellow are the most popular.

Popcorn's main virtue, besides its great taste, is that it is low in fat and high in fiber, making it a healthier alternative to potato chips and other fatty snacks. That's assuming, of course, that you air-pop it or use only a small amount of oil. The addition of a lot of butter or fake butter and salt turns it into a nutritional disaster.

The best way to keep fat to a minimum is to buy superior popcorn that doesn't need tons of butter and salt to taste good. If you buy bagged microwave popcorn, get the reduced-fat, reduced-sodium kind, which has less of that icky chemical "butter" flavor and is better for you. Keep in mind when reading labels that popcorn packagers think a 2.85-ounce bag yields 3 servings. We think they're joking.

In popcorn, you usually get what you pay for. Buy it from a store where the stock is likely to rotate fairly often. Look for bright kernels with a good sheen and no broken black tips, which can signify sloppy harvesting. Experiment with different brands to find a corn that's flavorful and has good "poppability."

Popcorn will keep for several months if stored properly. If it's in a plastic bag, transfer it to an airtight tin or a plastic or glass container. Keep it in a cool place no more than 60° to 65°, such as the refrigerator or freezer.

To pop corn, use a well-seasoned 3- or 4-quart pan (cast iron is good). Heat a tablespoon or two of oil until it just begins to smoke. Add the popcorn—about 3 tablespoons per person—to the pan. Shake the pan back and forth, holding it just off the burner, until the first kernel pops, then put the pan back on the burner. Do not cover the pan tightly, but leave some room for steam to escape. Cook the corn over medium heat, shaking the pan now and then, until the popping slows considerably. Dump into a bowl, salt lightly, and serve.

If you eat a lot of popcorn, you might want to buy one of those aluminum pans with a built-in stirrer and steam vents. Follow the manufacturer's directions.

To pop corn without fat, use an electric air popper and follow the manufacturer's directions. You can also buy special poppers for the microwave oven. Note, though, that popcorn (other than microwave popcorn sold in bags with heat susceptors) never pops as well in the microwave as it does on the stove top.

Corn, Cornmeal, and Popcorn

Southern Chicken Shortcake

Kentucky Burgoo with Corn Dumplings

Southwestern Corn Bread "Pizza" with Tomato, Peppers, and Pine Nuts

*Roasted Quail and Mushroom Sauce over Polenta
with Dried Tomato Bits*

Polenta with Uncooked Tomato Sauce

Cornmeal Mush with Sautéed Peppers and Turkey Sausage

Rosemary-Grilled White Polenta

Hush Puppies

Anadama Bread

Country Buttermilk Corn Bread

Double Corn Muffins

Raised Cornmeal Waffles

Spoon Bread with Sautéed Peaches

Indian Pudding with Raisins

Granola Popcorn

Southern Chicken Shortcake

Shortcakes often are sweet, but this savory version hits the spot. The corn bread can be made several hours ahead of time and reheated in a 300° oven or in the microwave on medium power just until warm; do not overheat.

Makes 4 servings

1 tablespoon unsalted butter or margarine

1 teaspoon canola oil

1 cup chopped onion

½ pound white mushrooms, sliced

½ pound brown mushrooms, sliced

1 green or red bell pepper, seeded and diced

2 cups diced, cooked, boneless, skinless chicken or turkey

1½ cups low-sodium chicken or vegetable stock

2 tablespoons cornstarch dissolved in ¼ cup cold water

½ teaspoon salt

½ teaspoon dried marjoram

¼ teaspoon freshly ground black pepper

4 pieces hot corn bread (see page 98)

In frying pan over medium heat, heat the butter and oil and add the onion. Cook, partially covered, until tender, stirring occasionally. Add the white and brown mushrooms and bell pepper. Continue cooking until tender, stirring as necessary. Add the diced chicken. Stir in the chicken stock, then the cornstarch mixture. Add the salt, marjoram, and pepper. Cook until the sauce thickens slightly, stirring occasionally.

To serve, cut through each square of hot corn bread to make 2 layers. Set 1 piece of corn bread on a plate. Cover it with the chicken mixture. Set the remaining piece of corn bread on top and drizzle with more of the chicken mixture. Serve hot.

433 calories, 12.5 g fat, 6 g saturated fat,
80 mg cholesterol, 4.5 g dietary fiber, 759 mg sodium

Kentucky Burgoo with Corn Dumplings

This famous Kentucky dish originally developed as a campfire stew made with wild game such as young squirrels, a hen or a rooster, and vegetables. Our variation—made simply with chicken, now that squirrel meat has fallen from favor—is made indoors and topped with cornmeal dumplings. The flavor is unique and interesting. This recipe can easily be doubled if you're having company.

Makes 4 servings

STEW

1 large chicken breast (about 1¼ pounds), boned, skinned, and diced

¼ cup yellow cornmeal

2 tablespoons canola oil

1 cup sliced onion

3 cloves garlic, minced

1 can (14½ ounces) crushed tomatoes

1 package (10 ounces) frozen corn

1 cup cooked lima beans

1 large carrot, peeled and sliced

1 cup low-sodium chicken stock

½ teaspoon salt

¼ teaspoon freshly ground black pepper

1 teaspoon honey

½ teaspoon ground cinnamon

¼ teaspoon ground allspice

¼ to ½ teaspoon hot red pepper flakes

DUMPLINGS

½ cup yellow or white cornmeal

½ cup unbleached all-purpose flour

1½ teaspoons baking powder

¼ teaspoon salt

2 tablespoons egg substitute, or 1 egg white, lightly beaten

⅓ cup skim or 1-percent milk

Preheat the oven to 350°.

To make the stew: Toss the chicken cubes with the cornmeal. Heat the oil over medium heat in a Dutch oven or similar ovenproof pan. Sauté the chicken pieces briefly until just browned, turning as necessary. Remove the chicken to a plate and set aside.

Spray the pan with nonstick cooking spray and sauté the onion and garlic, partially covered, over medium heat until the onion is soft, stirring occasionally. Add the tomatoes, corn, lima beans, carrot, stock, salt, pepper, honey, cinnamon, allspice, and hot red pepper flakes, to taste.

Add the chicken. Cover the pot and set in the oven. Bake for 1 hour or until all the ingredients are cooked and well blended. Taste to adjust the seasonings.

Thirty minutes before the stew is ready, prepare the dumplings. In a bowl, combine the cornmeal, flour, baking powder, salt, egg substitute, and milk. Carefully remove the burgoo from the oven and drop the batter by tablespoonfuls onto the stew. Cover and return it to the oven for 30 minutes or until the burgoo is ready and the dumplings are firm to the touch.

Ladle into bowls and serve hot.

---

609 calories, 20 g fat, 4 g saturated fat,
73 mg cholesterol, 13 g dietary fiber, 1,284 mg sodium

Southwestern Corn Bread "Pizza" with Tomato, Peppers, and Pine Nuts

This is also good with goat cheese instead of mozzarella.

Makes 4 main-dish servings; 8 appetizer servings

CRUST

1 cup stone-ground cornmeal
½ cup whole wheat flour
¾ teaspoon salt
2 teaspoons sugar (optional)
1 teaspoon baking powder

¼ cup egg substitute, or 1 egg
*   white, lightly beaten*
2 tablespoons olive oil
¾ cup buttermilk

TOPPINGS

2 cloves garlic, minced

½ medium red onion, thinly
   sliced

1 small yellow bell pepper, seeded
   and thinly sliced

1 jalapeño pepper, seeded and
   thinly sliced

1 medium tomato, thinly sliced
   and seeded

1 tablespoon finely chopped fresh
   cilantro

1 tablespoon pine nuts

2 ounces part-skim mozzarella
   cheese, grated (about ¾ cup,
   loosely packed)

To make the crust: Preheat the oven to 425°. Spray a 12-inch round shallow pizza pan or a 10-by-15-inch jelly-roll pan with nonstick cooking spray.

In a mixing bowl, combine the cornmeal, flour, salt, sugar, if desired, and baking powder. Add the egg substitute, oil, and buttermilk; stir just until mixed. Spread the batter evenly over the bottom of the prepared pan. Bake for 10 to 12 minutes or until the corn bread is firm and just beginning to turn golden on the edges.

Meanwhile, prepare the toppings: Spray a frying pan with nonstick cooking spray, and cook the garlic, onion, bell pepper, and jalapeño over medium heat, stirring frequently, until the onion softens. Remove from the heat.

When the crust is ready, arrange the sautéed vegetables evenly over the top. Add the tomato slices. Sprinkle with the cilantro and pine nuts, then the cheese. Return to the oven for 10 to 15 minutes, until golden. Let stand 5 minutes before cutting into wedges.

---

*338 calories, 12.7 g fat, 3 g saturated fat, 10 mg cholesterol,
7 g dietary fiber, 648 mg sodium*

Maize's Missing Ingredient

At the beginning of the twentieth century, hospitals and asylums in the South began filling up with victims of pellagra, a potentially fatal disease characterized by rough, reddened skin, weakness, diarrhea, and mental disorders. The disease was most prevalent in the cotton-growing states of the South. Earlier outbreaks of pellagra had also hit Europe and Egypt.

Medical researchers surmised that it was an infectious disease spread by insects. The U.S. Public Health Service enlisted Dr. Joseph Goldberger, a dedicated doctor and field researcher, to track down the cause.

Goldberger soon fingered the culprit: diet. Pellagra sufferers were very poor and their diet consisted largely of mush or grits made from degerminated corn, biscuits made with refined flour, boiled vegetables, and occasionally pork. When they added milk, eggs, and more meat to their diets, the pellagra cleared up.

To convince other doctors that diet was to blame, Goldberger rounded up twelve volunteers from prisons in Mississippi. He and his colleagues put the healthy convicts on a 6-month regimen of corn bread, salt pork, white rice, biscuits, gravy, grits, cabbage, sweet potatoes, and syrup. By the end of 6 months, five of the men had developed pellagra. To erase any further doubt, Goldberger and several volunteers injected themselves with pellagra-infected blood. None of them got the disease.

Pellagra tended to strike those who ate diets based largely on corn, although people who ate mostly millet or rice could get it too. Few poor people could afford milk, eggs, and meat. Goldberger experimented and discovered that eating inexpensive wheat germ, canned salmon, or brewer's germ could prevent pellagra.

Although Goldberger had found the cure for pellagra, for decades scientists continued to ponder two mysteries: Just what was corn missing that foods such as wheat germ and milk had? And why didn't pellagra decimate the native peoples of North and Central America, who had been living largely on corn for centuries?

Eventually, they discovered that pellagra results from the deficiency of B vitamins, especially niacin. Some grains, especially corn, are very low in tryptophan, an amino acid that the body turns into niacin. Degerminated corn is especially low in tryptophan. Degerminated, factory-milled corn did not become a staple of the southern American diet until the beginning of the twentieth century—about the time pellagra began to plague the South.

The Native Americans avoided pellagra by supplementing corn with a variety of other nutritious foods and by eating much of their corn in the form of hominy (see page 103). Soaking corn in lime increases the availability of tryptophan.

Pellagra no longer plagues the United States. Modern degerminated corn products are enriched with B vitamins. And most Americans, rich and poor, eat an overabundance of high-protein foods such as meat.

Roasted Quail and Mushroom Sauce over Polenta with Dried Tomato Bits

Polenta has again swept the country in popularity over the past few years and is especially popular in restaurant kitchens. It's actually a simple cornmeal food that can be dressed up with bits of dried tomatoes, onions, and a variety of spices. It can conveniently be prepared a day ahead of time and pan-fried just before serving.

Makes 8 servings

POLENTA

3 cups water
¾ cup yellow or white cornmeal
½ teaspoon salt
2 teaspoons sugar

1 tablespoon unsalted butter or margarine
½ cup reconstituted, dried tomatoes (see page 16), finely diced

SAUCE

1 tablespoon olive oil

2 teaspoons unsalted butter

4 large shallots, minced

1 cup fresh chanterelle mushrooms, sliced

1 cup fresh oyster mushrooms, sliced

1¼ cups dry white wine

1 cup low-sodium chicken stock mixed with 1 tablespoon cornstarch

Salt

Freshly ground black pepper to taste

ROASTED QUAIL

8 boned or partially boned quail

1 tablespoon olive oil

4 cloves garlic, minced

2 teaspoons chopped fresh thyme

2 teaspoons chopped fresh marjoram

Salt

Freshly ground black pepper

To make the polenta: Bring the water to a boil in a heavy pan. Slowly whisk in the cornmeal, salt, and sugar. Reduce the heat to simmer and continue whisking or use a wooden spoon until the polenta is smooth, thick, and free of lumps, about 25 minutes. The polenta will begin to pull away from the sides of the pan when stirred. Mix in the butter and chopped dried tomato. Pour the polenta into a 9-inch square baking pan, sprayed with nonstick cooking spray. Let cool, then cut into rectangles. Set aside.

To make the sauce: Heat the oil and butter in a frying pan over medium heat. Add the shallots and sauté until tender, stirring often. Add the mushrooms and cook until tender, stirring occasionally. Add the wine and cook until the liquid is reduced by half. Stir in the stock with the cornstarch, reduce the heat to a simmer, and cook for 10 minutes, stirring occasionally. Season with salt and pepper to taste. Set aside.

To make the roasted quail: Preheat the oven to 400°. Rub the quail with the oil and sprinkle with the garlic, herbs, and salt and pepper. Place in a roasting pan sprayed with nonstick cooking spray. On the stove top, brown the quail lightly on all sides. Place the quail in the oven and bake for 7 to 8 minutes or until the joints move easily and the juices run clear.

Just before serving, cook the polenta pieces over medium heat in a frying pan sprayed with nonstick cooking spray until they just begin to brown, then turn over and continue cooking until the polenta is heated through. Remove from the pan and place a piece of polenta on each dish. Set a hot quail on the polenta and drizzle the hot mushroom sauce over the quail. Serve immediately.

Without skin: 269 calories, 11 g fat, 3 g saturated fat,
71 mg cholesterol, 2 g dietary fiber, 391 mg sodium

Polenta with Uncooked Tomato Sauce

This quick sauce, really a tomato relish, is often used on pasta, but it's good with polenta as well. It's a great way to use up tomatoes when they all start to ripen at once. On a sultry summer night, this meal's a snap to make: Just slice off ready-made polenta, grill it, and top with the tomato sauce. Serve with a well-chilled white table wine or a glass of iced tea.

Makes 4 servings

2 pounds ripe tomatoes,
    preferably plum tomatoes
2 cloves garlic, minced
½ cup finely chopped red onion
2 tablespoons minced fresh basil
2 teaspoons minced fresh herbs,
    such as oregano, thyme, or
    sage

½ teaspoon salt
Freshly ground black pepper
Sugar (optional)
Red wine vinegar (optional)
8 slices polenta, about ¾ inch
    thick (about 1½ pounds total)
1 tablespoon olive oil

To make the sauce: Core and finely dice the tomatoes. Place in a glass or ceramic bowl and mix with the garlic, onion, basil, fresh herbs, salt, and pepper. If desired, adjust the tartness or sweetness by adding a dash of sugar and/or a splash of red wine vinegar. Cover and let stand at room temperature for 30 minutes to 1 hour, or refrigerate for up to 4 hours (bring to room temperature before serving).

Heat a charcoal or gas grill. Brush the polenta lightly on both sides with the olive oil. Grill over hot coals, turning once, until the polenta is golden and crusty, about

3 to 4 minutes per side. If you don't feel like firing up the grill, you can cook the polenta in a skillet, sprayed with nonstick cooking spray.

Place 2 pieces of the polenta on each plate and spoon the tomato sauce over the top. Serve immediately.

---

173 calories, 4.5 g fat, 0.5 g saturated fat, no cholesterol,
5 g dietary fiber, 289 mg sodium

Cornmeal Mush with Sautéed Peppers and Turkey Sausage

Mush, of course, is just the American name for polenta. To be more accurate, polenta is the Italian word for mush—Americans had corn first.

Long a breakfast favorite, especially in New England, cornmeal mush becomes a substantial meal when paired with peppers and lean sausage. For an interesting flavor, try one of the lean poultry "boutique" sausages available in specialty shops and large health food markets.

Makes 4 servings

MUSH

4 cups water
1 cup yellow or white cornmeal
½ teaspoon salt

¼ teaspoon ground white pepper
¼ cup minced parsley

SAUSAGE AND PEPPERS

4 lean turkey (or chicken)
  sausages

2 teaspoons canola oil

½ cup chopped onion

2 shallots, minced

2 large red bell peppers, seeded
  and thinly sliced

1 large yellow or green bell pepper,
  seeded and thinly sliced

½ cup sliced brown mushrooms
  (optional)

1 teaspoon minced fresh basil, or
  ½ teaspoon dried basil

¼ teaspoon salt

Freshly ground black pepper

1 tablespoon unsalted butter or
  margarine (optional)

To make the mush: Bring 3 cups of the water to a boil in a heavy saucepan. Add the remaining 1 cup of cold water. Whisk in the cornmeal, salt, pepper, and parsley. Continue cooking over medium-low heat until the mixture thickens, whisking often to prevent lumps from forming. Cover and reduce the heat to low; cook about 8 minutes.

Meanwhile, prepare the sausage and peppers: Heat a nonstick frying pan and cook the sausages on all sides until nicely browned. Pour off any fat and add the canola oil to the pan. Add the onion and shallots and cook over medium heat until tender. Stir the onion and shallots occasionally. Remove the cover, add the peppers, mushrooms (if using), basil, salt, and pepper, and continue cooking until the vegetables are tender, stirring occasionally. Set aside. If necessary, reheat before serving.

Remove the mush from the heat, stir in the butter, if using, and spoon into shallow bowls, and top with the sausage-and-pepper mixture.

---

267 calories, 12 g fat, 4.5 g saturated fat,
34 mg cholesterol, 5 g dietary fiber, 473 mg sodium

Rosemary-Grilled White Polenta

This recipe is from Don Hysko of Peoples Charcoal Woods in Cumberland, Rhode Island, which makes natural hardwood charcoal. The rosemary sprigs not only produce a fragrant smoke but also imbed themselves into the polenta, charring and producing pockets of intense flavor.

This is excellent with grilled pork tenderloin, beef, or poultry.

Makes 8 side-dish servings

9 cups water
2 teaspoons sea salt
3 tablespoons olive oil, plus more
  for grilling

2 cups white cornmeal
2 tablespoons unsalted butter or
  margarine, at room temperature
Handful of fresh rosemary sprigs

Bring the water to a boil in a large, very heavy pot (cast iron is best). Add the salt and 3 tablespoons of the olive oil. Very slowly, stir in the cornmeal. Cook, stirring, until the polenta pulls away from the sides of the pot as you stir, about 15 to 20 minutes. It should be smooth, thick, and creamy.

Stir in the butter, and spoon the polenta into a 9-inch square pan. Smooth the top, and let cool. The polenta will stiffen as it cools. After it cools for about 2 hours, cut into squares. (If waiting longer than 2 hours, refrigerate.)

Prepare a charcoal wood fire (medium heat) and place the fresh rosemary sprigs directly on the grilling rack. Lightly brush the polenta with more olive oil as needed. Immediately place the polenta squares on the grill, directly on the rosemary sprigs. Grill for 4 minutes per side, or until the polenta is golden and the rosemary is charred.

Serve warm.

---

197 calories, 11 g fat, 3 g saturated fat, 8 mg cholesterol,
3 g dietary fiber, 544 mg sodium

Hush Puppies

Every once in a while, we crave deep-fried foods, and this old southern favorite really hits the spot. Hush puppies traditionally accompany batter-fried catfish. (At least one story claims they were invented when the cook in a fishing camp fried up some of the cornmeal batter and threw it to the dogs to quiet them.) If your conscience bothers you, serve them with grilled fish. Coleslaw (make it low-fat) is another traditional partner.

So that the hush puppies absorb as little fat as possible, use plenty of oil and make sure it's nice and hot. We use canola oil because it's low in saturated fat. It does give off a fishy smell when heated to deep-frying temperatures. (Like fish, canola oil is rich in omega-3 fatty acids.) In this case, that just adds to the authenticity. You can, however, use corn oil instead.

Makes 6 servings

1 cup yellow cornmeal

2 teaspoons baking powder

1 tablespoon sugar

2 tablespoons unbleached all-
  purpose flour

¾ teaspoon salt

⅛ teaspoon ground white pepper

¼ cup egg substitute, or 1 egg,
  lightly beaten

1 to 2 dashes of hot red pepper
  sauce, plus more as needed

2 tablespoons minced onion

½ cup skim milk, or as needed

Canola or corn oil for frying

In a mixing bowl whisk together the cornmeal, baking powder, sugar, flour, salt, and pepper. Stir in the egg substitute, hot pepper sauce, onion, and enough milk to make a smooth, somewhat stiff batter.

Heat about an inch of oil to 350° to 375° in a heavy skillet, a wok, or a large, shallow saucepan. Slide—do not drop—a tablespoon of the batter into the hot oil, cooking 3 to 4 hush puppies at a time. Cook only a few seconds, until the hush puppies turn a golden brown. Turn them over using two forks and cook until brown on all sides, only a few seconds. Continue until all of the hush puppies are cooked. Drain well on paper towels.

Serve immediately, with additional hot sauce on the side.

*173 calories, 7.5 g fat, 0.5 g saturated fat, no cholesterol,
2.5 g dietary fiber, 454 mg sodium*

Anadama Bread

This New England classic tastes best served slightly warm, with a dab of apple or other fruit butter.

Makes 1 loaf; about 10 servings

½ cup yellow or white cornmeal,
   plus as needed
1½ cups boiling water
¾ teaspoon salt
¼ cup dark unsulfured molasses
1½ tablespoons unsalted butter or
   margarine

1 package (2¼ teaspoons) active
   dry yeast
¼ cup warm water (110° to 115°)
1 teaspoon sugar
2 cups bread flour
1 cup whole wheat flour
1 egg white, lightly beaten with 1
   teaspoon water

In a large bowl, combine the cornmeal, water, and salt. Blend in the molasses and butter; let cool slightly. Meanwhile, proof the yeast in the warm water mixed with the sugar. Add the yeast mixture to the cornmeal mixture, then stir in the bread flour and whole wheat flour to make a soft, somewhat sticky dough. Turn the dough out onto a lightly floured pastry cloth and knead by folding it back and forth with the help of the pastry cloth.

Put the dough in a bowl, cover with plastic wrap or a warm, damp kitchen towel, and let rise in a warm place for about 1½ hours or until doubled.

Punch down the dough and turn it out onto a pastry cloth. Let the dough stand for 15 minutes. Flatten the dough with a rolling pin or the palms of your hands, and roll the dough into a loaf shape, tucking the ends under if necessary.

Again cover the dough with plastic wrap and let rise in a warm place for 1 hour or until light, or nearly doubled in bulk.

Preheat the oven to 375°. Brush the bread with the egg white mixture and sprinkle with cornmeal.

Bake the bread in the center of the oven for 40 minutes or until it is firm and golden brown and sounds hollow when tapped. Let the bread cool on a wire rack.

*196 calories, 2.5 g fat, 1 g saturated fat,
5 mg cholesterol, 3 g dietary fiber, 172 mg sodium*

Country Buttermilk Corn Bread

For tender corn bread, do not overbeat the batter; just mix until all the ingredients are moistened. For a touch of extra color and sweetness, add a chopped red bell pepper to the batter. For some southwestern-style heat, add two or three seeded and finely chopped jalapeño peppers.

Makes 8 servings

1¼ cups unbleached all-purpose
   flour
2 teaspoons baking powder
¾ teaspoon baking soda
¾ teaspoon salt
2½ tablespoons sugar
1 cup yellow or white cornmeal

3 tablespoons unsalted butter or
   margarine, melted and cooled
1¼ cups buttermilk
½ cup egg substitute, or 1 egg
   and 2 egg whites, lightly
   beaten

Preheat the oven to 425°. Place an 8-inch square baking pan sprayed with nonstick cooking spray in the oven to preheat.

In a large bowl, combine the flour, baking powder, baking soda, salt, and sugar. Stir in the cornmeal. Blend the butter into the buttermilk and egg substitute. Add to the dry ingredients and stir only until the batter is mixed.

Pour the batter into the hot pan. Bake in the center of the oven for about 30 minutes or until the corn bread is firm and a tester inserted in the center comes out dry.

Cut into 8 rectangles while still warm.

*212 calories, 5.5 g fat, 3 g saturated fat,
13 mg cholesterol, 2 g dietary fiber, 432 mg sodium*

Double Corn Muffins

These muffins celebrate corn as both a grain and vegetable. If you like your muffins with "domes," fill the liners to the top.

Makes 12 regular or 10 large (high-domed) muffins

1 cup white or yellow cornmeal

1 cup unbleached all-purpose flour

1 tablespoon baking powder

2 tablespoons sugar

¼ teaspoon salt

¼ cup vegetable shortening, melted and cooled

1 egg

1 egg white

1 cup skim or 1-percent milk

1 cup fresh corn kernels, or 1 can (8 ounces) corn, drained

Preheat the oven to 400°. Line a 12-cup muffin pan with paper liners.

In a large mixing bowl, combine the cornmeal, flour, baking powder, sugar, and salt. Stir in the cooled shortening, egg, and egg white. Stir in the milk and corn kernels. The batter will be firm and coarse; do not overmix.

Fill the muffin liners three-quarters full. Bake in the center of the oven for 20 to 25 minutes, until crusty and firm. Let cool on a wire rack. These muffins are best served warm.

157 calories, 5 g fat, 1 g saturated fat, 18 mg cholesterol, 2 g dietary fiber, 150 mg sodium

Raised Cornmeal Waffles

A yeast batter makes waffles exceptionally light and flavorful. Note that yields will differ depending on the kind of waffle iron you use. We tested these on a standard, two-part iron.

To freeze the waffles, let them cool on wire racks, then place them in the freezer in a single layer. When frozen, place in airtight plastic bags and return to the freezer. Reheat the waffles in a toaster oven at 300° or in a widemouth toaster set on low to medium.

Makes 12 to 14 waffles

2½ cups water

½ teaspoon salt

⅔ cup yellow or white cornmeal

1 cup cold skim or 1-percent milk

2½ tablespoons packed light
   brown sugar

¼ cup unsalted butter or
   margarine, melted and cooled

½ teaspoon vanilla

1 package (2¼ teaspoons) active
   dry yeast

2¼ cups unbleached all-purpose
   flour

⅓ cup egg substitute

¼ teaspoon baking soda

In a saucepan, bring 1½ cups of the water to a boil with the salt. Meanwhile, whisk the cornmeal into the remaining cup of water until smooth. Gradually stir or whisk the cornmeal mixture into the boiling water. Reduce the heat to low and cook, stirring or whisking frequently, for 8 to 10 minutes, until the cornmeal is thickened and smooth. Remove from the heat and let cool for 5 minutes.

Stir the cold milk, brown sugar, butter, and vanilla into the cornmeal. Test the cornmeal; it should be lukewarm but not hot. If it is still hot, let cool longer. Whisk in the yeast and flour to make a smooth batter.

Pour the batter into a deep bowl, cover with plastic wrap, and let stand 45 minutes to 1½ hours or until the batter has risen high in the bowl and looks spongy.

Preheat a nonstick waffle iron that has been sprayed with nonstick cooking spray. Stir the egg substitute and baking soda into the waffle batter.

Spoon the batter into the waffle iron, using ¼ to ⅓ cup per waffle, depending on the type of iron. Bake according to manufacturer's directions or until steam is no longer coming out of the waffle iron. Repeat with the remaining batter.

Serve the waffles with raspberry preserves and fresh raspberries or drizzled with maple or berry syrup.

141 calories, 4 g fat, 2 g saturated fat, 9 mg cholesterol,
1 g dietary fiber, 113 mg sodium

Spoon Bread with Sautéed Peaches

Spoon bread, a southern staple, is a custardy corn bread that's generally served as a side dish, plain or sprinkled with a small amount of sharp cheese.

But we like it as dessert, too. Here it pairs with peaches for a sublime dessert. If peaches are out of season, substitute four medium-small bananas, sliced and sprinkled with lemon juice.

Makes 4 servings

3 egg whites

1 tablespoon unsalted butter or
    margarine, melted and cooled

⅓ cup white cornmeal

1 cup skim milk

½ cup buttermilk

½ cup egg substitute, or 3 egg
    yolks

½ teaspoon salt

⅛ teaspoon white pepper

1 teaspoon baking powder

½ teaspoon baking soda

1 tablespoon unsalted butter or
    margarine

4 peaches, peeled and sliced

3 tablespoons packed dark brown
    sugar

1 tablespoon rum (optional)

Preheat the oven to 375°.

Beat the egg whites until stiff but not dry; set aside.

In another mixing bowl, combine the melted butter with the cornmeal, milk, and buttermilk. Stir in the egg substitute, salt, pepper, baking powder, and baking soda. Fold in the egg whites.

Pour the mixture into a sprayed heavy 8-inch ovenproof frying pan or a 1-quart ovenproof casserole. Bake for about 40 minutes or until a tester inserted in the center comes out clean and dry.

Heat the butter in a frying pan over medium heat. Add the peaches and sauté, then sprinkle with the brown sugar and rum, if desired. Turn the peaches over and cook only until hot.

Remove the spoon bread from the oven and divide it among individual plates. Top with the warm sliced peaches and serve hot.

182 calories, 6 g fat, 4 g saturated fat, 18 mg cholesterol,
1.5 g dietary fiber, 612 mg sodium

Indian Pudding with Raisins

Barbara serves Indian pudding (with vanilla ice cream) for dessert at her annual Thanksgiving dinner. It's rich, filling, and authentic—both the Native Americans and the early European colonists used corn in various puddings.

Makes 8 servings

3 cups 2-percent milk

3 tablespoons unsalted butter or
   margarine, cut into small
   pieces

½ cup plus 1 tablespoon yellow
   cornmeal

½ cup packed dark brown sugar

½ cup dark unsulfured molasses

4 eggs, well beaten

¾ teaspoon ground ginger

½ teaspoon ground cinnamon

¼ teaspoon ground nutmeg

¼ teaspoon salt

⅓ cup golden raisins

Preheat the oven to 300°. Spray or grease a 1½- to 2-quart ovenproof casserole; set aside.

In a heavy saucepan, bring the milk and butter to a boil over medium heat. Whisk in the cornmeal, pouring it in slowly. Cook, stirring or whisking occasionally, until the cornmeal begins to thicken, about 5 minutes. Remove the pan from the heat and stir in the sugar, molasses, eggs, ginger, cinnamon, nutmeg, salt, and raisins. Pour the pudding mixture into the prepared pan and set it in the center of the oven. Bake for 2 hours. The pudding should be firm to the touch, and a tester inserted in the center should come out clean.

Serve the warm pudding in shallow dessert dishes, plain or with vanilla ice cream or sweetened whipped cream.

263 calories, 9 g fat, 4.5 g saturated fat,
125 mg cholesterol, 1.5 g dietary fiber, 159 mg sodium

Granola Popcorn

To pop corn without any fat, use an air popper or a special popper designed for the microwave.

Makes 8 servings

6 cups plain popped corn
3 tablespoons unsalted butter or
   margarine, melted
3 tablespoons warm honey
3 tablespoons packed dark brown
   sugar

¾ cup slivered almonds
1 cup old-fashioned oats
1 cup dark raisins
½ cup sunflower seed kernels
½ cup dried cherries or
   cranberries

Preheat the oven to 300°.

In a large mixing bowl, toss the popcorn with the butter, honey, sugar, almonds, oats, raisins, sunflower seeds, and cherries.

Spoon the mixture into a 2-quart ovenproof casserole. Bake the popcorn for 30 minutes, stirring once or twice. Spread on a baking sheet to cool. Put the popcorn in a bowl and serve.

*333 calories, 16 g fat, 4 g saturated fat,
12 mg cholesterol, 5 g dietary fiber, 7 mg sodium*

Hominy, Masa, and Grits

Hominy

When the European settlers arrived in the East, the native peoples offered them bowls of a tasty and nutritious corn porridge that the settlers called hominy, after the Algonquin word *uskatahomen*. The Algonquin and Iroquois showed the English how to make hominy by soaking corn kernels in a lye solution (made by letting wood ashes leach into rainwater), then rinsing them and rubbing off the hulls. The resulting corn was soft and had a slightly smoky flavor. Although the settlers and natives likely were not aware of it, hominy also had a nutritional advantage over plain corn; the alkaline bath freed up more of its niacin.

In Central America and what is now the American Southwest, the Native Americans treated corn in a similar manner, soaking it in lime, then mashing it under a stone roller to produce thin breads called tortillas. They also turned masa, or hominy dough, into other corn cakes, plain and filled, in various shapes and sizes.

The early colonists constructed hominy blocks, a noisy semi-improvement on the mortars and pestles the Algonquins used to grind corn. The corn was put in a huge wooden mortar and a section of tree trunk was hung from an overhanging limb to make a pestle.

To make hominy, modern processors prepare the corn much as the Native Americans did for centuries. They heat the kernels in a solution of lime (calcium carbonate), then rinse off the hulls. The hominy is then canned or dried. Dried hominy, readily available in the Southwest and other centers with large Hispanic populations, is often labeled by its Spanish name, *posole* (puh-ZO-lay), which also refers to a popular Mexican hominy soup. Plain dried whole corn that is not hominy is called *chico*.

Masa

Masa, the dough used to make corn tortillas, is ground hominy. Fresh masa, used in making tortillas, tamales, and other Central American favorites, is available in *tortillerias* and is essential to making light, fresh-tasting tortillas and tamales. However, many cooks favor dried masa mixes, for their convenience. They are shelf stable and need only the addition of water to make masa. Quaker Oats Masa Harina is the oldest and most widely available brand, but supermarkets in heavily Hispanic areas will generally carry a choice of two or three dry, or "instant," masa mixes. They can differ from each other in how finely they're ground and in whether they're made of yellow or white corn.

Making tortillas from these mixes is easy; just follow the directions on the package. If you want to make blue corn tortillas, be sure to purchase blue *masa*, not plain blue cornmeal, which will make tortillas that fall apart.

Grits

"Hawg 'n' hominy"—salt pork and dried corn—kept many a colonist alive through the brutal eastern winters. Samp, dried corn that was pounded and cooked into a porridge, was another staple. Cracked and broken hominy was referred to as grits, a food that was to become a defining element of southern cuisine. Grits still are one of the most distinctive foodstuffs of the South, where they are eaten as breakfast, as a side dish, in puddings, and in casseroles. In fact, "hawg 'n' hominy"—that is, country ham and grits—still makes a glorious southern breakfast.

Within a century, the early hominy blocks of the American colonies gave way to water-powered gristmills, which ground the kernels of corn between large stones. The resulting grits contained the oily germ and were very perishable.

Today, most mass-produced grits are degerminated—that is, they've had the corn germ removed—to extend shelf life. And although recipes and menus may refer to "hominy grits" and residents of Charleston, South Carolina, refer to grits as just plain "hominy," modern grits are made not of hominy but of plain corn.

To make grits, processors steam or soak the corn kernels to loosen the hulls, which are then removed along with the germ. The broken endosperm is passed through rollers to cut it. The coarser bits are packaged as grits, the finer grind as cornmeal, and the finest grind as corn flour.

In the South, some gristmills still produce stone-ground grits that contain the germ, or "heart." Grits aficionados praise their deep, true-corn flavor. They do take longer to cook than the mass-produced grits and are more perishable.

Grits are available throughout the country, although the biggest selection is in the South. They're ground from both yellow and white corn, but most southerners prefer the more "refined" white grits. For our money, stone-ground grits with the "heart" in them taste the best. They are perishable, though, and should be stored in the freezer unless you're from South Carolina and will eat them up in a couple of weeks. Stone-ground grits are labeled polenta in health food stores.

Old-fashioned grits are widely available in supermarkets. To cook grits, slowly pour 1 cup grits into 4 cups lightly salted, boiling water. Simmer over low heat, stirring frequently, until creamy. Stone-ground grits will take 30 to 40 minutes, old-fashioned grits 12 to 15 minutes.

Hominy, Masa, and Grits

Southwest Hominy Soup

Grit Hotcakes with Spicy Bean Salsa

Lemon Grits with Shrimp and Sweet Onions

Layered Tortilla Casserole

Lamb and Vegetable Soft-Shell Tacos

Gorditas Filled with Vegetables and Cheese

Up to Their Necks in Grits

Once upon a time, a salesman who routinely called on one of the two supermarkets in the small town of St. George, South Carolina, remarked to the manager, "Y'all sure do eat a lot of grits around here."

That offhand remark inspired research and study, which turned up the fact that St. George, a town of 2,000 about 60 miles northwest of Charleston, indeed eats a phenomenal amount of grits—more per capita, in fact, than anybody else. St. Georgians eat grits as a side dish with shrimp, chicken, or pork chops. They eat grits plain with a bit of margarine or butter, or topped with red-eye (ham) or sawmill (flour-thickened) gravy. They serve grits with lightly fried eggs and stir them together. They bake grits in casseroles with sausage and cheese.

In 1985, the town decided to publicly celebrate its love of grits and launched the World Grits Festival with the help of Quaker Oats and Martha White, two major grits processors. The annual festival, which attracts more than 40,000 visitors, is held for three days in April.

One of its most colorful events is the "Rollin' in the Grits" contest, which is exactly what it sounds like. The first year, a children's wading pool was filled with watered-down instant grits. Contestants were weighed before and after wallowing in the pool, and whoever had the most grits clinging to them won. Some of the smarter kids wore clothing with plenty of pockets. This led to a contest rule: No clothing with pockets.

Now, the grits are mixed up in a large vat. Contestants are weighed on a cotton scale and have fifteen seconds to roll around in the grits. Then they're weighed again to see how much of the wet grits have clung to their clothing, skin, and hair. Some adults pick up as much as 27 to 28 pounds in the grits bath.

Great prizes, such as a cruise, a fistful of cash, or an expensive stereo system, help explain why otherwise sane people would do such a thing.

The festival also serves up an extremely popular grits-eating contest; a carnival; dancing; a corn-shelling contest (not as easy as it sounds, since the corn is dried); and a parade, complete with Miss World Grits, Miss

Junior World Grits, and Baby Miss Grits. And the American Legion
cooks and serves favorite combos: fish and grits, ham and grits, sausage
and grits, chicken and grits.

The monies from the festival enhance the town's cultural facilities,
including the "grits castle," headquarters for festival paraphernalia such as
T-shirts, mugs, buttons, and—of course—bags of freshly cracked grits.

For more information about the festival, write World Grits Festival,
P.O. Box 787, St. George, SC 29477; or call (803) 563-3255. And remember—no pockets allowed.

Southwest Hominy Soup

*Canned hominy, white and yellow, is available at large supermarkets and at Hispanic
food stores. Or, use* posole—*dried hominy—if it's available. Add it to the soup at the
beginning, when you're cooking the chicken.*

Makes 8 servings

1 cup chopped onion
1 chicken breast with the bone,
 about 1½ pounds, skinned and
 cut into 2-inch pieces, or 1
 pound pork tenderloin, cut
 into ¾-inch pieces
2 quarts water
1 can (29 ounces) hominy,
 drained
1 cup cooked chickpeas
 (garbanzos), drained (optional)
1 can (14½ ounces) crushed
 tomatoes

1 can (4 ounces) mild green
 chiles, drained
½ teaspoon salt
¼ teaspoon freshly ground black
 pepper
½ teaspoon chili powder
3 cloves garlic, minced
4 cups shredded lettuce
3 tomatoes, chopped
4 green onions, chopped
1 lime, cut into wedges

Place the onion, chicken pieces, and water in a pot and bring to a boil. Reduce the heat to a simmer and continue cooking, covered, until the chicken is tender, about 45 minutes. Add the hominy, chickpeas, tomatoes, chiles, salt, pepper, chili powder, and garlic. Continue cooking another 45 minutes, partially covered.

To serve, ladle the hot soup into deep bowls, and sprinkle each bowl with the lettuce, tomatoes, and green onions. Pass the lime wedges at the table.

*443 calories, 4 g fat, 0.5 g saturated fat,
19 mg cholesterol, 11 g dietary fiber, 767 mg sodium*

Grit Hotcakes with Spicy Bean Salsa

Grits are often eaten for breakfast but also make an excellent supper. The salsa can be prepared the day before for easy serving. If you are in a hurry, you can use about 2½ cups of canned black beans; drain them and rinse well.

Makes 4 servings

SALSA

1 cup dried black beans
1 quart water
4 cloves garlic, minced
2 cups chopped tomatoes
½ cup chopped fresh cilantro
½ cup chopped green onion
2 jalapeño peppers, seeded and
    chopped (see page 16)

3 tablespoons olive oil
⅓ cup fresh lime juice
1 teaspoon ground cumin
½ teaspoon salt
¼ teaspoon freshly ground black
    pepper

GRIT HOTCAKES

½ cup whole wheat flour

½ cup unbleached all-purpose
flour

¾ cup white hominy grits

1½ teaspoons sugar

¾ teaspoon salt

½ teaspoon baking powder

½ teaspoon baking soda

1½ cups buttermilk

2½ tablespoons unsalted butter or
margarine, melted and cooled

½ cup egg substitute, or 2 eggs,
lightly beaten

1 cup fresh or defrosted corn

1 tablespoon canola oil

To make the salsa: Bring the beans and water to a boil and cook for 2 minutes. Add the garlic. Reduce the heat to a simmer and continue cooking until the beans are tender, about 1 to 2 hours. Add more hot water to the beans as necessary to keep them covered with water during cooking. Let cool, and drain.

Put the beans in a bowl. Toss with the remaining salsa ingredients. Refrigerate until ready to serve. Toss the salsa and taste to adjust the seasonings before serving.

To make the hotcakes: Blend the flours, grits, sugar, salt, baking powder, and baking soda in a bowl. Stir in the buttermilk, butter, and egg substitute. Stir in the corn. Let the batter stand at room temperature for 20 minutes.

Heat the oil in a frying pan or on a griddle. Pour the batter into the pan, using about 3 tablespoons for each hotcake. Cook until the hotcakes are firm on the bottom and a golden color. Turn over with a spatula and continue cooking until golden on the other side. Divide the hotcakes onto plates and serve with the salsa.

---

*703 calories, 24 g fat, 7 g saturated fat, 23 mg cholesterol,
16 g dietary fiber, 980 mg sodium*

Lemon Grits with Shrimp and Sweet Onions

Shrimp and grits is a longtime favorite in the Carolinas and other parts south. We've added a dose of sweet onions to turn it into a hearty supper dish. This is perfect with a salad of young greens on the side. You can also add some fresh or frozen peas along with the shrimp.

The shrimp and onion mixture is also excellent spooned over polenta or rice.

Makes 4 servings

4 cups low-sodium chicken stock

Juice and grated zest from ½
   medium lemon

¾ cup old-fashioned grits

2 teaspoons unsalted butter

2 teaspoons canola oil

1 large Vidalia or other sweet
   onion, diced

1 tablespoon unbleached all-
   purpose flour

1 tablespoon minced fresh
   tarragon or basil, or 1 teaspoon
   dried tarragon or basil

½ teaspoon dry mustard

1 pound medium raw shrimp,
   peeled and deveined

¼ teaspoon salt

¼ teaspoon white pepper

Lemon wedges

Tarragon sprigs

In a heavy-bottomed saucepan, bring 3 cups of the chicken stock and the lemon juice and zest to a boil. Add the grits in a slow, steady stream, stirring constantly. Reduce the heat to low, cover the pan, and cook the grits for 12 to 15 minutes, until they are the consistency of porridge. Remove from the heat and let stand 5 minutes.

Meanwhile, heat the remaining 1 cup of stock in a microwave or on the stove top until boiling; remove from the heat and set aside.

Heat the butter and oil in a nonstick frying pan until the butter foams and begins to turn light golden in color. Add the diced onion and cook over medium heat, stirring frequently, for 5 to 7 minutes, until the onion is very soft. Sprinkle with the flour, tarragon, and mustard. Cook, stirring, for a few seconds, then gradually add the hot stock, stirring constantly. Add the shrimp.

Cook over low heat, stirring constantly, for 2 to 3 minutes, until the shrimp is opaque and the sauce is thickened and smooth. Remove from the heat and season with the salt and pepper.

To serve, spoon the warm grits in the center of each dinner plate, then top with the shrimp-onion mixture. Garnish with the lemon wedges and tarragon sprigs.

335 calories, 8 g fat, 2 g saturated fat, 178 mg cholesterol,
5 g dietary fiber, 304 mg sodium

Layered Tortilla Casserole

Variations of this casserole—sometimes referred to as a dip—never go out of style. It's homey, comfort food. This version is lighter than usual in both flavor and fat. The soft tortilla chips in the casserole contrast with the texture of the crisp tortilla chips served on the side.

For a vegetarian version, substitute 2 cups cooked pinto or black beans for the chicken.

Makes 4 main-dish servings

3 ounces (4 to 5 cups) low-fat baked tortilla chips, plus more for serving
2 cups shredded cooked boneless, skinless chicken breast
2 cups finely diced fresh or canned tomatoes

1 cup green or red salsa, preferably homemade
¾ cup (about 3 ounces) grated reduced-fat, mild-flavored cheese, such as Monterey Jack
⅔ cup nonfat sour cream
1 tablespoon minced fresh cilantro

Preheat the oven to 350°.

Spray a 10-inch pie or cake pan with nonstick cooking spray. Layer half the tortilla chips evenly on the bottom of the pan, breaking up any very large chips. Top with 1 cup of the chicken, 1 cup of the tomatoes, ½ cup of the salsa, and half of the cheese. Repeat the layers.

Bake for 25 to 30 minutes or until the cheese is melted and golden. Remove from the oven and spread the top with the sour cream, then sprinkle with the cilantro. Serve immediately, with additional tortilla chips.

282 calories, 7 g fat, 3 g saturated fat, 67 mg cholesterol,
3 g dietary fiber, 446 mg sodium

Lamb and Vegetable Soft-Shell Tacos

In the East, "soft-shell" means a blue crab that's molting. In the West, it means a taco in which the tortilla is heated through rather than deep-fried to crispness.

Makes 4 servings

2 teaspoons olive oil

½ pound lean lamb (such as
   sirloin or leg), trimmed of all
   fat and finely chopped

1 cup chopped onion

1 cup chopped green bell pepper

2½ cups fresh or defrosted corn
   kernels

1 large tomato, seeded and
   chopped, plus more as needed

1½ teaspoons minced fresh mint,
   or ½ teaspoon dried mint

½ teaspoon ground coriander

½ teaspoon ground cumin

½ teaspoon ground red pepper

½ teaspoon salt

8 corn tortillas

Shredded romaine lettuce

Heat the oil in a skillet. Add the lamb, onion, and green pepper. Cook over medium heat, stirring frequently, until the onion softens and the lamb is no longer pink. Stir in the corn, chopped tomato, mint, coriander, cumin, red pepper, and salt. Cook for 10 minutes, stirring frequently.

Heat the tortillas in a sprayed nonstick skillet until warmed through. Fill with the lamb and vegetable mixture. Top each taco with shredded lettuce and a little diced tomato.

Serve immediately.

---

351 calories, 9 g fat, 2 g saturated fat, 38 mg cholesterol,
8 g dietary fiber, 413 mg sodium

Gorditas Filled with Vegetables and Cheese

Gorditas, "little fat cakes," are favorite snacks in northern Mexico and among many Mexican Americans living in the United States. They are cooked on a griddle and/or fried in oil until they puff up, then split and stuffed with various fillings. Although they are not low in fat, these gorditas do have less fat and saturated fat than normal, since they're usually made with lard and often stuffed with pork or an abundance of cheese.

Roasted, peeled poblanos are available frozen in some stores, especially in the West and Southwest. Or buy fresh peppers and roast them (see page 16). The filling is also good made with greens; substitute 3 cups chopped kale, chard, or spinach for the zucchini.

Makes 12 gorditas; 6 servings

FILLING

3 cloves garlic, minced

1 medium zucchini (5 to 6 ounces), trimmed and finely diced

1 medium tomato, peeled, seeded, and finely diced

3 roasted, peeled medium poblano peppers, finely diced

½ cup water, vegetable stock, or tomato juice

2 tablespoons finely chopped fresh oregano, or ¾ teaspoon dried oregano, crumbled

¾ cup (about 3 ounces) loosely packed crumbled fresh Mexican cheese (queso fresco) or goat cheese

⅛ teaspoon salt

GORDITAS

2 cups dry masa mix
1⅓ cups warm water, or as
needed
¼ cup whole wheat flour
1 teaspoon baking powder

¼ teaspoon salt
2 tablespoons corn oil or canola-
corn oil blend, plus more for
frying

To make the filling: Heat a frying pan that has been sprayed with nonstick cooking spray. Add the garlic and sauté briefly, then add the zucchini, tomato, peppers, water, and oregano. Cook over medium heat, stirring occasionally, until the vegetables are soft and the liquid has cooked off. Remove from the heat and stir in the cheese and salt. The filling can be made in advance and refrigerated; rewarm gently before using.

To make the gorditas: Mix the masa with enough water to make a dough that's quite moist but not dripping wet. Combine the flour, baking powder, and salt, then add to the masa. Stir in the corn oil. Knead the dough lightly until it gathers into a ball. It should be soft and moist but not too sticky. If the dough is too dry, add a little more water; if too wet, add a little more masa.

Pour oil to a depth of about 1 inch in a deep, heavy frying pan, preferably cast iron. Heat to 350° to 375°.

Divide the masa into 12 pieces, and pat each into a disk about 2½ to 3 inches across and between ⅛ and ¼ inch thick. Place the disks on waxed paper. When the oil is hot, slide 3 or 4 gorditas into the oil. Fry, turning once, until golden and puffed up. Remove the gorditas from the oil with a slotted spoon and drain on paper towels. Keep the gorditas warm in a 200° oven while you fry the remainder.

With a sharp knife, split each gordita most of the way through to make a pocket. Fill with the warm vegetable-cheese mixture. Serve warm.

362 calories, 20 g fat, 6 g saturated fat,
14 mg cholesterol, 7 g dietary fiber, 308 mg sodium

Rice, from East to West and Back

A sia is the cradle of rice, but America has nurtured the world's most popular grain for three centuries. The American rice industry began in the 1690s, when seed from Madagascar and India was planted in South Carolina. Rice thrived in the humid climate and swampy terrain. By the American Revolution, South Carolina was exporting about 30,000 pounds of rice a year, mostly to Britain.

Thomas Jefferson, author of the Declaration of Independence and an avid gardener and amateur botanist, wondered why the French preferred Italian rice over American. He reasoned that Italians must be growing a better variety. In his attempts to find the best rice, he brought in seeds from Europe, Africa, and Southeast Asia. One of his correspondents alerted Jefferson as to why American rice might seem inferior and mushy—it wasn't being cooked right. The water should be brought to a boil first, wrote Ralph Izard in a letter to Jefferson, and the rice cooked a shorter time than the meat.

Today, the United States exports nearly half its rice crop to 100 different countries. Ninety percent of the rice Americans eat—including what we buy in Japanese, Chinese, and Korean groceries—was grown in the United States.

And after all these centuries, a lot of us *still* don't know how to cook it.

Rice

We can remember when rice in the grocery store pretty much came in one color—white—and two kinds, plain and parboiled (converted). You boiled 1 cup of rice with 2 cups of water. It smelled like nothing and the best way to describe its flavor was inoffensive.

The last time we checked a large, well-stocked supermarket, we had a choice of white long-grain, Valencia, converted, instant brown and white, Texmati, Wild Pecan, popcorn rice, brown rice in medium and long grains, Japanese short-grain rice, arborio rice for risotto, and Thai jasmine rice. Not to mention all the "gourmet" rice mixes and Rizcous, rice's answer to couscous.

Consumption of rice in the United States has risen dramatically, from a little more than seven pounds per person in 1975 to an estimated twenty pounds in 1995. No doubt a lot of the credit goes to the influx of immigrants from countries where rice is, so to speak, the daily bread. The surge of interest in Louisiana's Creole and Cajun cooking, which prominently feature rice, didn't hurt.

Most of the world eats rice. Plenty of rice. Although wheat may be on its way to overtaking it, rice is the number-one grain eaten in the world. Thought to have originated in Asia, rice is a daily staple in all of Asia and much of the Middle East and is eaten to a lesser extent in Europe, Africa, and the Americas.

The American rice industry was centered in South Carolina until the end of the nineteenth century. The Civil War and the invention of harvesting machines that could not be used in South Carolina's swampy soil hurt the industry, and hurricanes put an end to it in 1910.

Meanwhile, Asian rice varieties were thriving in the Mississippi Valley. Today, Arkansas grows more rice than any other state, trailed by California, Louisiana, Texas, Missouri, and Mississippi. Florida recently began growing rice as well. The United States produces close to 200 million pounds of rice a year and exports about 45 percent of that.

Most rice is eaten, either as rice or in processed foods. It's also widely used in brewing; per person, we consume about a fifth of our rice in beer.

Rice, *Oryza sativa*, grows best in fairly warm, humid climates with lots of moisture. It comes in many varieties but generally falls into four categories, based on cooking properties. Long-grain rice has kernels that are four to five times longer than they are wide and cooks up dry and fluffy. Medium-grain rice is two to three times longer than it is wide, and a bit stickier than long-grain. Short-grain has very fat, almost round, grains and is still stickier. Waxy rice, also called sticky or glutinous rice, is very opaque and cooks up into a dense, sticky mass.

The ratio of two starches, amylose and amylopectin, determines whether a rice is dry or sticky. Amylose makes long-grain rice cook up fluffy and separate; medium, short, and waxy rices have a higher percentage of amylopectin.

Brown rice is the grain with all or part of its bran coating intact. White rice is rice that has been polished. Brown rice usually includes some green grains among the brown; this is normal, since the grains do not ripen evenly.

Here's a guide to some of the varieties.

Short-Grain Rices

Arborio: A fat, short-grain rice with an opaque core, arborio absorbs a lot of liquid and gives off starch to make a creamy sauce. It is used primarily for risottos and makes a good breakfast porridge. Traditionally imported from Italy, arborio now is grown in California from Italian seed and, recently, in Texas. American arborio is available in brown and white, although because of the bran coating, the brown arborio does not get as creamy. It's best used for dishes such as paella and sushi; the white arborio is fine for risottos.

Richvale Red: Developed and grown exclusively by Lundberg Family Farms, this is a short-grain red rice with a nutty, musky flavor. It does not clump as much as other short-grains when cooked and is good in stuffings.

Waxy, sweet, sticky, or glutinous rice: These are all names for rices that are opaque and turn into a sticky mass when cooked. Sticky rice, whole or ground, is used primarily in making stuffings, rice cakes, dumplings, and puddings.

Japanese sushi rices: Depending on the brand, these rices may be labeled short-grain or medium-grain. The grains cling together, making them ideal to use in sushi, but are not as sticky as waxy rice.

Medium-Grain Rices

Valencia or Valenciana: A medium-grain rice used in Spanish dishes, especially paella, Valencia can be used in risottos and sushi as well. It's an excellent rice to use for rice puddings.

Black Japonica: This actually is a Lundberg blend of two rices, a black short-grain Japanese-style rice and a mahogany-colored medium-grain rice, which grow in the same field. It's an aromatic, slightly spicy mix.

Long-Grain Rices

Long-grain rice is the most popular type in the United States and in many other countries as well. It comes in both regular varieties—the familiar boxed rice we all grew up with—and aromatic rices, which give off a nutty fragrance when they cook. All long-grain rices cook up fluffy, with separate grains. They are good all-purpose rices, whether served plain or with other ingredients.

Basmati: Considered one of the world's finest rices, basmati has a deep, "popcorny" aroma when it cooks and is unique in that it swells lengthwise, not widthwise, during cooking. It cooks up very dry, with distinctly separate grains. Basmati is native to India and Pakistan. Most American "basmatis" actually are Della rices and do not swell lengthwise. An exception is Kasmati, a fairly new RiceTec variety that is a basmati developed from Indian seed. Like the Indian rices, it is aged after harvesting to deepen its aroma and it lengthens during cooking.

Della types: This is a broad category referring to an aromatic rice developed by Louisiana State University. A cross between basmati and regular long-grain rices, it has much of basmati's aroma and flavor and cooks up dry. It swells widthwise, not lengthwise, during cooking. Some examples of Della types include Texmati, Louisiana "popcorn" rices, Konriko Wild Pecan Rice, and Creole Rose. Della-type rices are sold in both brown and white.

Jasmine: Native to Thailand, this long-grain rice is similar to basmati in aroma and flavor but softer and stickier, making it a good rice for chopsticks (the Thais, however, use forks). It's widely served in Southeast Asian and Chinese restaurants. True jasmine rice is imported from Thailand. RiceTec now grows an American jasmine–long grain cross in Texas; it's sold under the Jasmati brand.

Wehani: Another Lundberg product, this is an aromatic mahogany rice with a musky, nutty flavor. It's good in pilafs and stuffings.

Parboiled or converted: Parboiling is a technique developed centuries ago in India. Converted rice is soaked under pressure, steamed, and dried. This gelatinizes the starch and ensures the grains stay separate when cooked. It retains more nutrients than regular white rice.

Instant or quick-cooking: This is white or brown rice that has been pre-cooked; you basically are rehydrating it. To our mind, this mushy, "twice-cooked" rice is not worth the bother.

You should have little trouble finding just about any kind of rice you want. Most supermarkets carry the basic long-grain rices in white and brown, plus usually a few medium- or short-grain varieties, and at least one aromatic variety. Many supermarkets also carry Italian arborio, jasmine, and/or Japanese sushi rice.

A well-stocked health food store will carry basmati in white and brown, plus some of the specialty rices such as jasmine. And, of course, Asian and Middle Eastern markets carry the rices favored by their customers.

White rice keeps forever in a cool cupboard. Brown rice has more oils and should be used within 6 months or kept in an airtight container in the refrigerator or freezer.

There seem to be as many ways of cooking rice as there are rice cooks. Rice is rinsed, soaked, simmered, baked, steamed, and microwaved. We've even seen directions for cooking it in a large amount of water, pasta style, draining it, then steaming it—which strikes us as both overly complicated and a good way to kill both nutrients and flavor.

In trying to determine the best way to cook rice, we looked both at the quality of the cooked rice *and* nutrition. And basically, we came up with three rules of thumb.

First, ignore package instructions that call for cooking 1 cup of long-grain rice in 2 cups of water. That's usually too much water.

Second—and this borders on heresy in some quarters—do not rinse or soak rice. Asian cooks usually rinse rice several times, then cook it with a fairly small amount of water. This method does produce beautifully cooked rice. There is only one problem with it: Processors enrich rice by coating it with a mixture of B vitamins (and iron) after it's polished. B vitamins are water soluble. So when you rinse enriched rice, you pour vitamins right down the drain.

Like all rules, this has exceptions. If the rice contains bits of sticks, stones, or rice hulls—true of some imported rices—it must be rinsed. But all American rices, and many imported ones, are very clean.

Sticky rice must be soaked for several hours or overnight before being steamed. And true basmati rice (not Texmati or other crosses) is soaked in cold water to cover for 20 to 30 minutes. This helps the rice cook up very dry and lacy. The rice is drained, but the soaking water is reserved. The rice is cooked in the soaking water (plus some fresh water if necessary) to retain flavor and nutrients.

Of course, tradition can outweigh nutrition. If you can't imagine not rinsing rice because your mother did and her mother and grandmother before her did, go ahead and rinse.

Third, quit peeking. Whether you're cooking rice in a rice cooker, a steamer, or a saucepan on the stove top, you're essentially steaming it. When you keep nervously checking to see how it's doing, you allow steam to escape. Do not peek until the rice is near the end of its cooking time.

The best way to cook rice, hands down, is with a rice cooker. If you cook a lot of rice, this appliance, which cooks the grain over low heat and shuts off when the water has been absorbed, is indispensable. Follow the manufacturer's directions.

The next best way is to steam it. Bring 1½ to 1¾ cups water to a boil in the top of a double boiler. Stir in 1 cup long-grain rice and a little salt, if you like. Fit the top of the double boiler over the bottom of the double boiler, cover tightly, and steam the rice over simmering water for 20 to 25 minutes for white rice or 45 to 55 minutes for brown rice, or until it has absorbed the water. Adjust the heat as necessary so the water below the rice is simmering, not boiling up the sides of the pan. The advantage of this method is that it keeps the rice off the burner; it's sometimes hard to get the flame or coil low enough. Remove the top of the double boiler and let the rice stand, covered, for 5 minutes.

To cook rice on the stove top, use a heavy-bottomed pan. Bring 1½ to 1¾ cups water (and optional salt) to a boil. Stir in 1 cup rice. Turn the heat down to very low, cover the pan tightly, and cook for 15 to 20 minutes for white rice, 20 to 25 minutes for parboiled rice, or 45 to 50 minutes for brown rice, or until the rice has absorbed the liquid. Remove from the heat and let stand, covered, for 5 minutes.

If you have the oven on for another dish, try baking the rice. Add 1½ to 1¾ cups of boiling water or stock per cup of rice, cover tightly, and bake at 350° for 25 to 30 minutes for white rice, 30 to 40 minutes for parboiled rice, and 1 hour for brown rice.

We don't like to microwave rice. Microwaves cook unevenly, and often the rice tends to get mushy by the time it fully absorbs the water.

Rice

All-American Paella

Hoisin Turkey on a Bed of Brown Rice

Steamed Rice Balls, or Lion's Head

Vegetarian Brown Fried Rice

Fried Rice Wontons in Soup

Shrimp Brown Fried Rice

Eggplant Stuffed with Cracked Wheat and Brown Rice

Sizzling Rice Soup

Cold Tofu and Vegetables over Sushi Rice

Creole Red Beans with Sausage and Yellow Rice

Two-Rice and Wheat Berry Pilaf

Mushroom Risotto

Risotto with Crab and Artichokes

Jeweled Rice Pudding

All-American Paella

This is one of those pull-out-all-the-stops recipes designed for entertaining. Paella often involves some tricky timing, to get the rice cooked through without overcooking the seafood. We've made the process easier by preparing and cooking as many of the ingredients as possible ahead of time, and starting the rice on top of the stove. Because we're using brown rice, the paella takes a long time to cook. That can actually be an advantage if you have guests over; you have plenty of time to serve up appetizers or funny stories while the rice bakes.

This recipe is highly adaptable. Feel free to experiment with the best seafood and sausage that's available in your region. For example, one of our tests of this recipe was a western variation, with trout and buffalo sausage.

Makes 8 servings

16 small littleneck or cherrystone
  clams and/or black mussels,
  in the shell
6 to 8 ounces raw seafood of your
  choice: sea scallops, lobster
  meat, lumpfish, crab, crawfish,
  and/or shucked oysters
1 pound salmon, trout, or catfish
  filets
½ pound medium shrimp
1 pound boneless, skinless
  chicken breasts, cut into bite-
  size pieces
½ pound spicy lean sausage, such
  as chorizo, andouille, or
  Italian sausage
½ cup uncooked wild rice
1 tablespoon olive oil
2 cups finely diced onion

2 tablespoons minced garlic
1 jalapeño pepper, seeded and
  minced
2 red bell peppers, seeded and
  diced
1 cup diced fresh or canned
  tomatoes, drained (reserve the
  juice)
1½ to 2 cups low-sodium chicken
  stock
½ cup white wine, clam juice, or
  additional chicken stock
½ teaspoon saffron threads,
  crushed
½ teaspoon salt
1½ cups uncooked brown arborio
  rice or medium-grain brown
  rice
Chopped fresh parsley

Prepare all the seafood several hours ahead of time: Scrub the clams and/or mussels, and trim the beards, if any, from the mussels. If using lobster meat or crawfish, cut into bite-size pieces. If using crab, pick over and discard any bits of shell.

Skin the fish and remove any bones. Cut into bite-size pieces. Peel and devein the shrimp.

Place the prepared seafood on a clean plate or plates, cover all but the clams and/or mussels with plastic wrap, and store on a lower shelf of the refrigerator.

Also ahead of time, cook the chicken and sausage. Cut the chicken and sausage into bite-size pieces. Heat a large frying pan that has been sprayed with nonstick cooking spray. Add the chicken and sausage and cook, turning once, until nicely browned and just cooked through. Remove the chicken and sausage to a paper towel–lined plate, cover with plastic wrap, and refrigerate.

When ready to make the paella, preheat the oven to 375°. Remove the prepared seafood, chicken, and sausage from the refrigerator. Set aside. If using scallops and/or shucked oysters, drain and rinse, and set aside. Place the wild rice in a bowl and add hot water to cover. Set aside.

Heat the oil in a 12-inch-deep, ovenproof frying pan or large shallow casserole. Add the onion, garlic, jalapeño, and red bell peppers. Cook over medium heat, stirring, until the onion softens, about 5 minutes. Stir in the tomatoes and cook for 1 minute.

Add the reserved liquid from the tomatoes to 1½ cups of the stock and the wine. Add additional stock if necessary to make a total of 2½ cups liquid. Add the liquid to the frying pan or casserole, along with the saffron and salt. Bring to a boil. Stir in the brown rice and drained wild rice. Return to a simmer. Cover tightly and cook over low heat for 15 minutes.

Put the covered frying pan or casserole in the oven. Bake for about 30 minutes or until the rice has absorbed much of the liquid but still looks soupy. Tuck the clams and/or mussels into the rice, putting them near the edges of the pan or casserole. Tuck the chicken and sausage in the rice as well. Scatter the seafood and fish over the top of the rice; do not stir. Cover tightly and cook another 30 to 40 minutes, until the seafood and fish are cooked through and the rice is tender and has absorbed all the liquid. Remove from the oven and let stand 5 minutes. Stir all the ingredients together, then arrange the clams and/or mussels atop the rice mixture. Sprinkle with parsley. Serve hot.

With clams, salmon, scallops, and chorizo: 539 calories,
20 g fat, 5.5 g saturated fat, 140 mg cholesterol,
3.5 g dietary fiber, 676 mg sodium

Hoisin Turkey on a Bed of Brown Rice

This is a fast, delicious way to use turkey that's left over from Thanksgiving or any other occasion. Hoisin sauce, a sweet, thick sauce made of fermented soybeans, is available in Asian markets and some large supermarkets.

Makes 4 servings

1 tablespoon canola oil
4 cloves garlic, minced
½ teaspoon minced fresh ginger
4 green onions, chopped
1 can (6½ ounces) sliced water
  chestnuts, drained

2 cups diced cooked boneless,
  skinless turkey
3 tablespoons hoisin sauce
3 cups hot cooked brown rice

Heat the oil in a wok or frying pan. Add the garlic, ginger, and green onions, partially cover the pan, and cook over medium heat, stirring occasionally, about 1 minute. Stir in the water chestnuts, turkey, and hoisin sauce. Stir-fry just until the turkey is heated through.

Spoon the hot rice onto plates and top with the turkey mixture. Serve hot.

342 calories, 8 g fat, 1.5 g saturated fat,
53 mg cholesterol, 3.5 g dietary fiber, 278 mg sodium

Steamed Rice Balls, or Lion's Head

When the meatballs are steamed, the rice soaks up liquid and expands to cover the meat. Cover the meatballs until just before you are ready to steam them so that the rice will not dry out. The rice must soak overnight in cold water.

For really lean pork, have the butcher grind pork tenderloin, trimmed of all fat, or grind it yourself in a meat grinder or food processor.

Makes 16 rice balls; 4 servings

1 cup glutinous rice

3 dried shiitake mushrooms

¾ pound leanest ground pork

3 tablespoons minced cooked
   shrimp

8 water chestnuts, minced

1½ tablespoons soy sauce

1 teaspoon dark sesame oil
   (optional)

¼ teaspoon salt

½ teaspoon sugar

⅛ teaspoon freshly ground black
   pepper

Soak the rice, covered, in 3 inches of cold water overnight. The rice will become plump as it absorbs the water. Drain the rice just before you are ready to use it. Spread the rice on a double thickness of paper towels and pat dry.

Soak the shiitakes in boiling water for 20 minutes or until softened. Discard the stems and finely mince the caps. In a large bowl, mix together the pork, shrimp, minced shiitakes, water chestnuts, soy sauce, sesame oil, salt, sugar, and pepper. Shape into 16 small balls. Roll each meatball in the rice so the rice sticks on all sides.

Place a wire rack or a steamer that has been sprayed with nonstick cooking spray or covered with lettuce leaves in a wok or pot that has been filled with boiling water to just below the rack. Set the rice balls on the rack. Reduce the heat to medium, cover tightly, and steam for 20 minutes or until the pork is cooked through and the rice is tender. The rice will expand to cover the meatballs.

Serve hot, with hot mustard or wasabi.

---

377 calories, 5.5 g fat, 2 g saturated fat,
55 mg cholesterol, 1 g dietary fiber, 500 mg sodium

Vegetarian Brown Fried Rice

Fried rice is a classic dish that we happen to enjoy immensely. We have tried it on Tyler Street in Boston, on Wentworth Street in Chicago, on Alameda in Denver, and on Grant Street in San Francisco. The following recipe is our version of a vegetarian fried rice. Chinese restaurants always use white rice, but we like the nutty flavor of brown rice.

For best results, the cooked rice should be very cold. We recommend cooking the rice the day before, cooling it, freezing it, then defrosting it shortly before cooking.

Makes 4 main-dish servings

2 tablespoons canola oil

½ cup egg substitute, or 2 eggs,
lightly beaten

½ teaspoon salt

2 cloves garlic, minced

4 green onions, chopped

2 cups fresh bean sprouts, rinsed
and drained

½ cup grated carrot

½ cup fresh or defrosted green
peas

3 tablespoons reduced-sodium soy
sauce

½ teaspoon sugar

⅛ teaspoon freshly ground black
pepper

3 cups cooked, very cold brown
rice

½ teaspoon dark sesame oil
(optional)

Heat 1 tablespoon of the oil in a frying pan or wok. Pour in the egg substitute and sprinkle with ¼ teaspoon of the salt. When the eggs have set, turn the omelet over using 2 spatulas. Cook lightly; avoid browning the eggs. Remove the omelet, and with a pair of kitchen scissors, cut into thin strips. Reserve.

Clean out the pan, spray, and heat the remaining 1 tablespoon oil over high heat. Sauté the garlic and green onions only until soft, stirring occasionally. Add the bean sprouts, carrot, and peas, one vegetable at a time, stir-frying for a few seconds after each addition. Add the soy sauce, the remaining ¼ teaspoon salt, and the sugar, pepper, and rice. Stir-fry, breaking up lumps in the rice. Add the egg strips and continue stir-frying until the rice is hot, about 4 to 5 minutes. Mix in the sesame oil if using.

Spoon the fried rice into a large bowl or individual rice bowls. Serve hot. This is good alone or as a side dish.

292 calories, 8.5 g fat, 1 g saturated fat, no cholesterol,
5.5 g dietary fiber, 738 mg sodium

Fried Rice Wontons in Soup

Leftover fried rice makes a good wonton filling. The wontons could be served on a small plate as an appetizer or simmered in stock as they are here.

Wonton wrappers, small squares of egg dough, are available at Asian groceries and large supermarkets. The wrappers dry out quickly, so keep them covered with a damp cloth at all times if possible.

Makes 4 servings

8 wonton wrappers	**¼ teaspoon sugar**
¾ cup cooled brown fried rice	**1 teaspoon dark sesame oil**
(page 126)	**(optional)**
2 tablespoons whole wheat flour	**1 cup trimmed, chopped spinach**
1 tablespoon canola oil (optional)	**2 egg whites, lightly beaten**
6 cups low-sodium chicken stock,	**1 tablespoon dry white wine**
preferably homemade	

Prepare each wonton separately. Place a small bowl near the wonton wrappers. Spoon about 2 teaspoons of the fried rice in the center of a wonton wrapper. Dip your finger in the water and run it around the edges of the wrapper. Seal the edges together, shaping the wonton into a triangle. Set the wonton on a plate that has been sprinkled with the flour. Repeat with the remaining wonton wrappers and filling. Keep the finished wontons covered with a damp cloth so they don't dry out.

Bring a small pan of water to a boil over medium heat. Reduce the heat to a simmer and slide the wontons into the water a few at a time. Cook for a few minutes, until the wrappers are cooked through and pliable. Remove with a slotted spoon and set on a plate and repeat with the remaining wontons. Let cool.

Heat the oil in a frying pan. Fry the wontons slightly a minute or so on each side, just until golden. Set aside. This step is optional but worth it to make the wontons more crispy.

In a pot, bring the stock to a boil over medium heat. Add the sugar, sesame oil, spinach, egg whites, and wine. Reduce the heat.

Place 2 wontons in each soup bowl. Ladle the stock over them and serve hot.

---

201 calories, 8 g fat, 0.5 g saturated fat,
10 mg cholesterol, 1 g dietary fiber, 213 mg sodium

Shrimp Brown Fried Rice

You can substitute or add barbecued pork or turkey sausage to the fried rice. For the best results, use rice that's very cold. (See the recipe for Vegetarian Brown Fried Rice on page 126.)

Makes 4 to 6 servings

½ cup dried shiitake mushrooms

2 tablespoons canola oil

½ cup egg substitute, or 2 eggs, lightly beaten

½ pound raw small shrimp, shelled, rinsed, and patted dry

1 egg white, lightly beaten

1 teaspoon dry white wine

1 teaspoon cornstarch

4 green onions, chopped

1 cup bean sprouts, rinsed and drained

½ cup grated carrot

½ cup diced celery

2 tablespoons reduced-sodium soy sauce

½ teaspoon sugar

¾ teaspoon salt

4 cups cooked, very cold brown rice

Soak the shiitakes in boiling water for 20 minutes, or until softened. Trim and discard the stems, and mince the caps. Set aside.

Heat 1 tablespoon of the oil in a frying pan or wok. Pour in the egg substitute. When the eggs have set, turn the omelet over using 2 spatulas. Cook lightly; avoid browning the eggs. Remove the omelet, and with a pair of kitchen scissors, cut into thin strips. Reserve.

In a bowl, toss the shrimp with the egg white, wine, and cornstarch.

Clean out the pan, and heat the remaining 1 tablespoon oil over high heat. Add the shrimp and stir-fry for only about 30 seconds. Remove the shrimp, leaving any liquid in the wok. Reserve the shrimp. Add the shiitakes, green onions, bean sprouts, carrot, and celery. Stir-fry about 1 minute. Add the soy sauce, sugar, salt, and rice. Stir-fry the rice, breaking up lumps, for 4 to 5 minutes, until hot. Stir in the shrimp and cook just until heated through.

Spoon the fried rice into a large bowl or individual rice bowls. Serve hot.

400 calories, 10 g fat, 1 g saturated fat, 86 mg cholesterol,
5 g dietary fiber, 836 mg sodium

Eggplant Stuffed with Cracked Wheat and Brown Rice

Various stuffed-eggplant dishes abound on Middle Eastern restaurant menus. The addition of small whole olives and rosemary gives this dish a decidedly Mediterranean flavor.

Makes 4 servings

2 medium eggplants
¾ cup medium-grain cracked
   wheat
1½ tablespoons olive oil
¾ cup chopped onion
4 cloves garlic, minced
1 cup cooked brown rice
8 small oil-cured black olives

½ teaspoon salt
½ teaspoon dried, crushed
   rosemary
¼ teaspoon freshly ground black
   pepper
1 tablespoon red wine vinegar
Chopped fresh parsley

Preheat the oven to 350°. Make a few small cuts in each eggplant, and set the eggplants on a baking sheet in the center of the oven. Bake about 40 minutes or until soft. Let cool. Cut the eggplants lengthwise. Scoop out most of the pulp, leaving the skins intact. Coarsely puree the pulp and set aside.

While the eggplants are baking, soak the cracked wheat in 1½ cups boiling water for 30 minutes. Drain well.

Heat the oil in a frying pan, and cook the onion and garlic, partially covered, over medium heat until soft, stirring occasionally. Add the eggplant and mix well. Mix in the cracked wheat, rice, olives, salt, rosemary, pepper, and vinegar. Continue cooking over medium heat until all the ingredients are heated through. Let cool.

Gently spoon the filling into the eggplant skins, being careful not to pack it down. Set the stuffed eggplants on a baking sheet. Bake in the center of a preheated 350° oven until hot, about 10 minutes.

Serve sprinkled with parsley.

274 calories, 7 g fat, 0.5 g saturated fat, no cholesterol,
12 g dietary fiber, 342 mg sodium

Sizzling Rice Soup

This noisy dish is another favorite in Chinese restaurants. Hot soup is poured over fried rice cakes to produce the distinctive sizzle. We have adapted it using brown rice, although you can use white rice if that's what you have on hand. You can make the rice cakes in advance.

Usually, the rice cakes are deep-fried. We have reduced the amount of oil considerably to make a lighter version of this classic dish.

Makes 4 servings

2 teaspoons canola oil

3 cups cooked, very cold brown rice

6 cups low-sodium chicken or vegetable stock

½ teaspoon salt

1 tablespoon cornstarch

2 tablespoons water or chicken stock

1 cup shredded cooked boneless, skinless chicken breast

¾ cup fresh snow peas, trimmed and cut in half

½ cup drained, canned straw mushrooms (optional)

2 green onions, cut lengthwise and then into 1-inch shreds

½ teaspoon dark sesame oil

Heat the oil in a frying pan. Pat the rice evenly over the bottom of the pan to make a single large pancake. Cook over medium heat until golden brown on the bottom. Pat the pancake firmly with a spatula, making it as thin as possible. Spray the top of the pancake lightly with nonstick cooking spray. With 2 spatulas, quickly turn the pancake over. (It will break, but that's okay.) Cook on the remaining side until it turns golden brown. Remove to a plate, breaking the rice cake into 2-inch pieces. Set aside.

Note: It is important that both the soup and the rice be hot. Heat the stock and salt to simmering. Mix the cornstarch with the water and stir into the stock, then stir in the chicken, snow peas, mushrooms, and onions. Stir in the sesame oil. Place the rice cakes in the bottom of a terrine or serving bowl, and at the table, carefully ladle the hot soup over the rice cakes. Serve at once.

---

287 calories, 7 g fat, 1 g saturated fat, 18 mg cholesterol,
3.5 g dietary fiber, 291 mg sodium

Cold Tofu and Vegetables over Sushi Rice

This refreshing dish is inspired by a classic Japanese box-lunch favorite. In fact, it makes an excellent summer lunch to tote to work—even if you carry it in a plastic container instead of a lacquered box. Note that the tofu and vegetables need to be refrigerated for several hours or overnight.

Vary the vegetables as you like. You might prefer to cook the carrot briefly in the marinade; a microwave is handy for this. Or try a combination of spinach lightly cooked and marinated in soy and a little sugar, shiitake mushrooms cooked and marinated in soy, and lightly blanched summer squash or zucchini marinated in rice vinegar with a little sugar and soy. Or give this a California touch by adding a few avocado slices (sprinkle with lemon juice so they don't discolor too badly). Skip the tofu, or substitute 1 egg, lightly beaten and cooked, omelet style, then cut into strips.

Seasoned rice vinegar, which already contains salt and sugar, is sold at many supermarkets.

Makes 2 large servings; 3 average ones

TOFU AND VEGETABLES

½ seedless cucumber, cut into
   paper-thin slices
2 tablespoons plain rice vinegar
2¼ teaspoons sugar
1 medium carrot, cut into fine
   strips

½ teaspoon soy sauce
4 ounces soft or medium tofu,
   drained and cubed

SUSHI RICE

1 cup Japanese rice

1⅓ cups water

5 tablespoons plain or seasoned rice vinegar

4 teaspoons sugar (if using plain vinegar)

¼ teaspoon salt (if using plain vinegar)

2 green onions, thinly sliced

Thinly sliced pickled ginger (for sushi) and/or pickled daikon radish (optional)

Toasted seaweed (nori), cut into fine strips (optional)

Enoki mushrooms, rinsed (optional)

To make the tofu and vegetables: Lightly salt the cucumber slices and put in a colander to drain for about 30 minutes or until limp. Rinse the cucumber, and place in a glass or ceramic bowl with the vinegar and 2 teaspoons of the sugar. Toss to coat. Refrigerate several hours or overnight.

Toss the carrot strips with the soy sauce and the remaining ¼ teaspoon sugar in a small glass bowl. Refrigerate for several hours or overnight.

Place the tofu cubes in a bowl of ice water and refrigerate several hours or overnight.

To make the rice: Bring the rice and water to a boil in a heavy-bottomed saucepan. Reduce the heat to very low and cook the rice, tightly covered, for 15 to 20 minutes, until the rice has absorbed the liquid. Remove from the heat and let stand 5 minutes.

While the rice is standing, heat the vinegar; if using plain vinegar, add the sugar and salt and cook until the sugar dissolves. Pour the hot vinegar over the rice and quickly stir it in with a wooden paddle or spoon. Cover the rice and refrigerate until cool.

To assemble: Mound the rice on 3 plates or in 3 containers. Arrange the cucumber slices and carrot strips evenly over the rice. Top with the drained tofu. Sprinkle with the green onions. If desired, garnish with pickled ginger and/or daikon, toasted seaweed, and mushrooms.

Keep cold until serving.

Based on 3 servings: 300 calories, 1.5 g fat,
no saturated fat, no cholesterol, 2 g dietary fiber,
251 mg sodium

Creole Red Beans with Sausage and Yellow Rice

We have substituted leaner spicy turkey sausage for the traditional andouille sausage, but you may use andouille if you wish. Also, it's really not necessary to soak the beans overnight, which robs them of some nutrients. (In fact, most cultures that eat a lot of beans don't soak them.)

The beans can be prepared the day before. Reheat before serving time.

Makes 4 large servings

BEANS

1½ cups dry red beans, picked over and rinsed

About 1 quart water or low-sodium vegetable or beef stock

½ cup chopped celery

3 cloves garlic, crushed

2 large bay leaves

¼ teaspoon ground red pepper

¼ teaspoon dried thyme

¼ teaspoon freshly ground black pepper

½ teaspoon salt

2 teaspoons canola oil

½ cup chopped onion

¾ pound spicy turkey sausage, cut into ½-inch slices

1 cup chopped tomatoes

YELLOW RICE

1¾ cups water

1 cup long-grain white rice

1 teaspoon ground turmeric

Put the beans in a heavy pot and cover with 2 inches of water. Bring the water to a boil and continue cooking the beans for 2 to 3 minutes. Reduce the heat to medium-low. Add the celery, garlic, bay leaves, ground red pepper, thyme, and black pepper.

Cook until the beans are tender, 2 to 3 hours. Stir the beans occasionally. Add hot water as necessary to keep the beans covered. Add the salt when the beans are tender and have absorbed the water. Discard the bay leaves.

While the beans are cooking, heat the oil in a frying pan. Sauté the onion and sausage, stirring often, over medium heat until the sausage is cooked through. Set aside.

When the beans are cooked, stir in the sausage mixture and tomatoes.

Also cook the rice while the beans are cooking. In a saucepan, bring the water to a boil. Stir in the rice and turmeric. Cover, reduce the heat to very low, and cook 15 to 20 minutes. Remove the rice from the heat and let stand for about 5 minutes before serving.

To serve, spoon the rice onto individual plates and ladle the beans over the rice. Serve hot.

---

600 calories, 16 g fat, 5 g saturated fat, 65 mg cholesterol,
17 g dietary fiber, 829 mg sodium

Two-Rice and Wheat Berry Pilaf

One of the convenient ways to work more grains into your diet is to cook whole grains such as wheat berries and wild rice in big batches, then refrigerate or freeze them. If you have wild rice and wheat berries in your freezer, and leftover brown rice from earlier in the week, this pilaf goes together in no time.

Makes 4 to 6 servings

1 tablespoon canola oil

1 tablespoon unsalted butter or
  margarine

2 cloves garlic, minced

1 cup chopped green onion

1 cup grated carrot

2 cups cooked brown rice, cooked
  in low-sodium chicken or
  vegetable stock instead of
  water

½ cup cooked wild rice

1 cup cooked wheat berries

½ teaspoon salt

¼ teaspoon freshly ground black
   pepper

1 cup chopped fresh tomatoes

¼ cup chopped fresh basil

Heat the oil and butter in a frying pan over medium heat. Add the garlic, onion, and carrot and cook, partially covered, until tender, stirring occasionally. Add the brown rice, drained wheat berries, salt, and pepper. Continue cooking until hot. Stir in the tomatoes and basil.

    Serve hot.

Based on 4 servings: 237 calories, 7.5 g fat,
1 g saturated fat, no cholesterol, 5 g dietary fiber,
290 mg sodium

Mushroom Risotto

Arborio rice hails from the Po Valley of northern Italy, although it is now grown in the United States as well. Arborio is high in starch and creates a creamy "gravy" as the rice cooks. Another starchy short-grain rice, such as Spanish Valencia or Japanese sushi rice, can be substituted.

*   This dish can be served as a main dish, with a mixed green salad and some crusty bread. Do not attempt to speed up the cooking process; constant stirring and slow cooking are essential to the texture.*

Makes 4 main-dish servings

4 cups low-sodium chicken or
   vegetable stock

1 tablespoon plus 1 teaspoon
   unsalted butter

2 tablespoons olive oil

⅓ cup chopped shallots

1 pound white or brown
   mushrooms, cleaned and sliced

1½ cups white arborio rice or
   other short-grain rice

⅓ cup freshly grated Parmesan
   cheese

Salt

Freshly ground black pepper

In a large pot, heat the stock to simmering, and keep on very low heat.

Melt the 1 tablespoon butter in a heavy frying pan or saucepan over low heat. Add the olive oil, shallots, and mushrooms. Cook slowly for 5 minutes, stirring as needed, until the shallots soften. Stir in the rice and coat with the butter and oil. Increase the heat, for just 30 seconds, to lightly toast the rice.

Quickly add ¾ cup of the stock and reduce the heat to low. Continue stirring until the stock is absorbed. Add ½ cup of the stock and cook, stirring often, until absorbed. Repeat with the remaining 2¾ cups stock. The rice should be cooked through and slightly firm. If necessary, add warm water, a tablespoon at a time, until the rice is tender.

Stir in the 1 teaspoon butter and the Parmesan cheese. Season to taste with salt and pepper.

452 calories, 15.5 g fat, 5 g saturated fat,
17 mg cholesterol, 2.5 g dietary fiber,
297 mg sodium

Risotto with Crab and Artichokes

Made with Dungeness crab, this delicacy pays tribute to the San Francisco area, which gives us Dungeness crab and artichokes. You could also give it a southeastern flavor by using blue crab meat.

A 1½-pound Dungeness crab will yield about a cupful of meat. If you buy a frozen, previously cooked crab, defrost it in the refrigerator.

Makes 4 servings

1 cup cooked Dungeness crabmeat

4 to 5 trimmed, cooked baby artichokes or canned or frozen artichoke hearts

4 cups low-sodium chicken stock, preferably homemade

1 tablespoon olive oil

3 tablespoons minced shallots

1¼ cups white arborio rice or other short-grain rice

½ cup dry white wine or additional chicken stock

2 teaspoons unsalted butter or extra-virgin olive oil

1 teaspoon minced fresh basil
   (optional)
½ teaspoon salt
Freshly ground black pepper

1 roasted red bell pepper, peeled,
   seeded, and cut into strips (see
   page 16)

Pick over the crabmeat, discarding any pieces of cartilage. Refrigerate until needed. If using fresh or canned artichokes, cut them into quarters. If using frozen artichoke heart halves, cut them in half lengthwise. Set aside.

Heat the stock to simmering and keep on a very low heat.

In a large, heavy-bottomed saucepan, heat the olive oil. Add the shallots and sauté briefly, then add the rice and stir for a few seconds to coat the rice with the oil. Stir in about ¾ cup of the hot stock and cook over medium–low heat, stirring almost constantly, until the stock is absorbed. Repeat four more times, until you have added 3 cups of stock in all. Then stir in another ½ cup of stock and the wine and cook, stirring, until they have been absorbed.

Check the rice; if it is completely cooked through but still firm in the center and is suspended in a creamy sauce, it is done. If it is still too firm or starchy in the center, add the remaining ½ cup of stock.

When the rice is done, stir in the butter, basil if using, salt, and pepper. Stir in the crabmeat and artichokes; cook just until heated through. Serve immediately, topped with the strips of roasted pepper.

364 calories, 7.5 g fat, 2 g saturated fat,
28 mg cholesterol, 1 g dietary fiber, 533 mg sodium

Jeweled Rice Pudding

It is always helpful to have a beautiful dessert that can be prepared a day before serving time. This is an Americanized variation on a classic Chinese rice pudding. The "jewels" are the raisins, dates, apricots, and candied fruit.

Makes 8 to 10 servings

1 pound glutinous rice, soaked in
   cold water overnight or until
   the rice has swollen
1½ tablespoons unsalted butter or
   margarine
½ cup sugar
⅓ cup chopped candied orange,
   lemon, and/or lime
¼ cup candied pineapple
   (optional)
¼ cup quartered candied red
   cherries
¼ cup golden raisins
¼ cup chopped pitted dates
2 tablespoons chopped dried
   apricots

LEMON SAUCE

½ cup fresh lemon juice
1 teaspoon grated lemon zest
½ cup sugar
2 tablespoons cornstarch dissolved
   in ¼ cup cold water

Put the rice in a colander and set on a rack in a steamer over boiling water. Reduce the heat to medium, cover the steamer, and cook for 20 minutes or until the rice is soft.

Place the rice in a deep bowl and mix in the butter and sugar. Spray a 6-cup bowl or mold with nonstick cooking spray. Arrange the candied fruit, raisins, dates, and apricots in a decorative design on the bottom and up the sides of the bowl. Gently spoon in the rice, being careful not to disturb the fruit design. The recipe can be prepared the day before up to this point and refrigerated.

When ready to serve, cover the pudding tightly with aluminum foil and steam over hot water for 35 minutes or until heated through. Add extra hot water to the steamer as necessary.

While the pudding is steaming or earlier in the day, prepare the sauce: Combine the lemon juice, zest, and sugar in a small saucepan over medium heat. Heat until the mixture comes to a boil, then reduce the heat to a simmer. Stir the cornstarch mixture into the sauce. Continue cooking and stirring until the mixture thickens slightly and turns clear. Set aside. Serve hot.

To serve, invert the molded rice pudding onto a serving dish and bring to the table with the lemon sauce.

Based on 10 servings: 319 calories, 2 g fat,
1 g saturated fat, 5 mg cholesterol, 1.5 g dietary fiber,
26 mg sodium

Rice Flour, Rice Noodles, and Other Products

In the twentieth century, many of the immigrants to America have come from Asia. The resulting interest in Asian restaurants and cooking means not only that the number of Asian groceries has grown dramatically, but also that myriad rice products once found only in ethnic stores now show up in supermarkets, specialty shops, and health food stores. Here are just a few of them.

Any processed product, whether made from white rice or brown rice, will keep very well in a cool, dry place. Brown rice flour, however, is perishable and best frozen or refrigerated.

Most shoppers know rice cakes as those dry, puffed snack cakes available in the supermarket. Made of puffed brown rice, alone or with other grains, they are low in calories and free of fat (and, some would say, of flavor).

Asian rice cakes come fresh, frozen, or dried and are usually made of sticky rice that has been formed or cut into cakes. Mochi, a Japanese rice cake, is sticky rice that is pounded into a dense mass, then formed into balls or cakes. Brown rice mochi is widely available in health food stores, often in the freezer case. When heated, mochi puffs up. It's bland and slightly sweet on its own, and is usually served with sweet or savory fillings.

Crisp rice crackers, once a purely ethnic snack, have found their way into mainstream American stores. The Japanese-style rice crackers often are slightly sweet and flavored with seaweed.

Rice flour is made from finely ground rice and is used to make noodles, pastries, and dumplings. Rice flour sold in Asian markets is always white; in health food stores, you'll find brown rice flour.

Rice flour cooks up crunchy and crisp. It helps make coatings such as tempura batter crispy and lends crunch to traditional Scottish shortbread. It also makes a crackly-crunchy crust on bread, as we once learned from an instructor at the Cooking and Hospitality Institute of Chicago. Mix white or brown rice flour with enough water to make a thin paste, then brush it on top of the loaf just before baking. Rice flour contains no gluten and has a fine, sandy texture. It should be used very sparingly in baked goods.

Dried rice noodles, also called rice sticks, are brittle and translucent, like bean thread noodles. They're usually sold in two thicknesses: very thin, like vermicelli, and about the width of linguine or fettuccine. They're used mostly in stir-fried dishes and soups. The thin noodles sometimes are deep-fried.

If you frequent Thai restaurants, you'll recognize the thin noodles as the basis for *mee krob*, deep-fried noodles that are coated with a sweet sauce; and the thicker noodles as the basis for *pad Thai*, noodles that are stir-fried with peanuts, fish sauce, sugar, dried shrimp, and other ingredients.

Before using rice noodles in stir-fries or soups, you must soak then in warm water to cover for 10 to 20 minutes or until they soften. Drain. The thin rice noodles can also be deep-fried until crisp; do not soak them first.

In Chinese and Southeast Asian markets, you'll find fresh rice noodles, which are fairly thick and often come in large, folded sheets. Native to southern China, they're wrapped around fillings, egg-roll style, and are also cut into pieces and used in some stir-fried dishes, such as the Thai dish *pad sieuw*.

Health food stores also stock brown rice pasta, which has found a loyal following among people who are allergic to wheat or other grains.

Extremely thin, translucent, and brittle, rice papers are dried wrappers made of rice flour, water, and salt that are essential for making fresh Vietnamese spring rolls. They're available in markets that stock Southeast Asian ingredients. They usually bear the imprint of the bamboo trays they've dried on. To soften rice papers, slide them into a shallow bowl of warm water for a few seconds, then carefully remove and lay flat on a clean, thin kitchen towel.

Rice powder is rice, usually the sticky variety, that is soaked, toasted, and then ground. You can make it easily at home by soaking sticky rice, toasting it in a skillet until golden, then grinding it in a spice grinder or blender and sifting it through a sieve to make a fine powder. Rice powder, which can also be made from unsoaked long-grain rice, is used as a flavoring for some southern Asian dishes, especially Vietnamese.

Rice syrup is a sweetener, available in health food stores, made by adding an enzyme to a slurry of brown rice to convert the starches into sugar (malt). The liquid is drained off and cooked to produce a golden, mild-flavored syrup that's similar to corn syrup in thickness and intensity of sweetness. The perception is that it's more healthful than refined white sugar, perhaps because it's made from organically grown brown rice and not as heavily processed. Use rice syrup to sweeten tea or substitute it for corn syrup, honey, or molasses in recipes.

Rice vinegar is an essential flavoring in Asian cooking; a mild vinegar, it is also very good in salad dressings. Rice vinegar seasoned with sugar and salt is used to flavor rice for sushi. Both plain and seasoned rice vinegars can be found in many supermarkets.

Some Chinese dishes also call for black vinegar, a rice vinegar that tastes similar to Worcestershire sauce. It's available in Chinese groceries.

Rice wine is used extensively in Chinese and Japanese cooking. The Japanese flavor dishes with sake, a very dry rice wine, or mirin, a sweet cooking wine. The most popular of the Chinese rice wines is shao-hsing, which has a deep color and a rich, sherrylike flavor. These wines are worth seeking out, but if you run out, substitute vermouth, dry white wine, Scotch, or even grappa for sake. Dry sherry or dry white wine makes a good substitute for Chinese rice wine.

Rizcous is brown rice pasta that has been granulated, like couscous. It is the brand name for a product from Lundberg Family Farms that is found in health food stores, specialty shops, and some supermarkets. It can be used interchangeably with couscous.

Rice is an ingredient in some types of miso (Japanese) and chang (Korean), fermented pastes made of soybeans and other grains. Miso and chang are used to enhance the flavor and nutrition of soups and stews. Like yogurt, miso and chang contain live cultures. They should be added to soups at the last minute. Miso is also a staple of health food stores.

Rice bran is the coatings of bran removed when rice is polished white. Like all brans, it's a nutritious addition to muffins, cakes, cereals, and such. Rice bran also is made into an oil. Finely ground rice polishings, taken from the mostly bran-less rice in its final stage of polishing, are used in baked goods. Like oat bran, rice bran has been shown to lower cholesterol.

Rice Flour, Rice Noodles, and Other Products

Southeast Asian–Inspired Chicken Noodle Soup

Stir-Fried Rice Sticks and Vegetables with Chinese Five-Spice

Vegetarian Hot Pot with Rice Noodles and Soba

Fresh Rice Noodles with Beef and Broccoli

Liz Davis's Wheat-Free Peanut Butter Cookies

Mochi-Pineapple "Sandwiches" with Macadamia Caramel

Southeast Asian–Inspired Chicken Noodle Soup

Dried rice noodles of varying widths are often labeled rice sticks in Asian groceries or supermarkets. For this recipe, use the noodles that are about the width of fettuccine. If you have fresh or dried lemongrass on hand, use a couple of stalks of it, instead of the lime juice, to flavor the soup.

This soup contains relatively little broth in proportion to the noodles.

Makes 4 servings

½ cup dried padi straw
    mushrooms, or ½ cup sliced
    fresh mushrooms
6 ounces rice sticks
2 quarts low-sodium chicken
    stock, preferably homemade
1 to 2 small chile peppers, seeded
    and sliced
One 1-inch piece of fresh ginger,
    sliced
1 to 2 cloves garlic, or 1 shallot,
    sliced
3 tablespoons fish sauce

1 tablespoon fresh lime juice
¼ teaspoon sugar (optional)
½ pound fresh green beans, cut
    on the diagonal into long, thin
    pieces
1 medium carrot, cut into
    matchstick-size pieces
2 cups shredded cooked, boneless,
    skinless chicken breast
Freshly ground black pepper
Sliced green onions (optional)
Shredded fresh cilantro or mint
    (optional)

If using dried mushrooms, soak in cool water to cover for 20 minutes, until softened. Place the rice sticks in a large bowl and add warm water to cover; soak for 20 minutes, or until softened.

While the mushrooms and noodles are soaking, bring the stock, chiles, ginger, garlic, fish sauce, lime juice, and sugar, if using, to a boil. Reduce heat to a simmer and cook for 10 minutes. Add the mushrooms, green beans, carrot, and chicken and simmer for 5 minutes. Season with pepper to taste.

Serve hot, garnished with green onions and cilantro, if desired.

331 calories, 6 g fat, 0.5 g saturated fat,
37 mg cholesterol, 4 g dietary fiber, 740 mg sodium

Stir-Fried Rice Sticks and Vegetables with Chinese Five-Spice

Chinese five-spice powder, available at Asian food stores and large supermarkets, is a combination of cinnamon, cloves, white pepper, anise, and fennel. For this stir-fry, use the thin rice sticks that are about the width of angel's hair or vermicelli.

Makes 4 servings

¼ *pound dried rice sticks*

½ *cup low-sodium vegetable stock*

1½ *tablespoons cornstarch*

3 *tablespoons reduced-sodium soy sauce*

½ *teaspoon Chinese five-spice powder*

1 *tablespoon canola oil*

4 *cloves garlic, minced*

4 *green onions, halved lengthwise, then cut into 1½-inch pieces*

1 *cup julienned celery*

1 *cup fresh bean sprouts, washed and drained*

1 *cup red pepper strips*

1 *cup sliced water chestnuts, drained*

½ *teaspoon salt*

Soak the rice sticks in boiling water for 10 to 15 minutes or until softened. Drain and rinse in cold water. Cut the noodles into 2-inch lengths with kitchen scissors. Drain and set aside.

In a cup, stir together the stock mixed with the cornstarch, soy sauce, and five-spice powder. Set aside.

Heat the oil in a sprayed nonstick frying pan or wok. Add the garlic and green onions and stir-fry until softened. Add the celery, bean sprouts, red pepper strips, and water chestnuts, one vegetable at a time, then the salt. Stir-fry for about 1 minute. Stir in the drained noodles and continue stir-frying until the ingredients are combined and heated through. Stir in the sauce and continue cooking until the sauce thickens. Spoon the mixture into a deep bowl and serve immediately.

191 calories, 4 g fat, 0.5 g saturated fat, no cholesterol,
3.5 g dietary fiber, 676 mg sodium

Vegetarian Hot Pot with Rice Noodles and Soba

Putting together your own hot pot is fun—and you don't have to make advance reservations at a Chinese or Japanese restaurant. Best of all, you just prepare the food and the guests do the cooking at the table. It does require an appliance that will keep the broth hot, however, such as an electric wok, fondue pot, or deep chafing dish.

Using spoons or small wire ladles, guests add the raw food to the pot, cook it, then spoon it out and dip it into the sauces.

After the food is eaten, spoon the broth into bowls and enjoy the soup.

Hijiki, a sea vegetable, looks like dark curly shreds. To prepare it, soak it for 15 minutes in hot water. Drain and rinse. Cover with water and bring to a boil for 15 to 20 minutes.

Makes 6 servings

SAUCES

¼ *cup shredded fresh ginger*
½ *cup cider vinegar*
3 *tablespoons dry mustard*

2 *tablespoons dry white wine or water*
1 *teaspoon dark sesame oil*

HOT POT

¼ pound thin rice sticks, soaked in hot water for 10 minutes or until softened, then cut into 2-inch lengths

½ pound cooked soba (buckwheat noodles; see page 204)

1 package (10 ounces) fresh spinach, washed, drained, trimmed, and chopped

1 package (10½ ounces) firm tofu, drained and cut into ½-inch cubes

6 green onions, cut lengthwise and shredded

2 tomatoes, seeded and chopped

½ cup wheat sprouts, rinsed and drained (optional)

1 cup snow peas, trimmed (optional)

1 cup cooked, drained hijiki

2 quarts low-sodium vegetable or chicken stock (if desired, include some of the cooking liquid from the hijiki)

(optional)

Salt

Freshly ground black pepper

Garlic, chopped

To make the two sauces: Combine the ginger and vinegar; transfer to a small bowl. Cover and refrigerate until ready to use. To make the mustard sauce, put the mustard in a small bowl and mix in enough wine to make a smooth paste. Stir in the sesame oil. Cover and refrigerate until ready to serve. Stir both sauces before serving.

To assemble the hot pot: Arrange the noodles, spinach, tofu, green onions, tomatoes, sprouts, peas, and hijiki on separate plates and place on the table. Heat the stock and set it in an electric pot in the center of the table with the food and the sauces around it. Have spoons and small ladles, along with small bowls or plates, on the table for your guests.

Instruct your guests to choose their own ingredients and put them in the soup. Cover and heat the soup. Your guests then remove the cooked foods and enjoy them with the sauces. Continue this process two or three times. At the end of the meal, ladle the broth into bowls and enjoy. You might want to pass salt, pepper, and chopped garlic at the table.

236 calories, 5 g fat, no saturated fat, no cholesterol, 3 g dietary fiber, 199 mg sodium

Fresh Rice Noodles with Beef and Broccoli

Large sheets of rice noodles, a specialty of southern China, come packaged fresh or frozen in stores that carry Chinese and Southeast Asian ingredients. Their Chinese name is **sha he fan**.

These noodles form the basis of one of Virginia's favorite Thai restaurant dishes— **pad sieuw**—*which inspired this recipe.*

For a vegetarian version, substitute 4 to 6 ounces of fried tofu for the beef.

Black soy sauce, which is flavored with molasses, is available in Asian groceries.

Makes 4 servings

1 pound fresh or frozen rice noodle sheets

¾ pound broccoli

6 ounces beef top round steak, trimmed of all visible fat

1½ tablespoons rice vinegar, or 1 tablespoon white wine vinegar

1 tablespoon fish sauce (optional)

2 teaspoons Chinese fermented black beans, mashed with 1 teaspoon water

2 tablespoons black soy sauce, or 1½ tablespoons regular soy sauce and ½ tablespoon unsulfured molasses

2 tablespoons sugar or rice syrup

5 teaspoons canola oil

1 tablespoon minced garlic

If the rice noodles are frozen, thaw in the refrigerator. Cut each rice noodle sheet into 4 to 6 pieces; you want noodles that average 2 to 3 inches long and are about half the width of a lasagna noodle. Set aside.

Trim 2 inches from the bottom of the broccoli stalk, then cut the stalk on the diagonal into very thin pieces. Cut the florets into thin pieces. Set aside.

Using a very sharp knife, cut the beef across the grain into pieces no more than ⅛ inch thick (this is easiest if the beef is partially frozen first). Set aside.

The noodles, broccoli, and beef may be prepared ahead of time; cover each and refrigerate separately.

Make the sauce by mixing together the vinegar, fish sauce, if using, black beans, soy sauce, and sugar.

Pour about a cup of water into a wok and bring to a boil. Add the broccoli and cook, tossing, for about 2 minutes or until the broccoli just begins to turn bright green. Drain and set aside. Wipe out the wok with a paper towel.

Heat 3 teaspoons of the oil in the wok. Add the beef and stir-fry for about 2 minutes or until no longer pink. Remove from the wok with a slotted spoon and set aside.

Add the remaining 2 teaspoons oil to the wok. Add the garlic and stir-fry for about 30 seconds. Pour in the sauce ingredients and bring to a boil. Add the noodles and stir-fry for 1 minute. Add the broccoli and beef and stir-fry for 1 to 2 minutes, until heated through. Serve immediately.

424 calories, 27 g fat, 4 g saturated fat, 35 mg cholesterol,
3 g dietary fiber, 400 mg sodium

Liz Davis's Wheat-Free
Peanut Butter Cookies

Liz Davis, the young woman who shared this recipe with us, cannot eat gluten. The daughter of a professional baker, Liz has created a repertoire of recipes, such as this variation on a classic cookie, made without wheat.

We love these cookies. The absence of wheat actually gives them a clearer peanut flavor and a marvelously crunchy-sandy texture. They are not low in fat, but they're worth an occasional indulgence.

Be sure to use potato **starch** *in this recipe, not potato flour, which is heavier. Potato starch can often be found in the European or kosher section of the supermarket. If you use soy flour, note that it has a strong flavor in the raw dough; baking smooths it out.*

Makes 2 dozen cookies

½ cup creamy peanut butter

½ cup vegetable shortening or
  unsalted butter

½ cup granulated sugar

½ cup packed light brown sugar

1 egg

¾ cup brown rice flour or soy
  flour

½ cup potato starch

1 teaspoon baking powder

1 teaspoon baking soda

½ teaspoon salt

Preheat the oven to 325°. Lightly spray a cookie sheet with nonstick cooking spray.

With an electric mixer on medium speed, beat the peanut butter with the shortening until light and creamy. Add the sugars and beat until fluffy, about 2 minutes. Beat in the egg just until mixed.

In a medium bowl, combine the brown rice flour, potato starch, baking powder, baking soda, and salt. Add to the sugar mixture and mix well.

Roll the pieces of dough into 1½-inch balls. Place on the prepared cookie sheet. Dip a fork in cold water and press the tines gently against the cookies to make a crisscross design and to flatten them slightly.

Bake for about 18 minutes or until golden. Let cool briefly on the cookie sheet, then remove to a wire rack. Store in an airtight tin. These cookies freeze well.

---

128 calories, 7.5 g fat, 2 g saturated fat, 9 mg cholesterol,
0.5 g dietary fiber, 123 mg sodium

Mochi-Pineapple "Sandwiches" with Macadamia Caramel

A rich, gooey dessert with no refined sugar and no butter—in fact, no dairy products at all? In this recipe, which pays tribute to the ingredients and heritage of the Hawaiian Islands, we flavor the caramel with a rich "milk" of macadamia nuts and rice drink.

Mochi's chewiness, typical of many Asian rice-based desserts, may not be to everyone's taste. For a "safer" and even easier dessert, set the pineapple slices on crunchy rice cakes.

Makes 4 servings

½ *cup rice syrup*

⅓ *cup vanilla-flavored nondairy*
rice drink

⅓ *cup roasted, salted macadamia*
nuts, or 3 tablespoons
macadamia butter

¼ *teaspoon vanilla*

⅛ *teaspoon salt*

4 ounces mochi

2 teaspoons corn or peanut oil

1 cored fresh pineapple (20
ounces)

Chopped candied ginger
(optional)

To make the caramel: Pour the rice syrup into a small, heavy saucepan. Bring to a furious boil, reduce the heat to medium, and boil for 3 to 5 minutes or until the rice syrup is very thick and the color of deep butterscotch.

While the syrup boils, puree the rice drink and macadamia nuts in a blender or food processor until the nuts are finely ground. Set aside.

Remove the boiled syrup from the heat. Carefully stir in the macadamia mixture, a little at a time. Stir in the vanilla and salt. The caramel may be made ahead of time and refrigerated; heat slightly before serving.

To prepare the mochi and assemble the dessert: Cut the mochi into 8 sticks, about 1 inch wide. Heat the oil in a nonstick skillet. Add the mochi and fry until golden on the bottom, then turn and fry for a minute on the other side. Cover the pan and cook over low heat for 7 to 8 minutes or until the mochi puffs up.

Meanwhile, remove and discard the pineapple core and cut the pineapple into 8 slices. Dice 4 of the slices. Set aside.

When the mochi is browned and puffed, remove from the heat. Arrange 2 sticks of mochi on each of 4 plates. Top with a slice of pineapple. Spoon the caramel sauce over the mochi and pineapple. Sprinkle with the diced pineapple and a little candied ginger, if desired, and serve immediately.

For a fancier presentation, garnish each plate with edible flowers.

Variation: Omit the mochi. Place a plain rice cake (regular size, not mini) on each plate. Top with a pineapple slice. Scatter the diced pineapple around the rice cake and spoon the caramel sauce over all.

290 calories, 12 g fat, 1.5 g saturated fat, no cholesterol,
3.5 g dietary fiber, 64 mg sodium

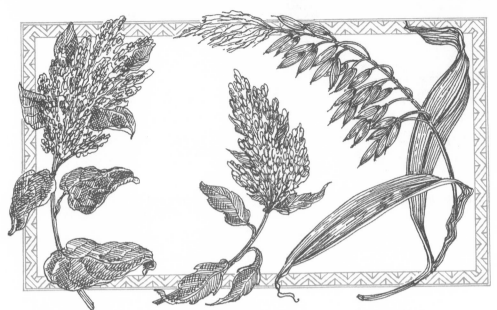

Native American Gifts, North and South

Besides corn, three other food grains we enjoy today are true-blue Americans—wild rice, amaranth, and quinoa. For centuries these grains have nourished the native peoples of North, Central, and South America.

Wild rice represents a small but precious legacy from our northern lakes. Amaranth, a grain sacred to the Aztecs, was recently resurrected for the natural-foods market and now shows up everywhere. And quinoa earned the title "mother grain" from the Incas for good reason: It provides more of the essential proteins than any other grain on earth.

Wild Rice

Wild rice is not really rice. And these days, hardly any of it is wild. Perhaps it would be better to call it by its Ojibwa name, *mahnomin,* which translates roughly to "gift from the creator."

Truly wild rice, a native of North America, is harvested by hand, as it has been for centuries. In late summer, the Ojibwa (also known as the Chippewa) gather it by maneuvering canoes through the tall grass. The harvester uses one stick, called a knocker, to bend down the grass and another stick to thresh off the grains. The wild rice is dried, then toasted to loosen the husks and develop the grain's distinctive tealike flavor. Traditionally the Ojibwa roasted it in kettles over wood fires, loosened the hulls by dancing on the rice in soft moccasins, and winnowed out the chaff by tossing the rice in birch baskets.

Today the Ojibwa use mechanized processing plants. But parching is still an art, said Dave Reinke of Manitok Wild Rice, a cooperative owned by the White Earth Band of the Ojibwa that harvests some 75,000 to 150,000 pounds of wild rice a year. "Proper parching improves the flavor and imparts a cooking quality." The White Earth processors still parch rice over wood.

Wild rice figures prominently in the lore of the Ojibwa, who once lived on the East Coast. Their prophets foretold a great journey that would end in a place where abundant food grew in the water. By the mid-1500s, they had migrated to northern Wisconsin and Minnesota and, like the Sioux and Fox who had lived there before them, quickly adopted wild rice as a staple food.

Wild rice thrives in the upper Great Lakes area, where the lakes and marshes have muddy bottoms for the seeds to anchor and mild currents that won't wash the seeds away. As the snow and ice melt in the spring and the lakes flood, oxygen and nutrients reach the seeds, which then sprout.

By Minnesota law, "lake rice" refers to true wild rice that has been harvested by hand; wild rice grown in paddies is labeled "cultivated." Minnesota requires rice sold in the state to be labeled with its place of origin.

About 99 percent of lake rice comes from Minnesota and Canada, although Wisconsin produces a small amount. Most of Minnesota's rice is harvested on the White Earth Reservation in the northwest part of the state and the Leech Lake Reservation in the northeast. To protect both the natural resource and the Ojibwa heritage, Minnesota allows no mechanical harvesting of lake rice and strictly regulates who can harvest lake rice and when.

Until the 1970s, wild rice resisted cultivation. Today, lake rice accounts for only about 10 percent of all the wild rice harvested in Minnesota. The other 90 percent, most of the "wild rice" you see in stores today, is cultivated in paddies, like regular rice. To grow wild rice, farmers flood the fields, as they do for regular rice. Just before harvesting, the fields are drained, and the rice is harvested mechanically. Minnesota usually is the largest producer of cultivated wild rice, producing some 5.5 million pounds annually, although it runs neck and neck with California for the number-one spot and wild rice is now cultivated in other states, including Idaho, Oklahoma, and Wisconsin.

Although it's elongated like rice and grows in water, wild rice, *Zizania aquatica*, is not closely related to rice. Also called Indian rice or water oats, this annual grass has strong, hollow stems that can reach up to ten feet in height and leaves that grow both under and above water.

Generally, paddy-grown rice is more consistent in flavor, color, and size than lake rice. Both cultivated and lake rice have a flavor reminiscent of black tea and hazelnuts. Lake rice can taste a little more tangy and smoky. Aficionados prize lake rice for its greater complexity. Reinke compares it to wine; the flavor depends on where and when the rice was harvested and how it was parched.

We have two words of advice on buying wild rice: Shop around. Prices depend on whether the rice is cultivated or wild, on the grade, on how good or poor the harvest is and—most of all—on whatever the seller can get. The Manitok cooperative sells lake rice for about $8 a pound, but we have seen lake rice advertised for over $30 a pound. Wild rice, whether cultivated or truly wild, will never be inexpensive. It is labor intensive and it loses 60 percent of its weight during roasting.

Rice grading means little, since each state or industry board seems to set its own rules. Grading generally reflects the size and color of the grain and how many broken bits are in the batch. It does not really reflect quality. Broken rice, in fact, cooks more quickly and is ideal for soups and stuffings.

We recommend buying wild rice by the pound from regional suppliers (see Mail Order Sources); it's less expensive that way than it is in tiny boxes. Wild rice will keep for several months in a cool, dry place, although for longer storage it's a good idea to freeze or refrigerate it in an airtight container.

Rinse wild rice before cooking. Because it varies in how much water it absorbs and how long it takes to cook, it's easiest to cook wild rice in plenty of water, then drain it. The general rule is to combine 1 cup wild rice with 3 to 4 cups water in a saucepan and bring the mixture to a boil over medium heat. Cover the pan, reduce the heat to low, and simmer for 45 minutes to an hour, or until the rice is tender and has split. Drain. The cooking time depends partly on whether you like your rice firm and chewy and only slightly split, or "butterflied" and tender.

We also tried another method, recommended by one wild rice seller, that worked well: Soak 1 cup of rice overnight in cold water to cover. Drain. Bring 2 cups fresh water to a boil. Add the soaked rice. Cover and simmer over low heat for 15 to 25 minutes or until the rice has absorbed the water and is tender. The rice retains more nutrients this way than when it's drained after cooking.

To cut the cooking time, you can use a pressure cooker. Bring 3 cups of water to a boil in the cooker. Add 1 cup rinsed wild rice. Cook for about 25 minutes after the cooker reaches pressure. If the rice is still too chewy for your taste, cook the regular way for another 5 to 10 minutes.

Cooked wild rice freezes well. Let it cool, then toss with a teaspoon or two of vegetable oil. Freeze it in an airtight container for up to 6 months, then thaw and use in pilafs, soups, and stuffings.

Some places that sell wild rice also sell it popped as a snack. Popped wild rice is not low in fat, but it is utterly delicious. You can make it yourself by deep-frying the wild rice until it pops.

Perhaps because they're both "water foods," wild rice and fish make a heavenly marriage. Wild rice makes excellent salads, pilafs, soups (use it like barley), and stuffings. Leftover cooked wild rice is great in omelets, stir-fried with vegetables like regular rice, or mixed into pancake or muffin batter.

Wild Rice

Wild Rice–Salmon Burgers with Cucumber-Yogurt Sauce

Pan-Fried Fish and Wild Rice

Wild and Brown Rice Pilaf with Asparagus and Morels

Wild Rice Salad with Cranberries and Candied Nuts

Wild Rice Waffles with Warm Strawberry Sauce

Wild Rice and Mandarin Orange Muffins

Wild Rice–Salmon Burgers with
Cucumber-Yogurt Sauce

To grind salmon, remove the skin and bones from the fillets or steaks, then grind the fish in a meat grinder or in a food processor fitted with the steel blade. Or ask your fishmonger to grind it for you.

These burgers are good with sliced tomatoes or served in whole wheat pitas.

Makes 4 servings

2 cups plain nonfat yogurt

1 clove garlic, minced

1 cup seeded, chopped cucumber

¼ teaspoon white pepper

2 cups (about 1 pound) uncooked
   ground salmon

1 cup cooked wild rice

½ cup minced green onion

⅓ cup whole wheat bread crumbs

1 tablespoon snipped fresh dill

¼ teaspoon freshly ground black
   pepper

1 tablespoon canola oil or
   unsalted butter

To make the sauce: In a small bowl mix the yogurt with the garlic, cucumber, and white pepper. Cover lightly and refrigerate until ready to serve. Stir the sauce before serving.

In a deep bowl, mix together the ground salmon, wild rice, green onion, bread crumbs, dill, and black pepper. Using clean hands, shape the mixture into patties, or use a hamburger press.

Heat the oil in a sprayed nonstick frying pan. Cook the burgers until lightly browned. Turn them over using a spatula and continue cooking 3 to 4 minutes longer, until cooked through. The burgers can also be grilled using a sprayed grill rack set on the grid over hot coals.

Put the burgers on individual plates and drizzle the sauce on top. Serve hot.

343 calories, 11.5 g fat, 1.5 g saturated fat,
65 mg cholesterol, 2 g dietary fiber, 219 mg sodium

Pan-Fried Fish and Wild Rice

If you make it with walleye or whitefish, this dish evokes the northern woods of Wisconsin and Minnesota. Make it with trout, and it conjures visions of the mountains and lakes of northern Idaho. All three states produce wild rice.

Makes 4 servings

1 pound walleye, trout, whitefish, or perch fillets
3 tablespoons yellow or white cornmeal
2 tablespoons unbleached all-purpose flour
½ teaspoon salt
¼ teaspoon freshly ground black pepper
¼ teaspoon onion powder
¼ cup egg substitute
2 tablespoons olive oil
½ cup finely chopped onion

1 cup cooked wild rice
1 cup cooked brown or white rice, or mixed rices
2 tablespoons dried blueberries or currants
1½ teaspoons finely chopped fresh rosemary, or 2 tablespoons finely chopped fresh parsley
Balsamic vinegar or fresh orange juice
Rosemary or parsley sprigs (optional)

Rinse the fish fillets and pat dry. Remove any stray bones. Set aside.

Mix the cornmeal, the flour, ¼ teaspoon of the salt, the pepper, and the onion powder. Dredge the fish in the egg substitute, then in the cornmeal mixture, shaking off the excess. Heat 1½ tablespoons of the oil in a skillet. Add the fish and fry on both sides until golden and just cooked through, about 5 minutes in all. Remove to a platter and keep warm in a 200° oven while you cook the rice.

Add the remaining ½ tablespoon oil to the pan and heat. Add the onion and cook until softened. Stir in the wild and brown rices, blueberries, remaining ¼ teaspoon salt, and chopped rosemary. Cook over medium heat, without stirring, until the rice forms a brown crust on the bottom. Stir the rice mixture, breaking up the crust into the rice. Spoon the rice onto a platter with the fish. Sprinkle lightly with balsamic vinegar, and garnish with rosemary sprigs, if desired.

Serve immediately.

With trout: 364 calories, 11 g fat, 1.5 g saturated fat,
45 mg cholesterol, 4 g dietary fiber, 321 mg sodium

Wild and Brown Rice Pilaf with Asparagus and Morels

Morels start popping up in May in the forests of the upper Midwest. Asparagus, a major crop in Michigan, comes in June. This is intended as a meatless main course. If you prefer, you can add a cup of diced cooked boneless, skinless chicken breast.

For a California version of this dish, substitute shiitakes for the morels and increase the amount of orange zest to 1 teaspoon.

Makes 4 main-dish servings

6 medium fresh morels, or about ⅓ ounce dried
1½ tablespoons olive oil
½ cup finely chopped shallots
½ teaspoon grated orange zest
¼ teaspoon dried marjoram
1 pound asparagus, trimmed and snapped into 1½-inch pieces

3 cups cooked long-grain brown rice
1 cup cooked wild rice
½ teaspoon salt
Freshly ground black pepper

If using fresh morels, soak in salted cold water to cover for 20 minutes, then drain, pat dry, trim and discard the stems, and coarsely chop the caps. If using dried morels, soak in warm water for 30 minutes or until softened. Drain, reserving the liquid. Trim and discard the stems; coarsely chop the caps. Strain the soaking liquid through cheesecloth or a coffee filter.

Heat the oil in a large sauté pan or stir-fry pan. Add the shallots and sauté for a minute, then add the orange zest, the marjoram, and ⅓ cup of the mushroom soaking liquid; or water if using fresh mushrooms. Add the asparagus in a single layer. Cover the pan tightly and cook the asparagus, stirring once, for 4 to 6 minutes, until it begins to turn bright green.

Stir in the brown rice and wild rice, tossing well. Cook over medium heat, stirring once or twice, until the rice is heated through. For an even better dish, let cook until the bottom of the rice begins to turn crusty, then stir this crust into the rice. Add the salt and pepper to taste. Serve warm.

296 calories, 7 g fat, 1 g saturated fat, no cholesterol,
6 g dietary fiber, 280 mg sodium

Wild Rice Salad with Cranberries and Candied Nuts

This delicious salad was created by Diane Venberg, marketing coordinator of Alfalfa's Seattle store and an accomplished vegetarian cook. (Alfalfa's is a chain of gourmet health food supermarkets owned by Colorado-based Wild Oats.) The addition of candied nuts lifts it out of the ordinary, and the Asian-accented dressing gives it a West Coast flair.

This sweet-tart salad makes an excellent side dish for Thanksgiving or other fall and winter holidays. The rices, dressing, and nuts can be prepared a day ahead of time, and the salad assembled the day of serving.

Makes 6 side-dish servings

DRESSING

1 tablespoon grated or minced
  fresh ginger
1 tablespoon mellow (light) miso
1 small clove garlic, minced

2 tablespoons canola oil
⅓ cup fresh orange juice
¼ cup plain rice vinegar
½ teaspoon sea salt

Salad

½ cup wild rice

1 cup long-grain brown rice

1 tablespoon maple syrup

1 tablespoon packed dark brown
  sugar or Sucanat (evaporated
  cane juice)

½ cup pecan or walnut halves

½ bunch green onions, chopped

1 cup diced celery

⅓ cup dried cranberries

⅓ cup dried currants

2 Bosc pears, peeled, cored, and
  sliced

To make the dressing: Place the ginger, miso, garlic, oil, orange juice, vinegar, and salt in a tightly covered bottle or jar and shake until well mixed. Set aside.

To make the salad: In a saucepan, bring 2 cups water to a boil. Add the wild rice, cover, reduce the heat to low, and simmer for 45 to 60 minutes, until tender. Drain any excess water. Meanwhile, cook the brown rice in another pan in 2 cups water, cooking 45 minutes or until tender. Place the rices in a mixing bowl and allow to cool. (The rices may be cooked a day ahead of time and refrigerated.)

In a small frying pan, heat the syrup and brown sugar until bubbly. Stir in the nuts and continue to cook just until the sugar caramelizes. Be careful not to let the mixture burn. Remove the nuts to a plate and let cool.

The day of serving, toss the rices with the green onions, celery, cranberries, and currants. Moisten the pears with a small amount of dressing. Add the remaining dressing to the salad and toss. Refrigerate until serving. To serve, mound the rice salad on a platter, and garnish with the pears. Sprinkle the candied nuts over the top.

367 calories, 12 g fat, 1 g saturated fat, no cholesterol,
8 g dietary fiber, 308 mg sodium

Wild Rice Waffles with
Warm Strawberry Sauce

This is a good recipe for leftover wild rice, or you could substitute cooked brown rice or a mixture of brown and wild rice. Use the ripest, juiciest strawberries you can find for the sauce. Or skip the sauce and serve these with maple or blueberry syrup or clover honey.

Makes 12 waffles; 6 servings

STRAWBERRY SAUCE

3 cups fresh strawberries

⅓ cup sugar

¼ cup fresh orange juice

½ teaspoon grated orange zest

½ teaspoon ground cinnamon

⅛ teaspoon freshly grated nutmeg

2 teaspoons cornstarch dissolved
   in 2 tablespoons cold water

WAFFLES

3 eggs, separated

1½ cups 1-percent or skim milk

1 cup unbleached all-purpose
   flour

¾ cup whole wheat flour

4 teaspoons baking powder

2 tablespoons sugar

½ teaspoon salt

¼ cup unsalted butter or
   margarine, melted and cooled

1½ cups cooked, cooled wild rice

½ teaspoon ground cinnamon

⅛ teaspoon ground nutmeg

⅛ teaspoon ground allspice

To make the strawberry sauce: Wash, hull, and slice the strawberries. Place in a small, nonaluminum saucepan. Mix in the sugar, juice, zest, cinnamon, and nutmeg. Bring to a boil over medium heat; reduce the heat to a simmer. Stir the cornstarch mixture into the sauce. Cook for 5 minutes, stirring occasionally, until the sauce is thickened and clear. Remove from the heat and set aside. (The sauce can be made ahead of time and refrigerated; warm over low heat before serving.)

To make the waffles: Beat the egg whites until they form stiff, glossy peaks; set aside. In another bowl, lightly beat the egg yolks. Stir in the milk, flours, baking powder, sugar, salt, butter, wild rice, and spices. Fold in the beaten egg whites. Let the batter stand for 15 to 20 minutes at room temperature. Stir the batter before using it.

Spray a waffle iron with nonstick cooking spray, and cook the waffles according to manufacturer's directions. Use about ⅓ cup of batter for each waffle.

391 calories, 12 g fat, 6 g saturated fat, 129 mg
cholesterol, 5 g dietary fiber, 463 mg sodium

Wild Rice and Mandarin Orange Muffins

When making these or any other muffins, stir the ingredients just until they are moistened and mixed together. Overbeating will turn the muffins tough.

Makes 10 muffins

1 cup whole wheat pastry flour
½ cup unbleached all-purpose
   flour
¾ cup sugar
1 tablespoon baking powder
1½ cups cooked, cooled wild rice
½ cup drained, crushed mandarin
   orange segments

¼ cup canola oil
½ teaspoon ground cinnamon
¼ teaspoon salt
¾ cup skim or 1-percent milk
¼ cup egg substitute, or 1 egg
   and 2 egg whites, lightly
   beaten

Preheat the oven to 350°. Line a regular muffin pan with paper liners. Set aside.

In a deep bowl, mix together the flours, sugar, baking powder, wild rice, orange segments, oil, cinnamon, salt, milk, and egg substitute, one ingredient at a time. Mix lightly; do not overbeat the batter.

Fill the muffin liners to the top. Bake in the center of the oven for about 20 minutes, until the tops of the muffins are firm to the touch and a tester inserted into the center of a muffin comes out dry.

Turn the muffins out onto a wire rack to cool slightly. The muffins are best served warm.

211 calories, 6 g fat, 0.5 g saturated fat, 1 mg cholesterol,
2.5 g dietary fiber, 174 mg sodium

Amaranth

It was quite a trip from the altar to the supermarket.

Until the Spaniards' arrival in 1519, the Aztecs so valued amaranth that it played a key role in their religious rituals. When their civilization fell under Hernando Cortés's sword, amaranth got mowed down with it. By the beginning of the twentieth century, grain amaranth had become a footnote to Central American agriculture. The Mexicans were still eating it, mixed with brown sugar syrup and made into candy, but only a scattering of farmers still grew it. It had already disappeared from the southwestern United States, where Arizona cliff dwellers had grown it in prehistoric times.

Now, amaranth is back in a big way. In the 1990s, we strolled the aisle of a Midwestern supermarket and saw, nestled among the cornflakes and frosted toasty stuff, a box of "ancient grain" cereal flakes made with amaranth. The health food stores fairly burst with amaranth in the form of flour, seeds, flakes, cookies, chips, and ready-to-eat cereals.

The residents of Mesoamerica and the Andes region were cultivating amaranth, which originated as a weed, well over 5,000 years ago. By the time of Columbus's arrival in the New World, it had grown to become a major food crop. It was highly nutritious, versatile (it can be grown for its leaves and stalks or its seeds), resistant to drought, and prolific (a single plant could yield as many as 500,000 seeds). It also stored well.

For religious rituals, the Aztecs mixed *huautli* (amaranth) with syrup and, sometimes, human blood, then molded the dough into cakes shaped like the Aztec gods. After the ceremonies, these cakes were broken up and distributed to the believers, who considered them the flesh and blood of their gods. Cortés and his troops, perhaps seeing blasphemy in this resemblance to their Catholic Eucharist, embarked on a campaign to wipe out such religious practices, killing and imprisoning Aztecs and burning and uprooting tens of thousands of acres of amaranth.

Once so prized that the Aztec emperor Montezuma annually collected 200,000 bushels of it for taxes, amaranth as a major food crop virtually vanished from Central and North America for the next four centuries.

It did thrive in both Europe and America as a flower and potherb. Known by such names as Joseph's coat, love-lies-bleeding, and cockscomb, ornamental amaranth grew in the gardens of the Virginia colonists and the Pennsylvania Dutch and brightened the pathways at Jefferson's Monticello. The amaranth that's grown for flowers has black seeds and is also eaten for its leaves. Grain amaranth has beige seeds.

In spite of the fact that marketers love to trumpet amaranth as an ancient American grain, it's not necessarily unique to the Americas, although it probably originated here. Its name comes from the Greek words for "immortal."

Inspired by data from a Michigan nutritionist that shows amaranth's great nutritional profile, the Rodale Research Institute in Pennsylvania took up the cause of amaranth in the 1970s, along with the agricultural research station at Ames, Iowa. They bred varieties suitable for U.S. agriculture. The drought-resistant crop grows well in eastern Colorado, Wyoming, Nebraska, and California.

Amaranth is not a cereal grain, but the seed of an herb. Its large family includes plants grown primarily for grain, those grown primarily for their leaves or stalks, and those grown as ornaments. A bit smaller than mustard seed, whole grain amaranth is light tan and tastes somewhat earthy and faintly peppery. It blends well with a variety of flavors. It cooks up into a gruel, but the seeds stay slightly crunchy.

Plain amaranth can be purchased as a whole grain, as a flour, and as a breakfast cereal. Health food stores and, increasingly, supermarkets carry plenty of products featuring amaranth. The whole grains keep very well in a cool, dry place. The flour is less stable and should be kept cool and used promptly.

To cook whole amaranth seeds, place 1 cup amaranth and 3 cups water in a saucepan. (Don't bother to wash it first; the grains are too small.) Bring to a boil over medium heat, cover, and continue cooking over medium-low heat for 20 to 25 minutes or until the grain has absorbed the water and is the consistency of mush. Stir occasionally, especially during the last 5 or 6 minutes of cooking, to keep the amaranth from lumping.

Cooked amaranth can be used as a side-dish alternative to mashed potatoes or as a main course. Like cornmeal, it can also be cooled in a pan, then sliced like polenta and grilled or fried, although it will not hold together as firmly as cornmeal. Leftover cooked amaranth also makes a good extender for meat loaves and similar dishes.

Amaranth will pop, and the Aztecs often enjoyed it this way. Popped amaranth is good in crumb-type piecrusts. Frankly, we're not sure popping amaranth is worth the bother—it's too easy to scorch, and it pops unevenly—but if you're curious, here's how it's done:

Heat a small, heavy, dry saucepan or skillet (not one with a nonstick coating) until very hot. Add 1 to 3 teaspoons amaranth seeds, just enough to cover the bottom of the pan. Put a lid on the pan, leaving it a little ajar, and pop the amaranth, shaking the pan back and forth constantly to keep it from burning. When the popping noise stops, remove the pan from the heat. This will take only a couple of seconds. Unlike popcorn, which contains more moisture, amaranth scorches easily; sometimes adding a tablespoon of water can help. Pop it quickly, and only a small amount at a time. Don't expect all of the seeds to pop.

Amaranth flour works well in a wide range of baked goods, from yeast breads to muffins. It is low in gluten and must be combined with wheat flour.

Amaranth

Chicken-Filled Amaranth Crepes with Avocado Sauce

Chicken in an Herbed Amaranth Crust

Amaranth in Acorn Squash

Amaranth with a Southwestern Flair

Amaranth Currant Rolls

Amaranth Bran Bread

Amaranth Date Muffins

Fresh Florida Fruit Tart with an Amaranth Crust

Chicken-Filled Amaranth Crepes with Avocado Sauce

Vibrant colors and deep flavors give this dish a sunny southwestern motif. You can roll the amaranth crepes around filling of your choice, if you prefer. To freeze, just stack them between sheets of waxed paper and wrap tightly. Rewarm them gently in an oven or the microwave.

Makes 6 servings

FILLING

3 cups diced cooked, boneless,
    skinless chicken breast
2 small tomatoes, seeded and
    chopped
1 cup cooked corn kernels, cooled
1 small red or green bell pepper,
    seeded and chopped
4 green onions, chopped

¼ cup chopped fresh cilantro
3 tablespoons nonfat mayonnaise
3 tablespoons nonfat sour cream
1 teaspoon ground cumin
¼ teaspoon salt
¼ teaspoon freshly ground black
    pepper

AVOCADO SAUCE

1 medium avocado, peeled

½ cup nonfat sour cream

CREPES

⅓ cup unbleached all-purpose
    flour
⅓ cup amaranth flour
¾ cup 2-percent milk
¼ cup egg substitute, or 1 egg
2 egg whites

2 teaspoons canola oil, plus more
    as needed
¼ teaspoon chili powder
Canola oil for frying the crepes
Chopped fresh cilantro (optional)
Chopped pimientos (optional)

To make the filling: Lightly toss all of the filling ingredients in a deep bowl. Taste and adjust the seasonings. Cover and refrigerate until needed.

To make the avocado sauce: Cut the avocado into 1-inch pieces and put it in a food processor or blender. Add the sour cream and process a few seconds until a smooth sauce is formed. Remove to a small bowl. Cover and refrigerate until needed.

To make the crepes: Combine the unbleached flour, amaranth flour, milk, egg substitute, egg whites, the 2 teaspoons of canola oil, and chili powder in a food processor or blender or in a bowl. Process a few seconds until smooth and all of the ingredients are combined, or whisk by hand. Pour the batter into a bowl, cover, and let stand at room temperature for 20 minutes before using it. Stir before using the batter.

Heat a nonstick 6- or 8-inch crepe pan. Brush lightly with additional canola oil, then pour 3 tablespoons of batter into the pan, swirling the pan so that the entire bottom of the pan is filmed with batter. Cook over medium heat until the bottom of the crepe is firm and beginning to color, usually less than 1 minute. Turn the crepe over using a spatula and—carefully—your fingers. Continue cooking until the crepe is cooked on the second side. Set the crepe on a plate and cover with a sheet of waxed paper or foil. Repeat until all of the crepes are cooked.

To assemble: Put a crepe on a dish. Spoon 2 to 3 tablespoons of the chicken filling down the center of the warm crepe. Roll up the crepe and set 2 crepes on each plate. Drizzle some of the avocado sauce over the crepes, then sprinkle with chopped cilantro and/or pimientos. Serve immediately.

---

354 calories, 13 g fat, 2.5 g saturated fat,
62 mg cholesterol, 5.5 g dietary fiber, 325 mg sodium

Chicken in an Herbed Amaranth Crust

We find that flaked amaranth cereal is a handy way to include this high-protein grain in the diet. Here, amaranth flakes take the place of cornflakes in an old-time favorite.

Makes 4 servings

1 cup finely crushed amaranth
  cereal flakes
½ teaspoon dried basil
½ teaspoon dried oregano
⅛ teaspoon freshly ground black
  pepper

2 egg whites
4 boneless, skinless chicken
  breasts (about 5 to 6 ounces
  each)

Preheat the oven to 375°. Spray a baking sheet with nonstick cooking spray.

Mix the amaranth crumbs with the basil, oregano, and pepper. Spread the crumbs in a shallow bowl and set aside. In a second bowl, beat the egg whites lightly, and set aside.

Wash the chicken pieces and pat dry with paper towels. One at a time, dip the chicken pieces in the egg whites, then roll them in the seasoned crumbs, patting the crumbs if necessary to hold them in place.

Arrange the chicken on the prepared baking sheet. Bake in the center of the oven for about 15 to 20 minutes or until the chicken is cooked through. To test the chicken, remove 1 piece and make a small cut to make sure the chicken is white inside.

Remove the chicken to individual plates and serve hot.

---

236 calories, 3 g fat, 1 g saturated fat, 103 mg cholesterol,
1 g dietary fiber, 146 mg sodium

Amaranth in Acorn Squash

Be sure to cook the squash until it is tender. If time is an issue, you can cook the squash ahead of time, prepare the filling, and refrigerate them separately. Add a few minutes to the baking time for the stuffed squash.

If you don't have any cooked barley or rice on hand, increase the amount of amaranth to ¾ cup and use 2¼ cups water.

If you want, you can sprinkle the filling with a little grated Monterey Jack cheese before baking.

Makes 4 servings

2 acorn squash, halved and
   seeded
½ cup whole grain amaranth
1½ cups water
½ cup cooked barley or rice
2 teaspoons unsalted butter or
   margarine

½ cup chopped green onion
¼ cup minced fresh parsley
1 teaspoon cumin seeds
½ teaspoon salt
⅛ teaspoon hot red pepper flakes
2 tablespoons sliced pimiento-
   stuffed green olives

Preheat the oven to 425°.

Set the squash halves, cut side down, in a pie plate or other ovenproof baking dish. Fill the pan with 1 inch of water. Bake the squash for 35 minutes.

While the squash is baking, prepare the filling. Put the amaranth and water in a small saucepan. Bring the mixture to a boil, cover, reduce the heat to medium-low, and continue cooking for 20 to 25 minutes or until the amaranth has absorbed the water. Toss the amaranth and barley in a deep mixing bowl. Add the butter, green onion, parsley, cumin, salt, red pepper flakes, and green olives and mix them together lightly.

Remove the squash from the oven and carefully turn the halves over. Reduce the heat to 350°. Gently spoon the filling into the squash. Add more water as necessary to the pan to keep it at the 1-inch level. Return the squash to the oven. Continue baking for 20 minutes or until the squash is tender.

Set the squash half on each plate. Serve hot.

222 calories, 3.5 g fat, 1.5 g saturated fat,
5 mg cholesterol, 11 g dietary fiber, 374 mg sodium

Amaranth with a Southwestern Flair

The slightly earthy flavor of amaranth makes it a natural with strong flavors such as garlic and hot peppers. Feel free to increase the hot red pepper flakes for more zip.

Makes 4 side-dish servings

½ cup whole grain amaranth

1½ cups water

1½ tablespoons canola oil or
   unsalted butter or margarine

2 cloves garlic, minced

1 cup chopped onion

1 yellow bell pepper or other
   pepper, seeded and thinly
   sliced

1½ cups chopped tomatoes

1 teaspoon chili powder

½ teaspoon ground cumin

¼ teaspoon salt

⅛ teaspoon hot red pepper flakes

To prepare the amaranth, place the grain and the water in a saucepan. Bring the mixture to a boil over medium heat. Cover and reduce the heat to medium–low. Continue cooking for about 20 minutes or until the amaranth has absorbed the water and is the consistency of gruel. Stir occasionally, especially during the last 5 minutes of cooking, to beat out any lumps that may form.

While the amaranth is cooking, prepare the vegetables. Heat the oil in a frying pan over medium heat. Sauté the garlic, onion, and pepper for about 5 minutes, stirring occasionally, until the vegetables are limp. Add the tomatoes, chili powder, cumin, salt, and hot red pepper flakes, and cook another 3 or 4 minutes. Stir in the cooked amaranth and cook another few minutes, until hot. Taste and adjust the seasonings. Serve hot.

*146 calories, 6.5 g fat, 0.5 g saturated fat, no cholesterol,
2.5 g dietary fiber, 148 mg sodium*

Amaranth Currant Rolls

If currants are not available, substitute dark or golden raisins.

Makes 12 rolls or 24 smaller rolls

1 package (2¼ teaspoons) active
   dry yeast

3 tablespoons honey

1½ cups warm water (110° to
   115°)

2 tablespoons canola oil

1 cup amaranth flour

1 cup stone-ground whole wheat
   flour

1¼ cups bread flour

1 teaspoon salt

2 tablespoons grated orange or
tangerine zest

½ cup currants

1 tablespoon unsalted butter or
margarine, melted and cooled

In a small bowl, combine the yeast, honey, and warm water, and allow it to proof; it will take about 5 minutes. Using a wooden spoon, stir in the oil, whole wheat flour, bread flour, salt, grated zest, and currants. Mix until all of the ingredients are combined and a soft, sticky dough is formed. Turn the dough out on a lightly floured board or pastry cloth. Knead the dough until it is smooth and soft.

Put the dough in a bowl, cover with plastic wrap, and let rise until doubled in size, about 1 hour or longer. Punch down the dough.

Divide the dough into 12 pieces. Roll the pieces of dough, one at a time, in your hand and shape into rounds. If you want to make smaller rolls, divide the dough into 24 pieces and shape them into 4-inch-long rolls. Place the dough on a sprayed baking sheet. Cover and allow to rise for 30 minutes.

Preheat the oven to 375°. Brush the rolls with the butter.

Bake the rolls in the center of the oven for 20 minutes or until the rolls are golden brown on the bottom and sound hollow when tapped on top. These are best served warm.

---

182 calories, 4 g fat, 1 g saturated fat, 3 mg cholesterol,
3 g dietary fiber, 180 mg sodium

Amaranth Bran Bread

This bread has a deep, nutty-earthy flavor. It's delicious with a smear of reduced-fat cream cheese.

Makes 1 loaf; about 12 servings

1 cup boiling water

½ cup 100% Bran or All–Bran
cereal

¼ cup canola oil, plus more as
needed

¼ cup molasses

1 teaspoon salt

1 package (2¼ teaspoons) active
dry yeast

1 teaspoon honey

¼ cup warm water (110° to 115°)

1 egg, lightly beaten

½ teaspoon baking soda

1 cup amaranth flour

3½ cups bread flour

1 cup dark raisins tossed with ¼
cup bread flour

In a large, heatproof mixing bowl, pour the boiling water over the cereal, oil, molasses, and salt. Let the mixture cool to room temperature.

In a second bowl, stir the yeast and honey into the warm water and let stand about 5 minutes, until foamy. Using a wooden spoon, stir the yeast mixture into cereal mixture. Stir in the egg and baking soda. Stir in the amaranth flour and bread flour. The dough should be damp and somewhat sticky, with just enough flour to hold it together. Knead the dough on a lightly floured surface until it is smooth but still damp.

Put the dough in a bowl, cover with a damp kitchen towel or plastic wrap, and let rise in a draft-free area until doubled in size, about 1½ hours.

Punch down the dough. Knead the floured raisins into the dough. Knead the dough a few minutes, until smooth and soft. Shape the dough into a round and set on a nonstick baking sheet. Cover and let the dough rise about 1 hour or until it has doubled in size.

Preheat the oven to 375°. Brush the top of the bread with additional canola oil and bake in the center of the oven for about 40 minutes or until the bread sounds hollow when tapped.

Let cool on a wire rack.

---

291 calories, 6 g fat, 0.5 g saturated fat,
18 mg cholesterol, 3.5 g dietary fiber, 241 mg sodium

Amaranth Date Muffins

Bake more of these light, moist, slightly sweet muffins than you need for breakfast, and freeze the remaining muffins for a handy dessert.

Makes 12 muffins

1¾ cups amaranth cereal flakes

1 cup whole wheat flour

⅓ cup packed light brown sugar

⅛ teaspoon salt

1 tablespoon baking powder

1¼ cups skim milk

¼ cup egg substitute, 2 egg
   whites, or 1 egg

3 tablespoons canola oil

½ cup chopped pitted dates

Preheat the oven to 400°. Line a muffin pan with paper liners; set aside.

Place the amaranth flakes, whole wheat flour, sugar, salt, and baking powder in a bowl. Mix in the milk, egg substitute, oil, and dates.

Spoon the batter into the muffin pan, to the top of the paper liners. Bake the muffins in the center of the oven for about 20 minutes, or until they are firm to the touch and a tester inserted in the middle of a muffin comes out dry. Let the muffins cool and remove from the pan. Serve warm or at room temperature.

132 calories, 4.5 g fat, 0.5 g saturated fat, no cholesterol,
2.5 g dietary fiber, 162 mg sodium

Fresh Florida Fruit Tart with an Amaranth Crust

Amaranth cereal flakes put a new spin on the old crumb crust. The crust is topped with tropical fruits that once were exotic but now grow routinely in Florida.

Makes 8 servings

½ cup egg substitute

1 egg white, lightly beaten

3 tablespoons sugar

1 tablespoon plus 1 teaspoon
   whole wheat flour

⅛ teaspoon salt

1 cup warm skim milk

1½ teaspoons vanilla

1 tablespoon rum

*3½ cups finely crushed amaranth
    flakes*
¼ cup packed light brown sugar
½ teaspoon ground cinnamon
⅛ teaspoon ground nutmeg
*3½ tablespoons unsalted butter or
    margarine, melted and cooled*

*6 cups sliced tropical fruit, such
    as bananas (sprinkle with
    lemon or lime juice to prevent
    slices from discoloring), star
    fruit, mangoes, and/or
    papayas*

To prepare the custard, combine the egg substitute with the egg white. Mix in the sugar, flour, and salt. Stir in the milk.

Cook the custard in the top of a double boiler over medium-low heat, stirring almost constantly, about 6 to 10 minutes or until the sauce thickens and coats a spoon. Remove from the heat. Stir in the vanilla and rum. Pour the custard into a bowl and cover with plastic wrap. Let cool.

While the custard is cooling, prepare the crust. Preheat the oven to 350°. Mix together the amaranth crumbs, brown sugar, cinnamon, and nutmeg. Stir in the melted butter. Press the crumb mixture firmly into a 9-inch tart pan with removable sides, or use a pie plate. Bake the crust in the center of the oven for 10 minutes. Let cool.

Just before serving, spread the cooled custard over the bottom of the crust. Arrange the fruit on top of the custard, overlapping and mounding it in a decorative way. Be creative and design the tart with the fruits you like best.

---

*259 calories, 7.5 g fat, 3.5 g saturated fat,
14 mg cholesterol, 4 g dietary fiber, 93 mg sodium*

Quinoa

What would make a struggling wheat farmer in southern Colorado decide to start growing "the mother grain" of the Incas?

"The Good Lord had me at the right place at the right time. That's the only real rhyme or reason I can figure," said Ernie Neu, who with his son Paul raises 130 acres of quinoa (KEEN-wah) in Colorado's San Luis Valley and sells the seed to everyone from Montana farmers who want to experiment with a new cash crop to chefs who want to dress it in chipotle vinaigrette and serve it with baby field greens.

"We can't produce enough. They want every grain we can grow," said Neu. He even grows black quinoa, a hitherto unknown variety. "It's probably a cross with one of our wild weeds," said Neu, who grows 4 or 5 major strains of quinoa and maintains a research plot with another 300 types. "It has a different taste. As rice is to wild rice, quinoa is to black quinoa."

Quinoa, *Chenopodium quinoa*, is not a cereal grain but a member of the goosefoot family, which also embraces beets, chard, spinach, and more than 200 other species of herbs, including lamb's quarters, a very nutritious plant that Americans call a weed. Nutritious and prolific, the goosefoots have a long history of cultivation in the Americas. At one point, goosefoot was a major food crop in what's now the eastern United States, but it gradually declined in favor of corn. Native to the Andes, quinoa has been grown for more than 5,000 years in South America. It was a major food staple for the Incas and still is for their descendants.

Neu began growing quinoa in 1984, when he was approached by Dave Cusack, a professor at the University of Colorado. Cusack, the son of a Colorado potato farmer and the husband of a Chilean woman, dreamed of a project that would unite the Andes and the Rockies. Early on, he joined the efforts of Steven Gorad and Don McKinley, founders of the Quinoa Corporation, to introduce quinoa to the United States. (The Quinoa Corporation eventually moved from Boulder, Colorado, to Torrance, California, where it markets quinoa imported from Bolivia.) Quinoa did thrive in test plots in the San Luis Valley, which had a soil, climate, and altitude similar to those of the Bolivian Andes. There was one problem: Residual pesticides from the livestock raising and farming in the valley tended to kill off the plants. Ernie Neu had begun growing wheat organically in the late 1970s and had one of the few patches of pesticide-free ground available in the area.

Further experimentation revealed that quinoa doesn't require high altitude, just a dry climate that cools down when it's time for the plant to set seed. The fact that it would set seed with little water caught Neu's attention; water is precious in the arid San Luis Valley. Today, quinoa grows in places as diverse as Montana and Phoenix (only in the wintertime, and whether it actually *thrives* in Phoenix remains to be seen, Neu said).

In 1985, Neu grew a little more quinoa, and in 1986, even more. In 1987, the first real commercial crop of quinoa—100,000 pounds—was harvested. And the market took off. Cusack was not around to see his efforts blossom; he was murdered in Bolivia in 1984. His dissertation adviser, John McCamant, took up where Cusack left off and is still one of Neu's partners. A handful of other farmers grow quinoa in southern Colorado, but to the best of his knowledge, Neu is the only one in North America who processes the seed.

Quinoa grows into a tall plant with leaves that look like notched spinach and seed clusters that can contain up to 100,000 seeds. The seeds come in different colors, but nearly all the quinoa sold in the United States is an ivory tan, with flecks of darker seeds (probably wild quinoa).

Uncooked, quinoa looks a bit like small sesame seeds. Cooked, it fluffs up and resembles couscous. Its texture, however, is both soft and crunchy, like caviar. The crunch comes from the germ that rims each seed in a white curlicue. Quinoa's flavor is hard to describe. It reminds us a bit of a cross between peanuts and buckwheat. If adobe had a flavor, we think it would be quinoa's: sun-baked and of the earth.

Quinoa comes closer to the "ideal" complete protein balance than any other grain and has higher levels of lysine than most cereals. This helps account for its popularity among today's vegetarians and with yesterday's Incas, who intuitively paired it with corn, which is very low in lysine.

Quinoa is readily available in health food stores as a whole grain, as a flour, and made into pasta. It's also used in ready-to-eat cereals and other processed foods.

You may have seen recipes that call for rinsing quinoa thoroughly in several changes of water. Unprocessed quinoa seed is coated with saponin, a bitter, suds-forming substance that acts as a natural insecticide. Quinoa sold in the United States, however, has had the saponin removed and needs only one good rinsing before it goes into the pot. Neu uses a modified rice polisher to rub off the saponin layer. South American quinoa has the saponin removed by a wet process and is then heated. The heat seems to kill the germ, meaning South American–processed quinoa will not sprout.

To cook, add 1 cup rinsed quinoa to 2 cups boiling water (add salt if you like), cover tightly, and cook over very low heat for 15 to 20 minutes, until the water is absorbed and the grain is tender-crunchy. Let stand a couple of minutes, then fluff with a fork before serving. Sometimes, quinoa will not absorb all the water; in that case, just drain it.

Some people like to toast quinoa before cooking it. Toasting is optional but brings out its nutty flavor. To toast it, do not rinse it first. Put it in the pan and toast over medium heat, shaking the pan back and forth frequently so the seeds don't burn. Add boiling water and cook 10 to 15 minutes.

Quinoa's earthy-nutty flavor marries beautifully with bold southwestern flavors: pine nuts, garlic, chiles, dried tomatoes, cinnamon. Use a little quinoa flour to provide an interesting flavor to breads, pancakes, and muffins. It is a fairly heavy flour and contains no gluten, so breads made with quinoa flour should contain plenty of wheat flour. Quinoa makes a good stand-in for buckwheat flour, although its flavor is milder.

Quinoa

Spiced Quinoa, Sweet Potatoes, and Root Vegetables

Tex-Mex Quinoa Pasta and Barley Salad

Quinoa and Couscous Tossed with Salsa

Quinoa-Stuffed Cherry Tomatoes with Yogurt Dressing

Quinoa Bread with Sunflower Seeds

Quinoa Corn Bread

Spiced Quinoa, Sweet Potatoes, and Root Vegetables

This spicy root vegetable and quinoa medley is good as a main dish or as a side dish.

Makes 4 servings

1 tablespoon olive oil
4 cloves garlic, minced
4 medium turnips, peeled and
    quartered
2 medium-large sweet potatoes,
    peeled and quartered
1½ cups peeled, diced rutabaga
½ cup pitted prunes
¼ cup dried currants
1½ cups low-sodium vegetable
    stock, or 1 cup canned
    vegetable broth diluted with ½
    cup water

1½ teaspoons ground cumin
½ teaspoon ground cinnamon
¼ teaspoon ground allspice
¼ teaspoon ground nutmeg
½ teaspoon salt
¼ teaspoon freshly ground black
    pepper
1 cup quinoa
½ cup chopped green onion

Heat the oil in a large frying pan over medium heat. Sauté the garlic, turnips, sweet potatoes, and rutabaga for 5 minutes, stirring occasionally. Stir in the prunes, currants, stock, cumin, cinnamon, allspice, nutmeg, salt, and pepper. Bring the mixture to a boil, then reduce the heat. Simmer, covered, until the vegetables are tender, about 25 to 30 minutes, stirring occasionally.

While the vegetables are cooking, prepare the quinoa. Put 1 cup rinsed and drained quinoa in a rice steamer with 1¾ cups water; cook according to manufacturer's directions for rice. Or put the quinoa in a pan with 2 cups boiling water, cover, and cook over low heat for 15 minutes or until the quinoa has absorbed the liquid and is tender. Stir in the green onion. Fluff the quinoa with a fork.

To serve, divide the quinoa among serving plates, and surround it with the hot cooked vegetables. Serve hot.

*315 calories, 6.5 g fat, 0.5 g saturated fat, no cholesterol,
10 g dietary fiber, 623 mg sodium*

Tex-Mex Quinoa Pasta and Barley Salad

Quinoa pasta is available at specialty markets and health food stores. A blend of quinoa flour and corn flour, it's a boon to people who cannot eat wheat, but it also tastes good in its own right.

Makes 4 large servings

1½ cups nonfat sour cream or
 plain nonfat yogurt
1 teaspoon ground cumin
1 teaspoon chili powder
½ teaspoon salt
1 package (8 ounces) quinoa
 pasta (shells or elbows),
 cooked according to package
 directions
1 cup cooked barley

1 cup reconstituted dried tomatoes
 (see page 16), chopped, or fresh
 cherry tomatoes, quartered
1 cup chopped green onion
3 jalapeño peppers, seeded and
 chopped (see page 16)
1 red bell pepper, seeded and
 chopped
1 cup shredded Monterey Jack
 cheese (optional)

In a small bowl, stir together the sour cream, cumin, chili powder, and salt. Let stand 15 minutes.

While the quinoa pasta and barley are still warm, combine them in a bowl. Mix in the tomatoes, onion, jalapeños, and bell pepper. Add the sour cream dressing and toss to coat. If using, add the shredded Monterey Jack cheese.

Serve the pasta salad warm (it's best this way) or at room temperature.

*333 calories, 2.5 g fat, no saturated fat, no cholesterol,
8 g dietary fiber, 620 mg sodium*

Quinoa and Couscous Tossed with Salsa

We find that quinoa is lighter in flavor if it is mixed with a small amount of a complementary grain. Also, adding a small amount of another grain enhances the texture of this dish. Like so many of our recipes, this can be served as a light lunch or dinner entrée, or as a side dish. The salsa can be prepared early in the day.

Makes 4 servings

1 cup chopped tomatoes
½ cup chopped onion
⅓ cup chopped fresh cilantro
1 teaspoon minced garlic
Juice of ½ lime
½ cup quinoa

½ cup whole wheat or regular
 couscous
½ teaspoon salt
¼ teaspoon freshly ground black
 pepper

To make the salsa: In a glass bowl, combine the tomatoes, onion, cilantro, garlic, and lime juice. Cover and refrigerate until ready to serve. Toss the salsa before serving.

To prepare the quinoa, bring 1 cup of water to a boil in a small pan. Stir in the quinoa; cover the pan. Reduce the heat to a simmer and continue cooking for about 15 minutes or until the quinoa is tender. Put the quinoa in a bowl. Let cool.

While the quinoa is cooking, prepare the couscous. Bring ½ cup water to a boil in a small saucepan. Stir in the couscous. Cover and remove from the heat. Let stand for 4 to 5 minutes, until the couscous has absorbed the liquid and is tender.

Fluff the couscous and mix it with the quinoa. Add the salsa, salt, and black pepper; toss thoroughly. For best taste, serve warm.

---

173 calories, 2 g fat, no saturated fat, no cholesterol,
5 g dietary fiber, 286 mg sodium

Quinoa-Stuffed Cherry Tomatoes with
Yogurt Dressing

This attractive dish is best served warm. You could also stuff cooked baby eggplants with the quinoa mixture. If you do not have any leftover cooked buckwheat (kasha) on hand, add cooked rice or couscous instead, or increase the amount of quinoa by 2 tablespoons and the vegetable stock by ¼ cup.

Makes 4 servings

12 large cherry tomatoes, or
    4 small regular tomatoes
¾ cup chopped green onion
½ cup chopped celery
1 teaspoon snipped fresh dill
¼ teaspoon freshly ground black
    pepper
1 cup low-sodium vegetable
    stock, or ½ cup canned
    vegetable broth diluted with
    ½ cup water

½ cup quinoa
⅓ cup cooked buckwheat (see
    page 204)
½ teaspoon salt
1 cup plain nonfat yogurt
2 tablespoons fat-free mayonnaise
1 teaspoon snipped fresh dill

Cut the tops off the tomatoes; scoop out the insides and set the tomatoes aside. Reserve the pulp.

Spray a frying pan with nonstick cooking spray and sauté the onion, celery, and reserved tomato pulp. Cook, covered, for a few minutes, until tender. Sprinkle with the dill and ¼ teaspoon of the pepper. Set aside.

To prepare the quinoa, bring the vegetable stock to a boil in a small pan. Stir in the quinoa and cover the pan. Reduce the heat to low and cook for about 15 minutes or until the quinoa is tender. Put the quinoa in a bowl. Let cool. Mix in the cooked buckwheat, the cooked tomato mixture, and the salt.

To make the dressing: Combine the yogurt, mayonnaise, and dill. Set aside, or cover and refrigerate until ready to serve.

With a teaspoon, stuff the tomatoes with the quinoa mixture. Divide the remaining quinoa mixture among 4 plates, and set the stuffed tomatoes on top. Drizzle with the yogurt dressing. Serve at room temperature.

*144 calories, 2 g fat, no saturated fat, 1 mg cholesterol,
3.5 g dietary fiber, 555 mg sodium*

Quinoa Bread with Sunflower Seeds

*Sunflower seeds add a pleasant crunch to this bread. If you don't have them, substitute
raisins or chopped nuts. Pine nuts are especially good.*

Makes 2 loaves; about 24 servings

3 cups warm water (110° to 115°)
**2 packages (4½ teaspoons) active
dry yeast**
**1 cup unbleached all-purpose
flour**
**⅓ cup plus 2 tablespoons honey,
preferably clover honey**
**¼ cup unsalted butter or
margarine, at room
temperature**

2 teaspoons salt
**1 cup bread flour or unbleached
all-purpose flour**
**4 cups stone-ground whole wheat
flour**
1 cup quinoa flour
1 cup sunflower seed kernels

In a glass bowl, combine 1 cup of the warm water, the yeast, and the flour, using a
wooden spoon. Cover with plastic wrap and let stand in a draft-free area for 30 minutes or until it has risen and is bubbly.

Mix together the remaining 2 cups warm water, the ⅓ cup honey, the butter, and
the salt. Stir the honey mixture into the yeast mixture. Then stir in the bread flour,
whole wheat flour, and quinoa flour, 1 cup at a time. Set aside 1 tablespoon of the
seeds to decorate the top of the loaves; mix the remaining seeds into the dough. The
dough should be damp and almost sticky. Knead the dough on a lightly floured
board for a few minutes, until the dough feels smooth yet soft. Put the dough in a
bowl, cover with plastic wrap or a damp kitchen towel, and set the dough to rise in
a draft-free area until doubled in size, about 1½ to 2 hours.

Punch down the dough and shape it into 2 loaves. Set each loaf in a 9-by-5-inch
loaf pan sprayed with nonstick cooking spray. Cover loosely and let rise until light.

Preheat the oven to 375°. Brush the tops of the loaves with the remaining

2 tablespoons honey and sprinkle with the reserved sunflower seeds. Bake in the center of the oven for 40 to 50 minutes or until the loaves sound hollow when tapped. Remove the breads from the pans. Let cool on a wire rack.

197 calories, 5.5 g fat, 1.5 g saturated fat,
5 mg cholesterol, 4 g dietary fiber, 181 mg sodium

Quinoa Corn Bread

The light earthiness of quinoa and the sweetness of corn make a winning combination that has been popular for centuries.

Makes 6 servings

1 cup yellow cornmeal
½ cup quinoa flour
½ cup unbleached all-purpose flour
½ teaspoon salt
1 cup 2-percent milk

2 egg whites, or 1 egg, lightly beaten
3 tablespoons canola oil
½ cup chopped red or green bell pepper

In a large mixing bowl, combine the cornmeal, quinoa flour, all-purpose flour, and salt. Mix in the milk, egg whites, oil, and red pepper. Do not overbeat the mixture.

Preheat the oven to 375°. Spray an 8-inch baking pan with nonstick cooking spray. Spoon the batter into the pan. Bake the cornbread in the center of the oven for 20 minutes or until it is firm to the touch and beginning to shrink away from the sides of the pan; a tester inserted into the center of the bread should come out dry. Let cool in the pan. Cut and serve while still warm.

244 calories, 9 g fat, 1 g saturated fat, 3 mg cholesterol,
3 g dietary fiber, 227 mg sodium

"Old Country" Favorites

Anyone who leaves home for a foreign land soon misses family, friends, and familiar foods—not necessarily in that order. From the Spanish, French, and English in the sixteenth and seventeenth centuries to the Ethiopians in the late twentieth century, the immigrants who made new homes in America tried to re-create the flavors they had known from the time they could first walk. Each new wave of immigrants adds bits of its culture and food lore to the great American stew pot, and everyone gets a taste. Irish Americans eat rye bagels. Chinese-American kids chomp on oatmeal cookies. Jamaican Americans dine on Italian fettuccine.

From a handful of native grains, America's bounty has grown to embrace a whole pantry full of them in various hues and flavors, just waiting for another adventurous cook to make them sing.

Barley

One of the oldest of the cultivated grains, barley grows everywhere from the Arctic Circle to the tropics. Barley is the world's fourth most important cereal crop, after wheat, rice, and corn. It's eaten in Ecuador and in Korea, in the Himalayas and along the Nile. Before early humans began growing wheat on a large scale, they made bread from barley.

American farmers grow plenty of barley—about seven million acres annually. But very little of it shows up as itself in the grocery store. More than half goes into animal feed; another 30 percent or so is malted, to be used in brewing and as a sweetener and flavoring in breakfast cereals and other foods.

That just goes to show that, in some things at least, Americans like to stick to tradition.

The first Dutch and British settlers brought barley to North America. They had little interest in eating it, though. They preferred to malt it for their wonderful beers and ales and to feed the rest to their animals. In those days beer was viewed as a nutritious grain beverage rather than something to get one into the proper frame of mind for Super Bowl Sunday. In fact, the Pilgrims who arrived on the *Mayflower* complained bitterly when some of their number grew ill and the ship's crew refused to share their beer. (It should be noted that beers back then more closely resembled "liquid bread" than most of today's mass-marketed brews.)

The Dutch and English, in turn, were themselves following in the tradition of the ancient Egyptians and Babylonians, who left behind texts comparing the virtues of various barleys for using in brewing beer.

Barley grows throughout the United States, but North Dakota, Idaho, Minnesota, Washington, and South Dakota are the major growing areas. The small amount of barley sold for human food goes mostly into soups, and barley is a standard ingredient in dry bean and grain soup mixes. Slightly sticky and chewy, barley gives soups body and sweetness, but it also makes excellent pilafs, salads, and stuffings.

Like wheat, barley (*Hordeum*) is a cereal grass that is planted in either the spring or the fall. Most barley grown in the United States falls into two botanically distinct types: six-row, the most commonly grown here, and two-row, which is more common in Europe and which boutique brewers claim makes a better malt. The names refer to the arrangement of kernels in the head. Hull-less barley, which, as the name implies, merely needs to be threshed like wheat, is a fairly new addition to the barley family.

Scotch or pot barley is the hulled, whole grain. Pearl or pearled barley is the grain with the bran layers polished off. In some Asian markets or specialty shops you'll find *hato mugi* barley, or Job's tears, a fat barley with a dark cleft down the middle. And in groceries that stock Ethiopian ingredients you might find black (really purple) barley.

Most barley sold in the United States ranges from light cream to tan in color and has a sweet, nutty flavor. It's somewhat bland on its own but makes a perfect foil for other ingredients.

About the only kind of barley you're likely to find in the average supermarket is pearl barley, on its own or as an ingredient in soup mixes. Health food markets carry hulled (whole-grain) barley, as well as barley flour, barley flakes, and, sometimes, barley grits and barley malt.

Barley flour long was a bread staple and is still used in flatbreads around the world. It's also an ingredient in Chinese longevity noodles. Barley flour can be used in all baked goods. It contains little gluten and is best mixed with wheat flour.

To cook pearl barley on the stove top, combine 1 cup barley with 2¾ cups lightly salted water or stock. Bring to a boil, reduce the heat to low, and cook, covered, for 40 to 45 minutes or until the barley has absorbed the water and is cooked through but still chewy. Stir once or twice during cooking. Uncover the barley and let stand 5 minutes before serving. If the barley is still too chewy for your taste after the allotted cooking time, add another ¼ cup of boiling water and cook another 5 to 10 minutes.

The same directions apply to quick-cooking barley, except that it will cook in 10 to 12 minutes. To cook hulled barley, use 3 cups water and cook for about an hour.

Because it's sticky and starchy, pearl barley makes a nice alternative to risotto. Use 5 cups stock to ¾ cup barley. Try it instead of rice in Mushroom Risotto (see page 136).

To microwave pearl barley, combine ¾ cup pearl barley with 2 cups water and ¼ teaspoon salt in a two-quart glass casserole. Cover and microwave on high (100 percent) until it comes to a boil, stir with a fork, then cook on high another 15 to 18 minutes. Let stand, covered, 5 to 6 minutes.

Cooked barley freezes well; just toss the cooled barley with a teaspoon of vegetable oil, place in a tightly covered container, and freeze. You can thaw it in a microwave, or put it in a casserole dish and reheat in a 350° oven for 10 minutes or until hot. Use it in soups or pilafs.

To cook barley grits as a breakfast cereal, add ⅓ cup grits to 1 cup lightly salted boiling water. Reduce the heat to low and cook, stirring often, for 10 to 20 minutes or until tender. Or place the barley grits and water in a deep microwaveproof bowl and microwave on high, stirring once, for 4 to 5 minutes.

Barley flakes are very similar to rolled oats in their cooking qualities. Add ½ cup barley flakes to 1 cup light salted boiling water. Reduce the heat to low and cook, stirring occasionally, for about 5 minutes. Or place the barley flakes, water, and salt in a deep microwaveproof bowl and cook on high, stirring once, for 2½ to 4 minutes.

Barley malt is a thick syrup made of malted barley. It's both sweet and slightly bitter, like dark molasses. You'll sometimes find powdered barley malt sweetener in health food stores; it is malted, dried barley mixed with maltodextrin (a corn sweetener). Malted barley is the main ingredient in malted milk powder, which you'll readily find in most supermarkets. Professional bakers often use a little barley malt in their flours as a dough conditioner—meaning yeasts love the stuff. There's no reason home bakers can't use the same trick. Use a little barley malt or malted milk powder instead of sugar in bread recipes. Malt also gives a marvelous flavor to pancake and waffle batters.

Barley

Barley and Mushroom Soup

Quick Root Vegetable and Barley Soup

Lima Bean and Barley Soup

Barley and Pasta with Ham and Leeks

Barley and Rice Salad with Shallots and Herbs

Warm Barley and Turkey Salad

Roasted Barley with White and Portobello Mushrooms

Barley and Shiitake Stuffing

Barley Rolls with Spinach and Feta

Malted Chocolate Barley-Oat Cake

Barley and Mushroom Soup

One of the many delightful aspects of dining in Chicago is visiting one of its many ethnic neighborhoods to find a good restaurant. We just happened to pass by a Polish restaurant on Milwaukee Avenue and stopped for soup. The barley-mushroom soup was so good that we have reproduced it here.

Makes 8 servings

½ cup dried boletus mushrooms
    (such as porcini, or those
    labeled Polish mushrooms)
2 tablespoons canola or corn oil
3 cloves garlic, minced
1 cup chopped onion
1 pound white mushrooms, sliced
2 quarts low-sodium vegetable
    stock, or 5 cups canned
    vegetable broth diluted with 3
    cups water

1 cup hulled or pearl barley
2 carrots, sliced
2 bay leaves
¾ teaspoon dried marjoram
1 teaspoon salt
½ teaspoon freshly ground black
    pepper
3 tablespoons snipped fresh dill

Reconstitute the mushrooms by soaking them in hot water for 20 to 30 minutes. The mushrooms will be soft and pliable when ready. Drain, rinse, and slice the mushrooms. Set aside. Heat the oil in a soup pot or other large pot. Sauté the garlic and onion over medium heat until tender, stirring occasionally. Add the wild and white mushrooms; continue cooking for about 2 minutes. Stir in the stock, barley, carrots, bay leaves, marjoram, salt, and pepper.

Bring the soup to a boil, reduce to a simmer, partially cover, and continue cooking for 1 hour or until the barley and vegetables are very tender and the flavors are blended. Stir in the dill, or reserve to sprinkle on top of the soup when serving.

Taste the soup to adjust the seasonings. Discard the bay leaves. Ladle the soup into shallow soup bowls and serve hot.

Variation: For a creamy, rich soup, heat 2 tablespoons butter or margarine in a small saucepan. Whisk in 2 tablespoons whole wheat flour until absorbed. Stir in

¾ cup skim milk and continue cooking over medium heat, whisking, until the sauce thickens. Stir the sauce into the soup and heat through.

---

155 calories, 4 g fat, 0.5 g saturated fat, no cholesterol,
6 g dietary fiber, 278 mg sodium

Quick Root Vegetable and Barley Soup

To clean the leeks, cut them in half lengthwise and rinse them under cold water, separating the layers so the water can reach the mud and sand. Then pat them dry.

Make 6 to 8 servings

3 tablespoons canola oil
2 cups chopped onion
1 large leek, white part only,
   thinly sliced
3 large carrots, diced
2 large parsnips, diced
3 quarts low-sodium vegetable
   stock, or 2 quarts canned
   vegetable broth diluted with 1
   quart water

1 cup pearl barley
1 teaspoon salt
1 teaspoon dried thyme
½ teaspoon freshly ground black
   pepper
3 bay leaves
3 tablespoons chopped fresh
   parsley (optional)

Heat the oil in a soup pot or other large pot. Sauté the onion, leek, and carrots over medium heat, partially covered, for 5 to 6 minutes, stirring occasionally.

Stir in the parsnips, stock, barley, salt, pepper, and bay leaves. Bring the soup to a boil, reduce the heat to a simmer, and continue cooking, partially covered, for 45 minutes or until all the vegetables and the barley are tender.

Taste the soup to adjust the seasonings. Remove and discard the bay leaves. Ladle the soup into bowls and sprinkle with the parsley, if using. Serve hot.

Based on 8 servings: 193 calories, 5.5 g fat,
0.5 g saturated fat, no cholesterol, 7.5 g dietary fiber,
285 mg sodium

Lima Bean and Barley Soup

For a faster version of this hearty winter soup, use a 10-ounce package of frozen baby lima beans. Barley miso, a paste of fermented soybeans and barley available in health food stores and Japanese or Korean markets, gives the soup a deeper, winey-salty flavor. If you use it, cut back on the amount of salt you add to the soup.

With a slice of rye bread, this very hearty soup will make a substantial meal.

Makes 6 to 8 servings

1 cup dried baby lima beans

2 tablespoons canola oil

2 cups chopped onion

½ pound sliced spicy chicken
  sausage, skin removed

2 quarts low-sodium chicken or
  vegetable stock

½ cup pearl barley

2 cups canned chopped tomatoes

1 teaspoon salt

½ teaspoon freshly ground black
  pepper

½ teaspoon dried marjoram

2 large bay leaves

1 tablespoon barley miso
  (optional)

Pick over the lima beans, discarding any stones and broken beans. If desired, soak the beans overnight in cold water to cover, then drain. (This is optional but can reduce the cooking time.) Put the beans in a pot, cover with water, and bring to a boil. Lower the heat and simmer for 1½ to 2 hours or until the beans are tender but still firm. Drain and set aside. The beans may be cooked ahead of time and refrigerated.

Heat the oil in a soup pot or other large pot. Cook the onion and sausage (breaking up the sausage), partially covered, over medium heat for 5 minutes, stirring occasionally. Add the stock, lima beans, barley, and the remaining ingredients except the miso.

Bring the soup to a boil, reduce the heat to a simmer, and continue cooking, partially covered, for 35 to 45 minutes, or until the barley is tender and the soup flavors are blended. If using the miso, stir a small amount of the soup into the miso to dissolve it, then add the warmed miso to the soup. Taste to adjust the seasonings. Remove the bay leaves.

Ladle the soup into shallow bowls and serve hot.

Based on 8 servings: 250 calories, 8.5 g fat,
2 g saturated fat, 23 mg cholesterol, 8 g dietary fiber,
624 mg sodium

Barley and Pasta with Ham and Leeks

This is a good way to use up leftover barley. Any shape of macaroni—elbow, bows, corkscrews, shells—works fine. You can substitute smoked turkey for the ham if you prefer. We like it with Pommery, a very coarse brown French mustard—or, as Virginia's daughter Lian calls it, "fancy mustard."

Makes 4 servings

4 ounces macaroni, preferably
   whole wheat
1 tablespoon olive or canola oil
2 medium leeks, white part only,
   cleaned and thinly sliced
1 medium carrot, finely diced
2 stalks celery, trimmed and
   finely diced
¾ cup low-sodium chicken stock
2 to 3 tablespoons brown seed
   mustard

2 tablespoons minced fresh
   parsley
½ teaspoon ground savory
⅛ teaspoon ground nutmeg
4 ounces chopped, lean, cooked
   ham
2 cups cooked barley
Salt
Freshly ground black pepper

Cook the macaroni in boiling water until al dente; drain.

While the pasta is cooking, heat the oil in a large, heavy saucepan. Add the leeks, carrot, and celery; cook over medium-high heat, stirring often, for 2 minutes. Add the chicken stock, mustard, parsley, savory, and nutmeg. Simmer for 5 minutes, until the stock is slightly reduced. Stir in the ham and barley and heat through.

Add the warm ham-barley mixture to the drained pasta. Toss well, season with salt and pepper to taste, and serve.

333 calories, 7.5 g fat, 1.5 g saturated fat, 12 mg
cholesterol, 7 g dietary fiber, 436 mg sodium

Barley and Rice Salad with Shallots and Herbs

Shallots taste like a more intense version of the onion. If, for some reason, you can't get them, substitute ½ cup finely chopped onion.

Makes 6 servings

1½ cups cooked, cooled hulled or pearl barley

1½ cups cooked, cooled white or brown rice (cooked in vegetable stock instead of water)

1 tablespoon olive oil

¼ cup thinly sliced shallots

4 cloves garlic, minced

1 cup seeded, chopped cucumber

1 cup chopped fresh tomatoes

½ cup thinly sliced Vidalia or red onion

½ cup grated carrot

2 tablespoons rice wine vinegar

¼ cup chopped fresh parsley

1 tablespoon chopped fresh basil, or 1½ teaspoons dried basil

Salt

Freshly ground black pepper

Combine the barley and rice in a large salad bowl. Set aside.

Heat the oil in a frying pan over medium heat. Sauté the shallots and garlic, stirring often, until the shallots are softened. Stir in the garlic and shallots with the barley and rice.

Add the cucumber, tomatoes, onion, and carrot to the salad bowl. Sprinkle the vinegar over the salad. Season with the parsley, basil, salt, and pepper to taste.

Serve warm or cold.

161 calories, 3 g fat, 0.5 g saturated fat, no cholesterol,
4 g dietary fiber, 100 mg sodium

Warm Barley and Turkey Salad

For convenience, this recipe uses fine pearl barley, sometimes labeled "instant" or "quick cooking." You can use 2 to 2½ cups of already cooked barley—any kind—if you have some on hand. This dish is good with a mixed green salad and crusty bread.

Makes 4 servings

1 cup water
1 cup instant (fine) pearl barley
¼ teaspoon salt or to taste
¼ cup low-calorie French or
  Italian salad dressing
1 cup trimmed fresh snow peas

½ cup chopped green onion
1 cup diced lean turkey pastrami
  or plain cooked turkey breast
¼ teaspoon freshly ground black
  pepper

In a large saucepan, heat the water to boiling; stir in the barley and salt. Cover, reduce the heat to medium, and cook for 12 minutes, stirring once or twice, until the barley is tender and has absorbed the liquid. Stir in the salad dressing, snow peas, onion, and turkey. Sprinkle with the pepper. Toss the ingredients well.

Serve warm or at room temperature.

266 calories, 4 g fat, 1 g saturated fat, 20 mg cholesterol,
9 g dietary fiber, 634 mg sodium

Roasted Barley with White and Portobello Mushrooms

Barley and mushrooms are a natural together, whether in soups or in casseroles like this one. You can sprinkle the dish with 2 tablespoons toasted pine nuts before serving if desired.

Makes 6 to 8 servings

2 tablespoons canola oil

2 teaspoons unsalted butter or
   margarine

3 cloves garlic, minced

1½ cups chopped onion

1 cup pearl barley

1 pound white mushrooms, sliced

½ cup diced portobello (or other
   hearty mushroom of your
   choice)

Salt

Freshly ground black pepper

2¾ cups low-sodium chicken or
   vegetable stock

Preheat the oven to 350°.

Heat the oil and butter in a frying pan. Sauté the garlic, onion, and barley over medium heat until the onion is soft, stirring occasionally. Add the mushrooms. Continue cooking, stirring occasionally, until the mushrooms are tender.

Spoon the mushroom-barley mixture into a 2-quart ovenproof casserole that has been sprayed with nonstick cooking spray. Sprinkle with salt and pepper. Stir in the stock. Set the casserole in the center of the oven. Bake, uncovered, for 30 to 35 minutes or until all of the stock has been absorbed and the barley is tender. Stir once or twice during baking.

Serve hot or at room temperature.

*Based on 8 servings: 166 calories, 5.5 g fat,
1 g saturated fat, 3 mg cholesterol, 5 g dietary fiber,
73 mg sodium*

Barley and Shiitake Stuffing

This stuffing is good for both chicken and turkey. It makes enough to stuff a chicken; to stuff a turkey, double the recipe.

Makes 4 servings

2¾ cups lightly salted water, or
  vegetable or chicken stock
1 cup pearl barley
1½ teaspoons canola oil
½ teaspoon olive oil
3 cloves garlic, minced
1 cup chopped green onion

½ cup chopped celery
½ cup reconstituted, chopped
  shiitake mushrooms
2 teaspoons dried tarragon
½ teaspoon salt
¼ teaspoon freshly ground black
  pepper

Bring the water to a boil in a saucepan. Stir in the barley, cover, and reduce the heat to a simmer. Continue cooking for 40 to 45 minutes or just until the barley is cooked through. Stir once or twice during cooking. Let the barley stand, uncovered, for 5 minutes.

Heat the canola oil and olive oil in a frying pan over medium heat. Sauté the garlic, onion, and celery, stirring occasionally, until soft.

Mix the barley with the cooked vegetables. Stir in the mushrooms, tarragon, salt, and pepper.

Use the barley mixture to stuff a chicken or fish. Or spoon into a 9-inch-square baking dish sprayed with nonstick cooking spray, and bake in a preheated 350° oven for 30 minutes. Serve hot.

215 calories, 3 g fat, 0.5 g saturated fat, no cholesterol,
9 g dietary fiber, 300 mg sodium

Barley Rolls with Spinach and Feta

Barley flour is found at health food stores. Because it has little gluten, it cannot be used on its own to make bread or rolls but should be used with wheat flour. It adds a slightly nutty taste to these attractive rolls.

These rolls freeze well. To reheat, cover them lightly and put in a preheated 350° oven for 6 to 9 minutes or until warm.

Makes 8 rolls

1 package (10 ounces) frozen
   chopped spinach, defrosted,
   well drained, and squeezed dry
½ cup finely crumbled feta cheese
2 tablespoons dried onion flakes
1 clove garlic, finely chopped
2 cups bread flour, plus more as
   needed
1½ cups barley flour

3 tablespoons sugar
½ teaspoon salt
1 package (2¼ teaspoons) active
   dry yeast
1½ cups warm 1-percent milk
   (110° to 115°)
¼ cup canola oil
¼ cup egg substitute, or 1 egg,
   lightly beaten

In a large bowl, combine the spinach, cheese, onion flakes, and garlic. Set aside.

In a deep mixing bowl or the large bowl of an electric mixer fitted with the dough hook, combine the bread flour and barley flour. Add the sugar, salt, and yeast. Stir in the milk, oil, and egg substitute. Mix until the ingredients are combined. Turn the dough out onto a lightly floured pastry cloth and knead until a soft dough is formed. Lift up the sides of the cloth to help you knead the dough at first. If necessary, add more bread flour, a tablespoon at a time, to make a soft but workable dough. Or knead in the mixer.

Put the dough in a bowl and cover loosely with plastic wrap or a damp kitchen towel. Set in a warm place and let rise until doubled in bulk, about 1 hour.

Punch down the dough and divide into 8 pieces. Roll out 1 piece of dough on a lightly floured pastry cloth to a circle about 4 to 5 inches in diameter. Sprinkle the top third of the rolled dough with 1 tablespoon of the spinach filling. Roll up the dough, jelly-roll style, then form into a coil, pressing the ends together. Set the roll on a sprayed baking sheet. Repeat with the remaining dough and filling. Cover the rolls loosely and let rise for 35 minutes or until light.

Preheat the oven to 400°. Bake the rolls for 18 to 20 minutes or until firm and golden brown. Let cool on a wire rack.

---

360 calories, 11.5 g fat, 3 g saturated fat,
16 mg cholesterol, 5.5 g dietary fiber, 362 mg sodium

Barley in the Bottle

Why do brewers need barley to make beer?

In a word, sugar. The yeasts that ferment the ales, pilsners, lagers, and stouts we love so well need sugar to survive. They get it from grain. Although just about any seed grain can be germinated to make sugars, barley makes an especially nice fermentable sugar, or malt.

Malt gives beer its mouth feel, color, and sweetness. In a well-crafted beer, malt's rich sweetness complements the bitterness of the hops. (Hop is not a grain but a climbing plant in the hemp family. The dried cones of the female flowers are used in brewing.)

When barley (or any other seed grain) sprouts, enzymes turn the starches into sugars designed to feed the emerging plant. So the first thing brewers or malting houses do is soak the barley, then let it sprout. The brewer or maltster dries the sprouted barley, cracks it, then roasts it. Malt is roasted at different temperatures and lengths of time, depending on the kind of beer desired. Generally, the lighter malts go into lagers and ales; the really dark ones provide the rich caramel color and flavor in robust beers such as porters and stouts.

The malt is then mixed with water to make the mash, and the dissolved sugar is drained off. The drained sugary liquid, or wort, is boiled with hops. Then yeast is added to the mixture and it is allowed to ferment into beer.

The malting process, along with the quality of the ingredients, is one of the main reasons good beers cost more than indifferent ones. Malting is labor-intensive and good malt is not cheap, so large, mass-market brewers usually cut the mash with other sugars and grains, such as rice and corn. Small-scale beer craftspeople also say two-row barley makes a better malt than the more common (and less expensive) six-row barley.

By the way, we met one home brewer who feeds his four-year-old daughter an unusual snack: crystal malt (a malt that retains a fair amount of unfermentable sugars and is used to give a good caramel sweetness to beers). She loves the malty, rich flavor of the crunchy grain, and he figures it is better for her than candy. It does make a nice snack: sort of an extra-malt version of Grape-Nuts.

Malted Chocolate Barley-Oat Cake

Chocolate and malt, which is derived from barley, were made for each other, and the combination makes this rich yet delicate cake irresistible. For the most intense malt flavor, use powdered barley malt sweetener (a combination of malted barley and maltodextrose), available in some health food stores.

Makes 12 servings

2 cups skim or 1-percent milk

1 cup quick-cooking oats

6 tablespoons unsalted butter, cut
    into small pieces

2 eggs, separated

1 egg white

½ cup barley flour

⅔ cup unsweetened cocoa powder

½ cup powdered barley malt
    sweetener plus 3 tablespoons
    all-purpose flour, or ¾ cup
    plain malted milk powder

½ teaspoon salt

½ teaspoon baking soda

¾ cup sugar

1 tablespoon vanilla

FOR DUSTING THE TOP

1 teaspoon unsweetened cocoa
    powder

2 tablespoons confectioners' sugar

2 teaspoons powdered barley malt
    sweetener, or 1 tablespoon
    plain malted milk powder

Preheat the oven to 350°. Spray a 10-inch springform pan with nonstick cooking spray.

In a microwaveproof bowl, combine the milk with the oats. Microwave on high, stirring once, for 3 to 4 minutes, until a thick, creamy porridge is formed. (Or bring the milk to a simmer on the stove top, stir in the oats, and cook 2 to 3 minutes, until thick.) Stir in the butter until melted. Let the mixture cool until warm but not hot.

While the oats cool, beat the 3 egg whites until stiff but still glossy; set aside. Whisk together the barley flour, cocoa, powdered barley malt, salt, and baking soda. Set aside.

Pour the oat-butter mixture into a mixing bowl. Beat in the sugar and vanilla. Beat in the egg yolks, one at a time. Beat the batter on medium speed for 2 minutes. Beat in the flour mixture just until mixed; the batter will be thick. Stir in about ½ cup beaten egg whites to lighten the batter, then gently whisk or fold in the remaining egg whites.

Pour the batter into the prepared pan. Bake in the center of the oven for 30 to 35 minutes or until the cake no longer looks dimpled and wet in the center (the cake may crack a bit on top). Do not use a tester to check for doneness; it will not come out clean.

Let cool. While the cake is still in the pan, wrap tightly in foil to store.

Shortly before serving, sift the cocoa with the confectioners' sugar and malt powder. Sprinkle evenly over the top of the cake. Remove the sides of the pan and serve the cake plain or with nonfat or low-fat frozen yogurt.

212 calories, 8.5 g fat, 4.5 g saturated fat,
53 mg cholesterol, 3 g dietary fiber, 237 mg sodium

Buckwheat (Kasha)

To many Americans and Canadians, buckwheat means gray but delicious pancakes. To Americans of Russian ancestry, buckwheat means a porridge, a side dish, or blinis (thin crepes) served with smoked fish or roe. To American of Japanese or Korean descent, buckwheat means noodles.

With its deep, toasted, grassy-earthy flavor, buckwheat is not a timid grain. It begs for strong flavors: the robust sweetness of dark maple syrup, the salty tang of caviar, the pungency of horseradish.

Buckwheat has been cultivated only fairly recently in human history. Central Asians were growing it in the tenth century A.D., and it arrived in Europe much later. It came still later to the United States, traveling mostly with Eastern European immigrants to the East Coast. In fact, many people know buckwheat more by its Russian name, kasha, than its English one. Kasha tends to be associated with Jewish cooking, perhaps because many of the Russian immigrants were Jewish.

Shortly after the turn of the century, U.S. farmers were growing nearly a million acres of buckwheat; sixty years later, acreage was about one-twentieth of that. New York, Pennsylvania, Michigan, and Minnesota are the main buckwheat-growing states. Farmers use most of the crop to feed animals and as "green manure," a plant that's plowed under to improve the soil. Most of the rest becomes flour.

Buckwheat makes legendary pancakes and crepes and is a prominent feature of many pancake mixes. It's also commonly found in multigrain flour mixes. Buckwheat groats (the whole kernels) have a distinctive triangular shape. They're sold with some of the bran coating removed. Raw groats are a light greenish-tan; the toasted groats, also known as kasha, turn a soft mahogany. They are sold whole and, in some markets, in medium and fine grinds.

One of the reasons modern cooks might be interested in rediscovering kasha is that it cooks in 10 minutes.

Buckwheat noodles, usually labeled by their Japanese name, soba, are a staple of northern Japanese and Korean cookery. They're made of buckwheat flour, water, and salt; sometimes they also contain wheat flour, yam flour, or green tea. The Japanese often serve them warm or cold in a simple broth, accompanied by garnishes of wasabi (green horseradish), seaweed, and scallions.

Some beekeepers plant buckwheat for their bees. The nectar-rich flowers bloom well into the fall and bees that pollinate them produce a dark, robust honey.

Buckwheat, *Fagopyrum esculentum*, is an herb, not a cereal grain, and is related to sorrel and rhubarb. It matures quickly and grows to a height of 2 to 4 feet. About 20 percent of its three-cornered seed is hull; the hulls make good mulch and animal bedding.

"Earthy" probably best sums up buckwheat's flavor. It's toasty, nutty, and grassy as well, with hints of cocoa.

Buckwheat groats, found in many supermarkets and health food stores, are traditionally cooked into porridges, savory or sweet; a grain-based sausage; soups; and savory side dishes. Kasha also makes a good breakfast cereal flavored with cinnamon and sugar. Puffed kasha is available as a ready-to-eat cereal.

Buckwheat tastes best toasted. If you buy raw groats rather than kasha, you should toast them in a dry skillet before cooking. Because kasha softens quite a bit during cooking, the groats are often heated in the pan with beaten egg or egg white before the liquid is added. This step is optional, but the egg white coats the grains and helps keep them from becoming mushy.

Add hot liquid, using 2 cups liquid to 1 cup buckwheat groats. Cook the buckwheat for 10 to 12 minutes, just until tender. To cook buckwheat as a porridge, use more water and cook for 20 minutes. To use buckwheat groats in soups or stews, add them during the last 15 to 20 minutes of cooking.

Buckwheat noodles are widely available in health food stores and Japanese and Korean groceries. To cook them, boil in lightly salted water for 5 to 10 minutes, depending on thickness, until cooked through but still slightly chewy.

Buckwheat flour carries a strong flavor and is low in gluten. It can be used in small amounts in yeast breads but is even better used in quick breads such as muffins, pancakes, and crepes. Buckwheat flour comes in dark, the most nutritious, and light, which has a milder flavor. Most likely you'll encounter only one kind in the store, probably the dark kind.

Buckwheat

Buckwheat Crepes with Spinach, Goat Cheese, and Roasted Garlic

Seafood One-Pot Meal

Blinis with Sour Cream and Midwest Caviar

Kasha and Lentil Salad

Roasted Buckwheat with Pears and Mandarin Oranges

Kasha Raisin Rolls

Buckwheat Corn Muffins

Buckwheat Crepes with Spinach, Goat Cheese, and Roasted Garlic

These crepes are a dark color and have an assertive, earthy flavor. The recipe will probably yield extra crepes. They're also good stuffed with other greens, such as kale or chard, or sweeter vegetables such as winter squash or sweet potatoes.

It's easiest to roast the garlic ahead of time. It will keep, tightly covered and refrigerated, for several days.

Makes 4 servings

4 heads (complete bulbs, not cloves) of garlic

CREPES

1 cup buckwheat flour

½ cup unbleached all-purpose flour

½ cup egg substitute, or 1 egg and 2 egg whites

2 cups skim or 1-percent milk

¼ teaspoon salt

2 to 3 teaspoons unsalted butter or margarine

SPINACH-CHEESE FILLING

1 tablespoon olive oil

¾ cup minced onion

1 package (10 ounces) fresh spinach, washed, drained, trimmed, and chopped

3 ounces goat cheese, crumbled

3 ounces (about ⅓ cup) light ricotta cheese

¼ cup snipped fresh dill, or 2 tablespoons dried

½ teaspoon salt

¼ teaspoon freshly ground black pepper

Plain nonfat yogurt (optional)

To roast the garlic: Preheat the oven to 275°. Remove some of the loose outer skin and carefully cut off the top ½ inch from each head of garlic. Wrap each head in aluminum foil, or use a garlic roaster, and set in the center of the oven. Roast the garlic 1 hour or until soft when squeezed. The garlic can be refrigerated.

To make the crepes: Mix together the buckwheat flour, all-purpose flour, egg substitute, milk, and salt in a blender or food processor or by hand with a whisk until smooth. Let stand for 20 minutes to tenderize the batter. Stir.

Spray a 6- or 7-inch crepe pan with nonstick cooking spray and melt about ½ teaspoon of the butter. When the pan is hot, add ⅓ cup of the batter. Tilt the pan so that the bottom of the pan is covered evenly. Pour off any excess batter. Cook the crepe quickly on both sides. Remove the crepe to a clean kitchen towel and let cool. Continue until all of the crepes are made; you should have 12 to 14 crepes. If the crepes start sticking, add small amounts of the butter to the pan. Discard any mal-formed crepes. When the crepes are done, stack them between squares of waxed paper or aluminum foil. Cover with foil and refrigerate until serving time, freeze, or use immediately. They will keep in the refrigerator, well covered, for 1 day.

To warm the crepes, place the stack in a 350° oven for about 10 minutes. If they're stacked between waxed paper—not foil—you can warm them in the microwave. Heat the stack of crepes on medium for 1 minute, then continue heating in 30-second increments as necessary, until gently warmed.

To make the filling: Heat the olive oil in a frying pan over medium heat. Add the onion, partially cover the pan, and cook until soft, stirring occasionally. Stir in the spinach, cover, and cook for 5 minutes or until the spinach has wilted. Remove the pan from the heat and stir in the goat cheese, ricotta cheese, dill, salt, and pepper. Set aside. Reheat to serve.

To assemble: Spoon 2 tablespoons of the warm filling on each warm crepe, roll, and set 2 crepes on each plate. Spoon 1 or 2 tablespoons of yogurt on top and serve with the roasted garlic. Instruct your guests to squeeze the garlic over the crepes.

423 calories, 13 g fat, 6 g saturated fat, 20 mg cholesterol,
7.5 dietary fiber, 664 mg sodium

Seafood One-Pot Meal

The increase in the number of Japanese restaurants, especially in America's large cities, is sparking interest in the hearty one-pot meals that are so important to Japanese cuisine.

Makes 4 servings

1½ pounds flat fish, such as flounder or tilapia
¼ cup white cornmeal
1 tablespoon canola oil
12 ounces dried Japanese buckwheat noodles (soba)
5 cups dashi (seaweed and fish stock) or low-sodium chicken stock
2 tablespoons reduced-sodium soy sauce
Salt

3 tablespoons Japanese rice wine (mirin)
1 package (10 ounces) fresh spinach, washed, drained, trimmed, and chopped
1 package (10½ ounces) firm tofu, drained and cubed
4 green onions, chopped
4 dried shiitake mushrooms, reconstituted and stems removed

Sprinkle the fish evenly with the cornmeal. Heat the oil in a skillet and fry the fish over medium heat, turning once, until the fish is opaque and somewhat firm and flakes easily. Cut it into 4 pieces and set aside.

Cook the noodles in lightly salted boiling water over medium heat until cooked through but not mushy, about 5 minutes.

In a second soup pot, bring the dashi, soy sauce, salt, and rice wine to a boil over medium heat. Add the noodles, spinach, tofu, onions, and mushrooms. Cook to heat through.

Place the pieces of fish in deep earthenware or regular soup bowls, and pour the hot soup over them. Serve immediately.

612 calories, 10.5 g fat, 1 g saturated fat,
82 mg cholesterol, 3 g dietary fiber, 1,128 mg sodium

Blinis with Sour Cream and Midwest Caviar

There is a large Russian population in Chicago, and to them we are grateful for the Midwestern blini, a small pancake usually served with sour cream and caviar.

We like to use fresh large red salmon roe and delicate tiny yellow whitefish roe from the Midwest. But you can serve these blinis with any kind of roe or caviar, or smoked whitefish or sturgeon.

Makes about 40 blinis; 8 servings

1 cup buckwheat flour
1 cup unbleached all-purpose flour
1 package (2¼ teaspoons) active dry yeast
2 teaspoons sugar
½ teaspoon salt
2 cups skim or 1 percent milk

1 tablespoon unsalted butter or margarine
1 egg
2 egg whites
2 cups nonfat sour cream
1 cup minced sweet onion
4 to 8 ounces salmon or whitefish roe, or caviar of your choice

In a glass bowl, combine ½ cup of the buckwheat flour and ½ cup of the all-purpose flour with the yeast, sugar, and salt.

Heat the milk and butter just until the butter has melted. Let cool to lukewarm (110° to 115°). Stir the milk mixture into the yeast and flour. Mix in the egg, egg whites, and remaining buckwheat flour and all-purpose flour. Stir with a wooden spoon. Cover with plastic wrap and set aside for 45 minutes. The mixture will almost double.

To cook the blinis: Spray a large frying pan with nonstick cooking spray, or coat lightly with oil. When the pan is hot, pour in the batter, using about 3 tablespoons for each pancake. Cook over medium heat until bubbles form on the pancakes. Turn them over using a spatula and a fork. Continue cooking until the blinis are a golden brown. Do not undercook.

To serve, put the sour cream, onion, and caviar in individual bowls. Serve the blinis on individual plates and allow your guests to help themselves to the garnishes.

*264 calories, 8 g fat, 2.5 saturated fat, 198 mg cholesterol,
2 g dietary fiber, 654 mg sodium*

Kasha and Lentil Salad

Don't overcook the lentils; they should retain their shape and be a bit chewy.

Makes 4 servings

1 cup roasted buckwheat groats
   (kasha)
2 cups boiling water
1 cup cooked lentils, rinsed in
   cold water and drained
1 cup diced red onion
1 red or yellow bell pepper, seeded
   and diced
1 cup diced celery

3 cloves garlic, minced
2 teaspoons minced fresh basil
¼ cup olive oil
⅓ cup cider or raspberry vinegar
3 tablespoons chopped pecans,
   walnuts, or other nuts
½ teaspoon salt
¼ teaspoon lemon pepper

Heat the nonstick frying pan over medium heat and toast the kasha until hot. Stir in the boiling water. Cover and reduce the heat to low. Continue cooking until the water is absorbed, about 10 minutes.

In a large bowl, combine the kasha and lentils. Add the onion, bell pepper, and celery, and toss. Then add the garlic, basil, oil, vinegar, nuts, salt, and lemon pepper. Mix well. Taste and adjust the seasonings. Serve cold or at room temperature.

*388 calories, 19 g fat, 2.5 g saturated fat,
0 mg cholesterol, 8.5 g dietary fiber, 296 mg sodium*

Roasted Buckwheat with Pears and Mandarin Oranges

This is good as a side dish to meat, poultry, or seafood. Usually buckwheat kernels are served savory, but we added bits of fruit for a change. If you want to make this into a main dish, just spoon grilled scallops or shrimp over the kasha.

Makes 4 servings

2 teaspoons olive oil
½ cup chopped onion
1 cup chopped white or portobello
   mushrooms
1 large firm pear, cored, peeled,
   and chopped
2 tablespoon fresh orange juice
   (or the reserved juice drained
   from the mandarin oranges)
1 cup medium-grain roasted
   buckwheat groats (kasha)

2 cups low-sodium vegetable
   stock, or 1¼ cups canned
   vegetable broth diluted with
   ¾ cup water
¼ teaspoon salt
¼ teaspoon freshly ground black
   pepper
1 cup mandarin orange slices,
   drained

Heat the oil in a sauté pan. Cook the onion over medium heat, partially covered, until soft. Stir once or twice. Add the mushrooms. Sprinkle the pear with the orange juice and add to the pan. Continue cooking for 1 to 2 minutes. Stir in the kasha, vegetable stock, salt, and pepper. Reduce the heat to a simmer, replace the cover, and cook about 10 minutes, or until the buckwheat is tender. Stir in the oranges. Serve hot.

---

239 calories, 4.5 g fat, 0.5 g saturated fat, no cholesterol,
6.5 g dietary fiber, 454 mg sodium

Kasha Raisin Rolls

You can substitute chopped walnuts, currants, or chopped dried figs (dusted with some of the flour) for the raisins. These dense rolls taste good with soup on a cold winter night.

Makes 24 small rolls

1 cup fine-grain roasted
   buckwheat groats (kasha)
2 cups boiling water
2 packages (4½ teaspoons) active
   dry yeast
½ cup warm water (110° to 115°)
1 teaspoon sugar
3½ to 4 cups bread flour
⅓ cup stone-ground whole wheat
   flour

1½ cups warm skim milk
½ teaspoon salt
3 tablespoons warm honey
½ cup raisins
1 egg white, lightly beaten
3 tablespoons flax seeds or seeds
   of your choice, such as sesame
   or poppy seeds

First, cook the kasha. Stir it into the boiling water, cover, reduce the heat to a simmer, and cook 10 minutes or until tender. Remove any lumps by pressing with the back of a fork. Let cool. The kasha may be cooked ahead of time.

In a glass bowl, combine the yeast with the warm water and sugar; allow to proof until foamy, almost 5 minutes. Stir in 3½ cups of the bread flour and the whole wheat flour, milk, salt, kasha, and honey. The dough should be soft and somewhat sticky. Mix in the raisins.

Put the dough in a mixing bowl; cover with a damp kitchen towel or plastic wrap. Set aside in a warm place to double in size, about 1½ hours.

Put the dough on a lightly floured pastry cloth. Sprinkle the dough with more bread flour if necessary to keep it from sticking. Roll out the dough using the pastry cloth as a guide by lifting the cloth up and pushing it down on the dough in a kneading motion until the dough can be kneaded easily, about 1 minute. Knead until smooth.

Spray 2 muffin pans with nonstick cooking spray. Divide the dough into 24 pieces. Roll each piece of dough into a ball. Set 1 ball in a cup of the muffin pan. Repeat with the remaining dough balls. Stir the beaten egg white and use it to brush the tops of the rolls. Sprinkle with the seeds.

Loosely cover the rolls and let rise for 45 minutes or until light.

Preheat the oven to 400°. Set the pans in the center of the oven and bake for 20 to 30 minutes or until the rolls are firm to the touch and a golden color. Let cool on wire racks. Serve warm.

---

54 calories, 0.5 g fat, no saturated fat, no cholesterol,
1 g dietary fiber, 55 mg sodium

Buckwheat Corn Muffins

Muffins are at their best eaten fresh and warm. Unless you have a group of people around to finish them off, freeze the leftovers and reheat to serve (see page 16). This is a savory, somewhat grainy muffin.

Makes 12 muffins

½ *cup yellow cornmeal*
½ *cup buckwheat flour*
½ *cup unbleached all-purpose*
  flour
1 *tablespoon baking powder*
½ *teaspoon ground cumin*
¼ *teaspoon salt*
¾ *cup frozen corn, defrosted and*
  drained

2 *tablespoons frozen apple juice*
  concentrate, thawed
½ *cup egg substitute, or 2 eggs*
1½ *cups skim or 1-percent milk*
⅓ *cup unsalted butter or*
  margarine, melted and cooled

Preheat the oven to 400°. Insert paper liners in a muffin tin.

In a deep bowl, combine the cornmeal, buckwheat flour, and all-purpose flour. Whisk in the baking powder, cumin, salt, and corn.

Mix in the apple juice concentrate, egg substitute, milk, and butter.

Spoon the mixture into the paper liners, filling them three-quarters full. Bake in the center of the oven for 15 minutes or until the muffins are firm to the touch and a tester inserted into the center of a muffin comes out dry.

Let the muffins cool on a wire rack. Serve warm.

128 calories, 5.5 g fat, 3 g saturated fat, 14 mg
cholesterol, 1 g dietary fiber, 164 mg sodium

Millet

In the United States and Western Europe, people know millet well. It's the small round tan seed we feed to our parakeets and the wild birds that visit our backyards in the winter.

In many countries, people may let birds eat millet—but only what they don't eat themselves. Millet, which probably originated in central Asia, is a staple grain throughout much of Africa. Millet is also eaten in the former Soviet republics, Eastern Europe, India, the Caribbean, Korea, the Himalayas, and some parts of China. For centuries the northern Chinese ate it as their primary grain, until wheat and rice supplanted it.

The Swiss who emigrated to America and became known as one contingent of the Pennsylvania Dutch also ate plenty of millet, at least until they arrived in America and discovered corn. Millet quickly fell by the wayside.

Millet seems to be one of those "peasant foods" that easily falls victim to affluence and technology. It ripens quickly, grows in fairly poor soils, and resists drought, making it ideal for poor agricultural areas. When technology allows them to better exploit marginal farmland, farmers simply move on to growing other, more popular and more easily harvested grains such as rice or wheat. Millet has hulls that are easy for birds to crack; humans, lacking beaks, have to pound the seed vigorously.

Hulled millet is not hard to find in the United States, but few Americans have cooked with it. That's too bad, because it cooks quickly, has a sweet, mild flavor, and is one of the most versatile grains around. Millet can stand in for mashed potatoes or rice. It makes an excellent breakfast porridge, polenta, or mush. It's one of the best grains for stuffing vegetables. It's equally good in searing spicy dishes and sweet puddings. Millet flour is good in cookies, crackers, and flatbreads. Uncooked millet seed can be added to breads and crackers to give them some extra sweetness and crunch. In fact, we're hard put to think of something you *can't* do with millet.

Millet grows in quite a few states and is widely used for poultry and livestock feed. Arrowhead Mills, the largest distributor of millet and millet flour to health food stores, gets its organically grown white proso millet from farmers in Kansas, Colorado, Nebraska, and South Dakota.

Millet, *Poaceae*, is the common name for several species of the grass family. Most of the millet grown in the United States for human food is proso, or common, millet, *Panicum miliaceum*, also called broomcorn millet. It grows to four feet tall and bears seeds on spikelets.

Hulled millet seeds are small, round, and golden yellow. Their flavor is sweet and mild, a little like a cross between toasted almonds and corn.

Whole grain millet and millet flour are readily available in health food stores and African, Indian, and Korean groceries. Health food stores also sell puffed millet as a ready-to-eat cereal.

Millet keeps well in a cool, dark place, but will go rancid over time, turning it bitter. Use it within 3 to 4 months, or refrigerate or freeze it in an airtight container.

Millet requires some care in cooking to keep it from turning into a dense mass with all the appeal of mortar. How you cook millet depends on whether you seek a porridgelike texture or a mass of light, fluffy, separate grains.

For porridge—which makes an ideal polenta, breakfast cereal, or substitute for mashed potatoes—add 1 cup rinsed millet to 3½ cups boiling water and simmer over low heat for 30 to 40 minutes, stirring occasionally, until the millet is soft and thick. You can pack this mixture into a loaf pan, chill and slice like polenta, use like mashed potatoes, or add a little maple syrup and milk for breakfast.

For light, fluffy millet with fairly distinct grains, rinse 1 cup millet and dry thoroughly. Heat 1 teaspoon oil in a heavy pan. Add the millet and cook over medium heat, stirring frequently, until the grain smells nutty and some of the grains are just beginning to turn a pale brown. The oil is optional but seems to help keep the grains from sticking too much. Slowly stir in 2 cups hot water or stock (careful—it'll splatter a bit) and a little salt (optional). Turn the heat down to very low, cover, and cook for 15 to 20 minutes, until the millet has absorbed the liquid. Remove from the heat and let stand 10 minutes. Fluff with a fork and serve immediately or use in the recipe. Millet cooked this way makes a good vegetable stuffing and can be served like rice or couscous, with spicy stews, with Chinese stir-fries, mixed with beans— you name it.

Millet flour is a starchy, low-gluten flour with a gritty texture similar to rice flour's. It's good in cookies and crackers. Use a small amount in breads, muffins, pancakes, and other baked goods.

Millet

Millet-Stuffed Peppers with Pizza Flavors

Millet, Cabbage, and Beef with Garlic and Sesame

Millet-Stuffed Roasted Onions

Millet Berry Muffins

Free-Range Chicken with Millet Stuffing

Peppered Millet Crackers

Millet Almond Crisps

Millet-Stuffed Peppers with Pizza Flavors

Tomato, garlic, and oregano give these the comforting flavor of pizza. The recipe is vegetarian as it stands; you could add a small amount of lean sausage if you like.

Makes 4 main-dish servings

FILLING

1 tablespoon olive oil
1 cup finely diced onion
3 cloves garlic, minced
½ pound mushrooms, cleaned
    and finely diced
½ teaspoon dried basil
¼ teaspoon dried oregano
1 cup uncooked millet

1½ cups boiling low-sodium
    vegetable stock, or ¾ cup
    canned vegetable broth diluted
    with ¾ cup water
½ teaspoon salt (omit if using
    canned vegetable broth)
Freshly ground black pepper
4 medium to large green bell
    peppers

SAUCE

1½ cups tomato sauce
½ teaspoon sugar (optional)
1 clove garlic, minced
¾ teaspoon dried oregano

¼ teaspoon hot red pepper flakes
¾ cup (2 ounces) loosely packed
    grated part-skim mozzarella

To make the filling: Heat the oil in a heavy saucepan. Add the onion, garlic, and mushrooms. Cook over medium heat, stirring frequently, until the mushrooms and onion have softened and much of the mushroom liquid has evaporated, 6 to 8 minutes.

Stir in the basil, oregano, and millet, then stir in the boiling stock. Bring back to a simmer, then reduce the heat to very low, cover tightly, and cook 20 to 25 minutes, until the millet has absorbed the liquid. Remove from the heat and add the salt (if using) and pepper.

While the millet is cooking, prepare the peppers. Cut each pepper in half length-wise and cut out the seeds, ribs, and stems. Place the peppers, cut side down, in a single layer in a microwaveproof baking dish. Add ½ cup water. Cover loosely with plastic wrap or waxed paper. Microwave on high, turning the peppers once, for 5 to 7 minutes, until the peppers are steaming hot and beginning to soften. Drain the peppers and place, cut side up, in a 9-by-13-inch glass baking pan or similar-size baking dish. (If you do not have a microwave oven, you can steam the peppers for 10 to 15 minutes to soften them.) Set aside.

When the millet is cooked, pack the mixture into the pepper halves. To make the sauce: In a small bowl, combine the tomato sauce, sugar (if using), garlic, oregano, and red pepper flakes. Pour evenly over the stuffed peppers. Sprinkle the mozzarella cheese over the peppers. (At this point, you may cover and refrigerate the peppers to be baked later.)

Preheat the oven to 375°. Cover the dish tightly with foil and bake for 20 to 25 minutes (add 10 to 15 minutes if the peppers have been refrigerated), until the peppers are just tender. Uncover and bake another 5 minutes. Serve hot.

226 calories, 7 g fat, 2 g saturated fat, 8 mg cholesterol,
5 g dietary fiber, 818 mg sodium

Millet, Cabbage, and Beef with Garlic and Sesame

Inspired by the flavors of Korean-American cookery, this quick skillet dish is for those who like some spice in their dinner. It could be made with lean ground turkey, but beef is more Korean. This makes delicious leftovers, which can be reheated the next day in the microwave.

Makes 4 servings

2 teaspoons canola oil
1 to 1½ tablespoons minced garlic
1 tablespoon minced fresh ginger

6 ounces 95-percent lean ground beef
4 cups shredded Chinese (Napa) cabbage

¼ *teaspoon salt*

¼ *teaspoon cayenne pepper*

2 *cups cooked millet*

1 *tablespoon reduced–sodium soy*
  sauce

3 *tablespoons apple juice or cider*

1 *tablespoon rice vinegar*

2 *teaspoons sugar*

½ *teaspoon dark sesame oil*

1 *teaspoon sesame seeds*

Heat the oil in a large, heavy skillet. Add the garlic and ginger. Sauté briefly, then stir in the beef. Cook, breaking up the beef into small chunks, until the meat is no longer pink. Add the cabbage, salt, and cayenne pepper. Cook, stirring frequently, just until the cabbage wilts. Stir in the millet, soy sauce, apple juice, vinegar, and sugar. Cook 2 to 3 minutes. Stir in the sesame oil and sesame seeds. Serve immediately.

---

299 calories, 10.5 g fat, 3 g saturated fat,
35 mg cholesterol, 2.5 g dietary fiber, 430 mg sodium

Millet-Stuffed Roasted Onions

These are a wonderful side dish to lean beef, pork tenderloin, or roasted turkey. You can even serve them as a light entrée for two.

Makes 6 side-dish servings

3 *large onions (1 pound total)*

Olive oil

2 *cups cooked millet*

¾ *teaspoon dried thyme*

2 *teaspoons dry sherry*

½ *teaspoon salt*

¼ *teaspoon freshly ground black*
  pepper

Preheat the oven to 350°. Lightly oil or spray an 8- or 9-inch baking dish.

Peel the onions and trim the ends. Cut in half crosswise. Remove the center part from each onion half, leaving a ¼- to ½-inch shell. Finely chop the onion you removed. Measure out 1½ cups chopped onion (reserve the remainder for another use). Brush the onion halves lightly with olive oil and place in the baking dish; set aside.

Heat 1 tablespoon oil in a skillet. Add the 1½ cups of chopped onion and sauté about 5 minutes, until softened. Stir in the millet, thyme, sherry, salt, and pepper. Cook, stirring, until heated through.

Stuff the onion halves with the millet mixture, mounding the mixture generously on top of each onion half. Brush lightly with more olive oil. Roast, uncovered, for 45 minutes or until the tops are nicely browned and the onions are tender. Serve warm.

*160 calories, 5.5 g fat, 1 g saturated fat, no cholesterol,
2 g dietary fiber, 181 mg sodium*

Millet Berry Muffins

Millet adds a delightful crunch to these muffins, which also make a delicious, unusual stuffing for chicken (see page 222). Or add a little grated lemon or orange zest to them, sprinkle the tops with cinnamon sugar, and serve for breakfast. (Adding a small amount of millet to a whole wheat bread adds a nice crunch. See page 35)

Makes 12 muffins

*1¾ cups unbleached all-purpose
  flour*
*1 cup fresh or frozen blueberries
  or raspberries (or both)*
½ cup uncooked millet
¾ cup sugar

1 tablespoon baking powder
¼ teaspoon salt
½ cup egg substitute, or 2 eggs
¾ cup skim or 1-percent milk
*2 tablespoons unsalted butter or
  margarine, melted*

Preheat the oven to 400°. Spray a 12-cup muffin tin with nonstick cooking spray, or line with paper liners.

Toss ¼ cup of the flour with the fresh (not frozen) berries and set aside.

In a large bowl, stir together the remaining flour and the millet, sugar, baking powder, and salt.

In a smaller bowl or large measuring cup, beat the egg substitute with the milk and butter. Stir the mixture into the dry ingredients just until mixed. Fold in the berries. Spoon the batter into the muffin tin, filling the cups about three-quarters full.

Bake in the center of the oven for about 25 to 30 minutes or until the muffins are golden brown and a tester inserted into the center of a muffin comes out clean. Serve warm.

---

214 calories, 8.5 g fat, 5 g saturated fat,
22 mg cholesterol, 1 g dietary fiber, 187 mg sodium

Free-Range Chicken with Millet Stuffing

This delicious stuffing is a great way to use up any leftover muffins.

Makes 6 servings

6 day-old Millet Berry Muffins
  (see page 221)
1 tablespoon unsalted butter or
  margarine
1 tablespoon plus 1 teaspoon
  olive oil
1 cup chopped onion
1 cup sliced fresh mushrooms
½ cup chopped celery

1 free-range chicken (3½ to 4
  pounds)
1 teaspoon dried, crumbled sage
¼ teaspoon garlic powder
¼ teaspoon salt
¼ teaspoon freshly ground black
  pepper
1 onion, sliced

Crumble the muffins into a bowl; set aside.

Melt the butter and the 1 tablespoon oil over medium heat in a frying pan. Add the onion, mushrooms, and celery and sauté over medium heat until tender, about 5 minutes, stirring as necessary. Let cool, then stir the vegetables into the crumbled muffins.

Preheat the oven to 350°. Trim any excess fat from the chicken, then set the bird breast side up on the counter, with the cavity facing you. Working from the cavity opening, carefully loosen the skin around the breast area. Carefully spoon the stuffing under the skin, then gently pat the skin back into shape. Brush the chicken with the 1 teaspoon oil and sprinkle with the sage, garlic powder, salt, and pepper.

Pour water or chicken stock to a depth of ¼ inch in a roasting pan. Lay the onion slices in the water or stock. Place a rack in the pan and set the bird on it, breast side up. Roast the chicken, uncovered, about 1 hour and 10 minutes or until the juices run clear when the bird is pierced with the point of a sharp knife and the joints can be moved easily.

Let the chicken stand 8 to 10 minutes before slicing. Slice the breast carefully so that a layer of the stuffing is connected to the slice of breast meat. Serve the bird so that your guests have slices of stuffed breast meat as well as dark meat slices.

Without skin: 401 calories, 18.5 g fat, 8 g saturated fat,
89 mg cholesterol, 1.5 g dietary fiber, 343 mg sodium

Peppered Millet Crackers

These fairly bland crackers get a boost from black pepper. They're good with just a dab of goat cheese. Be sure to grind the pepper fresh for the best flavor. Try to roll out the crackers as evenly as possible; if they're different thicknesses, the thinner ones may burn before the thicker ones are done.

If you like tongue-burning foods, replace half of the black pepper with cayenne pepper.

Makes about 50 crackers

1¼ cups unbleached all-purpose flour	**2 tablespoon cold unsalted butter or margarine, cut into small pieces**
¾ cup millet flour	
1¼ teaspoons salt	**3 tablespoons canola oil**
1 teaspoon sugar	**½ cup cold plain nonfat yogurt**
½ teaspoon coarse-ground black pepper	**2 tablespoons whole millet**

Preheat the oven to 400°. Lightly spray a baking sheet with nonstick cooking spray.

In a food processor, pulse the flours, salt, sugar, and pepper to mix. Cut in the butter and oil until the dough is crumbly. Add the yogurt and process just until the dough gathers into a ball on the blade.

Roll the dough out on a lightly floured work surface to ⅛ inch thick. Sprinkle the millet seeds evenly over the dough and roll the rolling pin over the dough to embed the seeds. Cut into 2-inch rounds. Reroll the scraps once, and repeat.

Bake for 10 to 12 minutes, until the crackers are golden tan. Watch carefully so they don't burn. Remove to wire racks to cool. Store in airtight tins.

---

34 calories, 1.5 g fat, 0.5 g saturated fat,
1 mg cholesterol, 0.2 g dietary fiber, 55 mg sodium

Millet Almond Crisps

In texture and sweetness, these cookie/confections remind us a bit of the lace cookies usually made with oatmeal, and the sesame candies found in Middle Eastern groceries. The millet makes them very crunchy. It's best not to make these on a humid day, when they can get too chewy instead of crisp.

For a very different flavor, replace the almonds with skinned, unsalted peanuts.

Makes about 60 cookies

1 cup whole almonds
2 tablespoons almond or canola
  oil
¼ cup unsalted butter
⅔ cup packed light brown sugar
⅓ cup light corn syrup

¼ teaspoon salt
1 teaspoon almond extract
½ teaspoon vanilla extract
1 cup uncooked millet
2 tablespoons unbleached all-
  purpose flour

Preheat the oven to 325°. Spray baking sheets with nonstick cooking spray.

In a food processor, nut grinder, or clean coffee grinder, grind the almonds until finely chopped. Add the oil and grind until the almonds form a coarse, sticky paste. Set aside.

Melt the butter in a heavy saucepan. Stir in the brown sugar, corn syrup, and salt. Cook over medium heat for about 2 minutes, until the mixture is bubbling hot. Stir in the almond extract, vanilla extract, and millet. Cook over medium heat, stirring, for about 5 minutes or until the mixture gives off a toasty-buttery aroma. Remove from the heat and stir in the almond paste, then the flour.

Drop by level teaspoonfuls onto cookie sheets, leaving at least 2½ inches between the mounds of batter (the cookies will spread). The batter thickens as it stands; you can then roll it into scant 1-inch balls. If the batter gets too thick, reheat slightly over low heat. Bake for 7 to 9 minutes, until the cookies are flat, bubbly, and golden.

Let cool on cookie sheets for 1 minute, then remove to wire racks to cool completely. Store in airtight containers.

55 calories, 2.5 g fat, 0.5 g saturated fat, 2 mg cholesterol,
0.5 g dietary fiber, 13 mg sodium

Oats

Call it timing. Call it luck. Call it the stuff of which marketers' dreams are made. In the 1980s, research showed that oat bran, an obscure foodstuff fed mostly to livestock, could help lower blood cholesterol. Researchers had known about oats' health benefits for years. But in an era when cholesterol numbers were replacing astrological signs as conversational openers, people were ready to pay attention. From 1985 to 1989, the number of oat bran products in grocery stores climbed from 8 to almost 200. Quaker Oats scrambled, often unsuccessfully, to keep the stuff on the shelves, while food processors put oat bran in chips, cookies, muffins, high-fat cereals, spongy white breads—even beer.

By 1990, the public had had more oat bran than it could swallow. A small study indicating that oat bran was no better than farina—and presumably any other low-fat food eaten instead of high-fat fare—finished the fad. Food processors busily scurried to produce the next edible "miracle," and some began touting rice bran.

It didn't work. The public love of health fads shifted from food to supplements—tryptophan, chromium, melatonin.

Ironically, oats and oat bran are making a comeback. The U.S. Food and Drug Administration has proposed allowing oats to carry labels proclaiming their role in helping to prevent heart disease, as part of a healthful diet. Oats are the first actual food, rather than nutrient (such as fiber or calcium), to be allowed this distinction. The product must contain 20 grams or more of oat bran to carry that claim—no beers or white breads need apply. Critics have attacked the proposal for setting an unhealthy precedent by supporting the dubious idea that particular foods can work magic.

All this hoopla over oats (which are, indeed, nutritious) is somewhat intriguing, since through the centuries, horses have eaten far more oats than people have. As the ditty goes, "Mares eat oats and does eat oats . . ." Historians believe the cultivation of oats followed hand in hand with the raising of horses. Even now, people eat only 5 to 10 percent of the U.S. oats crop. Most of the crop is turned into animal feed and straw.

Besides being sold as a breakfast cereal, oats are used by food processors. Oat flour is used as a fat stabilizer in dairy products such as ice cream. A recently developed product derived from oats, Oatrim, is used as a fat substitute.

Oats arrived in America around 1600 with colonists from the British Isles, who planted the grain in Virginia along with wheat, barley, and vegetables. The grain traveled through the northern states with Scottish, Welsh, and Swiss immigrants. Oats grow everywhere, but the northern Midwestern states grow the biggest commercial crops.

Like wheat, oats, *Avena*, come in white and red and are planted in either the spring or fall. They are threshed and winnowed like wheat but must be hulled. The hulled groats are long, narrow, and golden tan. Steel-cut oats, also called Scottish or Irish oats, are groats that are sliced into bits.

To make rolled oats, processors heat the grain kernels to loosen the husks, then remove the hulls. The whole groats are steamed and passed through steel rollers that turn them into flakes. Old-fashioned oats are rolled the thickest; quick-cooking and instant oats are rolled a little thinner and cut into finer pieces.

Oat bran is the outer coating of the grain. Whole and rolled oats still retain much of the bran. Oat flour is simply whole oats ground into a powder.

Oats have a sweet, pecanlike flavor that makes them especially suitable for breakfast porridge and desserts.

Whole oat groats are found in health food stores and, occasionally, supermarkets. They're suitable for pilafs, soups, and even salads. If you cook them in plenty of vegetable or chicken broth, they're a good stand-in for risotto. Steel-cut (Scottish) oats are traditionally used in scones and porridges. They, too, make a good "risotto." They're sold in some supermarkets and most health food stores.

Old-fashioned oats and quick-cooking oats make good breakfast cereals, granola, breads and scones, and extenders to stretch the meat (and boost the nutrition) in meat loaves and burgers, as well as the world's best cookies (for oat cookie recipes, see pages 293 to 294). We admit we don't understand the popularity of instant oats, which have sugar, salt, and flavorings added to them and cost considerably more than regular oats, while lacking the pleasantly rough-chewy texture.

Oat bran makes a good porridge—although to our mind, rolled oats have a better texture. It's also good in baked goods such as muffins. Oat flour, widely available at health food stores and found in some supermarkets, is good in pancakes, waffles, muffins, and other baked goods. In a pinch, you can make your own oat flour by whirling oats in a food processor or blender until finely ground. This flour will have a coarser texture than commercially milled flour.

Oats are rich in antioxidants and will keep practically forever in a cool cupboard. In fact, oat flour is used in some fatty foods such as peanut butter, margarine, and doughnut mixes to keep them from going rancid.

Oats taste wonderful toasted, and toasting cuts the cooking time for oat groats. Toast them briefly in the pan before cooking, or in the oven (see page 8).

All kinds of oats can be cooked either on the stove top or in the microwave. Whole oats also cook well in a pressure cooker.

To cook whole groats, toast them first, or soak for at least an hour in cold water. Bring 1 cup groats and 3 cups lightly salted water to a boil. Cook, loosely covered, over low heat for 40 to 50 minutes or until cooked through. Cook for the shorter time if you prefer the oats chewy, or longer if you like a softer, more porridgelike dish. To pressure-cook, use 3 cups water to 1 cup oats and cook for 20 to 30 minutes after reaching pressure (see page 9).

Regardless of whether you use the stove top or microwave, you can vary the consistency of porridge oats by which method you use. For porridge with a creamier consistency, combine the oats, cold water, and salt (optional), then bring to a boil. For chewier oats, bring the water to a boil before stirring in the oats.

To cook steel-cut oats, use 3 cups lightly salted water to 1 cup oats, and cook over low heat for 15 to 20 minutes after the water boils. In the microwave, cook on high for 13 minutes or until the oats have absorbed the liquid. Let stand, covered, for 2 minutes, stir, and serve.

To cook either old-fashioned or quick rolled oats, use 1 cup water to ½ cup oats; add a pinch of salt. Cook old-fashioned oats 3 to 5 minutes on the stove top after the water boils, or 3 to 4 minutes in the microwave (with cold water). Cook quick oats 1 to 2 minutes after the water comes to a boil, or 1½ to 2 minutes in the microwave.

Oats

Thirties-Style Oatmeal Meat Loaf

Oats with Oregano and Olives

Oat Sesame Bread

Oatmeal Pesto Bread

Oatmeal Maple Breakfast Bread

Oat Cheddar Scones

Oat Bran and Pumpkin Muffins

Cinnamon Oatcakes

Nectarine-Raspberry Crumble

Thirties-Style Oatmeal Meat Loaf

The oatmeal meal loaf was popular during the depression era in the Midwest and the East. Stretching the meat with oatmeal made this a practical way to feed a family. Now we add the oatmeal for flavor and nutrition.

Supermarkets routinely carry very lean ground beef, often labeled 95 percent lean. To get really lean ground pork, ask the butcher to grind pork loin or tenderloin that has been trimmed of fat. Or buy pork tenderloin and grind it yourself in a meat grinder or food processor.

This dish is good with brown rice and a steamed green vegetable.

Makes 8 servings

¾ *pound leanest ground pork*

¾ *pound leanest ground beef*

⅓ *cup chopped onion*

1 *cup uncooked oats (old-fashioned or quick-cooking)*

½ *cup wheat sprouts (optional)*

1 *teaspoon salt*

½ *teaspoon garlic powder*

¼ *teaspoon freshly ground black pepper*

1 *teaspoon coarse mustard*

¼ *cup ketchup*

¼ *cup egg substitute, or 2 egg whites, lightly beaten*

1 *cup skim or 1-percent milk*

Preheat the oven to 400°. Spray a 9-by-5-inch loaf pan with nonstick cooking spray.

Mix together the pork, beef, onion, and oats in a deep mixing bowl. Add the wheat sprouts (if using), salt, garlic powder, pepper, mustard, ketchup, egg substitute, and milk, and combine thoroughly.

With a spoon, pack the meat mixture into the prepared pan, smoothing the top. Bake in the center of the preheated oven for 1¼ hours or until browned on top and firm to the touch.

Slice the loaf and serve hot.

237 calories, 10.5 g fat, 4 g saturated fat,
66 mg cholesterol, 1 g dietary fiber, 445 mg sodium

Oats with Oregano and Olives

This savory porridge is the oat equivalent of risotto. It's an excellent side dish with lean grilled lamb, chicken, or fish. Or eat it as a main dish with a salad on the side.

Makes 4 servings

1 cup oat groats or steel-cut oats

3 cups hot low-sodium chicken or vegetable stock

¼ cup (about 2 ounces) flavorful black olives, such as kalamata

1 large clove garlic, minced

2 tablespoons finely chopped fresh oregano

⅛ teaspoon salt

Place the oats in a large, heavy saucepan. Toast over medium heat, stirring frequently, about 5 minutes or until the oats are golden and begin to make popping noises. Pour in the hot stock and bring to a boil. Turn the heat to low, cover loosely, and cook 20 to 30 minutes for steel-cut oats or 45 to 60 minutes for whole oats, stirring occasionally, until the oats are tender and "porridgey." Stir in the olives, garlic, oregano, and salt. Cook another minute or two, stirring. Serve hot.

191 calories, 5 g fat, 0.5 g saturated fat, no cholesterol,
3.5 g dietary fiber, 159 mg sodium

Oat Sesame Bread

This bread has a good sesame flavor and is excellent toasted. For a different flavor, substitute another flaked grain—spelt, rye, barley, wheat, Kamut, or triticale—for the rolled oats.

Makes 1 loaf; about 12 servings

1 cup old-fashioned or quick-
    cooking oats
½ cup oat bran
2 cups boiling water
1½ teaspoons active dry yeast
Pinch of sugar
¼ cup warm water (110° to 115°)
2 tablespoons dark sesame oil

1 tablespoon molasses
1 teaspoon salt
3½ to 4 cups bread flour
1 tablespoon egg substitute, or
    1 egg white beaten with
    1 teaspoon water
1 tablespoon sesame seeds

Place the oats and oat bran in a large, heatproof mixing bowl. Pour the boiling water over them and let stand, stirring once or twice, until the mixture is lukewarm.

Meanwhile, mix the yeast and sugar with the warm water in a small bowl; let stand 5 minutes or until the yeast foams up.

Add the yeast mixture to the warm oats. Stir in the sesame oil, molasses, and salt. Add 3½ cups bread flour, you should have a soft, sticky dough. Knead the dough with a heavy-duty mixer fitted with the dough hook, or by hand, for 5 to 10 minutes, until smooth and elastic. The dough should be soft and a bit sticky; add small amounts of flour as necessary to keep it from sticking all over the bowl or work surface.

Place the dough in a bowl, cover with a damp kitchen towel or plastic wrap, and set aside in a warm place to rise until doubled in bulk, which will probably take at least 2 hours.

Lightly spray a 9-by-5-inch loaf pan with nonstick cooking spray.

Punch down the dough. Form into a loaf and place in the prepared pan. Cover loosely and let rise again until the dough comes at least to the top of the pan, about 1 to 1½ hours.

Preheat the oven to 350°. Brush the top of the loaf with the egg substitute, then sprinkle the sesame seeds evenly over the top. Bake the bread for 30 to 40 minutes, until it is golden and sounds hollow when tapped on the bottom. Turn out onto a rack to cool completely before slicing.

217 calories, 4 g fat, 0.5 g saturated fat, no cholesterol,
2.5 g dietary fiber, 182 mg sodium

Oatmeal Pesto Bread

Pesto—the sauce of fresh basil ground with garlic, nuts, olive oil, and cheese—lends a touch of pungency to an otherwise sweet bread. This is a good bread to serve with spaghetti.

Makes 1 loaf; about 12 servings

1 cup boiling water

1 cup quick-cooking (not instant) oats, plus more as needed

1 package (2¼ teaspoons) active dry yeast

¼ cup warm water (110° to 115°)

3 egg whites, lightly beaten

3 tablespoons honey

¼ cup pesto sauce (commercially bottled or homemade)

3 to 3½ cups bread flour

½ cup amaranth flour (optional)

¾ teaspoon salt

Pour boiling water over the oats in the large bowl of an electric mixer. Let stand 10 minutes. Set aside.

Dissolve the yeast in the warm water and let stand 5 minutes, until foamy.

Blend 2 of the egg whites, the yeast mixture, the honey, and the pesto with the oatmeal. Gradually mix in the flour(s) and salt until a ball of soft dough forms. Remove to a lightly floured board and knead about 3 minutes, until smooth. Return the dough to a bowl, cover lightly, and let rise in a warm place until doubled, about 1½ hours.

Punch down the dough and knead the dough only a few minutes. Shape into a round loaf. Brush with the 1 egg white and sprinkle with uncooked oats.

Set the dough on a baking sheet sprayed with nonstick cooking spray. Let rise 1 hour or until light.

Preheat the oven to 375°. Bake the bread in the center of the oven for 45 minutes or until the bread is crusty and sounds hollow when tapped.

Let the bread cool on a wire rack.

*204 calories, 3 g fat, 0.5 g saturated fat, 2 mg cholesterol,
2 g dietary fiber, 183 mg sodium*

Oatmeal Maple Breakfast Bread

Maple syrup sweetens this lovely yellow-tan bread, which is excellent toasted for breakfast and spread with a smear of light cream cheese. If you actually keep it around long enough for it to get stale, turn it into French toast—topped with maple syrup, of course.

To make a bread that's suitable for turkey sandwiches, and as an accompaniment to more savory main courses, cut the amount of maple syrup to ⅓ cup and increase the skim milk to 1⅓ cups.

This recipe makes two loaves; the second can be tightly wrapped and frozen for up to three months.

Makes 2 loaves; about 16 servings

2½ cups old-fashioned oats

1 cup skim milk

⅔ cup pure maple syrup,
    preferably dark amber, plus
    more for brushing the bread

1 tablespoon walnut or canola oil

1½ teaspoons salt

4 teaspoons active dry yeast

¼ cup warm water (110° to 115°)

3 to 4 cups bread flour

⅓ cup coarsely chopped walnuts
    (optional)

Place 2 cups of the oats in a large bowl. In a saucepan or in the microwave, heat the milk, syrup, oil, and salt until steaming hot but not boiling. Pour over the oats and stir well. Let stand 10 minutes, until the oats have softened and the mixture is lukewarm.

Meanwhile, dissolve the yeast in the warm water. Let stand 5 to 10 minutes, until the yeast foams up.

Stir the yeast mixture into the oat mixture. Stir in enough bread flour—about 3 cups—to make a soft, slightly sticky dough. Knead with an electric mixer fitted with the dough hook, or by hand, until the dough is smooth and elastic. This will take about 5 minutes in the mixer, about 10 minutes by hand. Work in small amounts of additional bread flour, a tablespoon at a time, as needed.

Place the dough in a bowl, cover lightly with a damp kitchen towel or plastic wrap, and set aside in a warm place to rise until doubled in bulk, 1 to 2 hours.

Spray a 10-by-15-inch cookie sheet with nonstick cooking spray.

Punch the dough down and divide in half. Knead in the walnuts, if using, until incorporated in the dough. Round each half of dough into a loaf, tucking under the dough to form a tight ball.

Sprinkle 6 tablespoons of the oats over the baking sheet, concentrating the oats in the two places where you will set the loaves. Set the loaves on the baking sheet, leaving at least 3 inches of space between them. Brush the loaves lightly with maple syrup and sprinkle the remaining 2 tablespoons oats over the tops of the loaves.

Cover loosely with a kitchen towel and let rise in a warm place until very light, about 45 minutes to 1 hour.

Preheat the oven to 375°.

Bake the loaves in the center of the oven for 40 to 45 minutes or until they're golden and sound hollow when tapped on the bottom. Let cool on racks.

---

*Without walnuts: 188 calories, 2 g fat, 0.5 g saturated
fat, no cholesterol, 2.5 g dietary fiber, 210 mg sodium*

*With walnuts: 204 calories, 3.5 g fat (other nutrients
the same)*

Oat Cheddar Scones

These scones are good for breakfast topped with a bit of apple butter and accompanied by fresh apples. Or serve them with a big salad for a light dinner.

For chewier, more authentic scones, substitute steel-cut oats for the rolled oats. Soak them in the buttermilk for 30 minutes. If you'd rather not fool with baking individual scones, just spoon the batter into a sprayed 9-inch cake pan and cut the scone into wedges after it's cooled.

Makes 8 scones

1½ cups old-fashioned oats
1½ cups buttermilk
¼ cup egg substitute
¾ cup stone-ground whole wheat
  flour

¾ cup unbleached all-purpose
  flour
2 tablespoons packed dark brown
  sugar
2 teaspoons baking powder
½ teaspoon baking soda

½ teaspoon salt

2 tablespoons cold unsalted butter
  or margarine, cut into bits

¾ to 1 cup (about 3 ounces)
  loosely packed grated extra-
  sharp Cheddar cheese

Preheat the oven to 400°. Lightly spray a baking sheet with nonstick cooking spray.

In a small bowl, stir the oats with the buttermilk and egg substitute. Let stand 10 minutes to soften the oats.

In a food processor or a mixing bowl, combine the flours, brown sugar, baking powder, soda, and salt. Pulse several times to mix, or lightly rub the mixture through your fingertips to mix it and remove the lumps. Add the butter and pulse or rub until the butter is incorporated.

Stir the softened oats mixture into the flour with a fork, stirring just enough to mix the ingredients. Set aside 2 tablespoons of the grated Cheddar; stir the remaining cheese into the batter.

Spoon the batter onto the center of the baking sheet. Spray the back of a spoon with nonstick cooking spray and use it to pat the batter into a rough round about 8 inches in diameter. Sprinkle with the reserved Cheddar. With a large knife, sprayed with nonstick cooking spray, cut the batter into 8 wedges. Using the flat side of the knife, gently push the wedges apart so there is at least ¼-inch space between them. The batter will be very sticky; clean off and respray the knife as necessary.

Bake for 20 to 25 minutes or until the scones are golden and firm. As the scones firm up but before they're completely baked through, use the flat side of the knife to push them apart again. Serve the scones the same day they're baked.

*240 calories, 8 g fat, 4.5 g saturated fat,
20 mg cholesterol, 3.5 g dietary fiber, 397 mg sodium*

Oat Bran and Pumpkin Muffins

Muffins are flavorful, and they freeze well; therefore you can make them ahead of time and bring them to room temperature as needed.

Makes 12 muffins

1½ cups oat bran

½ cup plus 2 tablespoons packed
   dark brown sugar

½ cup whole wheat flour

2 teaspoons baking powder

1 teaspoon ground cinnamon

¼ teaspoon ground allspice

¼ teaspoon ground ginger

⅛ teaspoon ground nutmeg

¼ teaspoon salt

1 cup cooked, mashed pumpkin
   (canned is fine)

½ cup skim or 1-percent milk

2 egg whites, lightly beaten

2 tablespoons canola oil

Preheat the oven to 425°. Line a muffin pan with paper liners, or grease the muffin cups.

In a deep bowl, stir together the oat bran, sugar, flour, baking powder, cinnamon, allspice, ginger, nutmeg, and salt. Stir in the pumpkin, milk, egg whites, and oil. Stir just until the ingredients are combined; do not overbeat.

Spoon the batter into the muffin pan, filling the cups about three-quarters full. Bake the muffins in the center of the oven for 20 minutes or until the muffins are firm to the touch and a tester inserted into the center of a muffin comes out dry. Remove the muffins from the pan and cool on a rack. Serve warm.

125 calories, 3 g fat, 0.5 g saturated fat, no cholesterol,
3 g dietary fiber, 164 mg sodium

Cinnamon Oatcakes

Virginia's Scottish ancestry inspired these sandy-textured hybrids of shortbread and oat cakes. They have much less saturated fat than traditional shortbread and provide the fiber and nutrients of whole grains. Not too sweet, they make a good snack—or breakfast—with a cup of tea or glass of skim milk.

Makes 12 cookies

1 cup old-fashioned oats

1 cup stone-ground whole wheat
   flour

1 teaspoon ground cinnamon

¼ teaspoon salt

¼ cup confectioners' sugar

¼ cup cold unsalted butter, cut
   into 4 or 5 pieces

¼ cup canola oil

1 to 2 tablespoons cold skim milk

2 teaspoons sugar mixed with

½ teaspoon ground cinnamon

Preheat the oven to 350°.

Place the oats in a food processor. Process on high speed until finely ground. Add the whole wheat flour, cinnamon, salt, and confectioners' sugar; pulse two or three times to mix the dry ingredients.

Add the butter, the oil, and 1 tablespoon milk. Pulse several times to form a moist dough that holds together. If the dough is too crumbly, add another tablespoon of milk.

Press the dough over the bottom of a 9-inch cake pan. Sprinkle evenly with the cinnamon sugar. Use a sharp paring knife to score the dough into 12 wedges, cutting about halfway through.

Bake for about 20 minutes, until the cookies are firm. Let cool for 5 minutes, then cut into wedges along the score lines. Remove to a rack to cool completely. Store in a single layer in an airtight container. These cookies are fragile.

---

144 calories, 9 g fat, 3 g saturated fat, 11 mg cholesterol,
2 g dietary fiber, 46 mg sodium

Nectarine-Raspberry Crumble

In texture, this dessert falls somewhere between a crisp—fruit sprinkled with a topping of oats, brown sugar, flour, and seasonings that bakes up crunchy—and a cobbler, fruit topped with a softer biscuit topping. You could experiment with other juicy fruits, such as Bartlett pears, in place of the nectarines. Because there's no sugar in the fruit, it's best to use sweet fruits at the peak of the season.

Makes 8 servings

2 pounds firm but ripe
  nectarines, peeled, and sliced
2 cups fresh or defrosted and
  drained raspberries

1 cup quick-cooking (not instant)
  oats
2 to 4 tablespoons whole wheat
  pastry flour
½ cup packed light brown sugar

¼ *teaspoon salt*	⅓ *cup unsalted butter or*
¾ *teaspoon ground cinnamon*	*margarine, at room*
⅛ *teaspoon ground nutmeg*	*temperature*

Preheat the oven to 375°. Spray a 9-inch-square baking pan with nonstick cooking spray.

Toss the nectarines and berries together, then spoon into the prepared pan.

Mix together the oats, flour, sugar, salt, cinnamon, and nutmeg. Cut the butter into the oat mixture using a pastry knife or a food processor. Drop the oat mixture by spoonfuls over the fruit.

Bake in the center of the oven for 25 to 30 minutes or until golden on top. Serve warm, plain or with low-fat vanilla yogurt or ice cream.

---

223 calories, 9 g fat, 5 g saturated fat, 21 mg cholesterol,
5 g dietary fiber, 72 mg sodium

Rye

When you look at who brought rye bread to the United States—Germans, Poles, Russians, Scandinavians—you quickly notice a pattern. They all came from chilly climates.

That's no accident. Compared with other grains, rye is low in protein and not particularly loaded with nutrients. It does have one virtue that appealed to farmers in northern Europe: It doesn't mind the cold. In fact, rye will survive winter temperatures that dip well below zero and will start growing again when the thermometer registers a balmy 40° above. It will also thrive in fairly lousy soil. Rye kept popping up as a weed among the rows of wheat European farmers tried to grow with limited success. (They wanted gluten-rich wheat for breads.) Rye survived when wheat died. Before long, a good many of the peasants in northern Europe were practically living on rye bread, especially the dense *Schwarzbrot,* black bread, that was the ancestor of today's deli pumpernickels.

Those who immigrated to America from the British Isles brought rye, too, for a different reason: It makes good whiskey. That, no doubt, was another virtue much prized by those who lived in clammy climates.

Ironically, today the top rye-growing states are Georgia, Texas, and Oklahoma, although rye grows in every state. Rye is a minor crop in the United States. Most of it is planted for animal feed, pasture, or green manure. About a quarter of the crop is sold as human food—and nearly all of that is ground into flour for bread and crackers. Some of the rest goes into whiskey.

Rye bread enjoys the greatest popularity in the urban centers of the Northeast, especially New York City, where the delis feature light Jewish rye, black pumpernickel, and every possible shading in between. The upper Midwest also features a basketful of ryes: German cocktail rye, Polish rye with sauerkraut, Swedish limpa with candied fruit, and the salty rye of Finnish crackers.

Rye, *Secale*, is a close relative of wheat. The rye plant has slim seed spikes that produce dark, gray-brown kernels. It threshes off the plant, like wheat. Rye flour is classified as light, medium, and dark, suitable for different styles of bread. Rye has an assertive flavor with a trace of bitterness, like grassy walnuts.

Rye flour is readily available in supermarkets. Often you'll see a rye-wheat blend, which actually contains mostly white flour and a little rye flour. Although it's convenient for bread making, we usually recommend buying plain rye flour so you can control the amount in the bread. Although rye flour comes in dark, medium, and light, that's more of interest to commercial bakers than home bakers. Generally, you'll have your choice of one kind of rye flour—probably medium—in the supermarket or health food store. European delis may give you two choices. Stoneground rye has a rough-hewn texture that we like in rye breads.

Rye is also sold as whole kernels (berries), and flaked.

Rye flour and berries keep fairly well, although it's best to refrigerate or freeze them if possible.

Rye is a heavy flour and has little gluten. For the best breads, it should be mixed with wheat flour. Rye doughs usually are very wet and sticky; the liquid creates steam to help compensate for rye's heaviness.

To cook rye berries, soak 1 cup rye overnight in cold water and drain. Add to 3 cups boiling water, cover loosely, and cook over low heat for 45 to 60 minutes, until cooked through but still a bit chewy. Do not toast rye berries; toasting tends to bring out their bitterness. Add soaked or cooked rye berries to rye or multigrain breads for some extra texture.

To cook whole rye in a pressure cooker, use 3 cups water to 1 cup rye berries and cook for 25 to 30 minutes after the cooker comes up to pressure. To microwave them, combine 2½ cups cold water with 1 cup rye berries in a deep bowl. Microwave on high (100 percent) for 10 minutes, then reduce the heat to medium (50 percent) and microwave for 30 minutes or until cooked through.

To cook rye flakes, add ½ cup of the grain to 1 cup boiling water and cook for 2 to 3 minutes, or combine the rye flakes and water in a deep container and cook in the microwave on high (100 percent) for about 3 minutes or until tender. Uncooked rye flakes make a nice addition to the top of any type of rye bread; brush the loaf with a little egg or egg white so they adhere.

Pungent ingredients such as garlic, sauerkraut, onions, and strong cheeses go well with rye's hearty flavor. One classic Wisconsin sandwich consists of Limburger or brick cheese, mustard, and a slice of onion on dark rye. (Of course, it is washed down with beer.) Rye and buckwheat occupy similar positions on the flavor scale and can stand in well for each other. Rye, for example, goes well with smoked salmon. But sweet flavors can also offset it nicely—as in the candied fruit and anise of Swedish limpa, and the raisins and walnuts in the French-style rye that's so popular at boutique bakeries.

Rye

Rye Berry Stir-Fry with Pepper Strips

Lower East Side Pumpernickel

Cocktail Rye Loaf

Mock Sourdough (Light Rye)

Rye Burger Rolls with Caraway Seeds

Rye Garlic Bagels

Limpa Bread

Rye Berry Stir-Fry with Pepper Strips

Here rye, commonly associated with Eastern European cookery, gets an Asian accent. Other firm, chewy grains, such as wheat berries, oat groats, or whole-grain Kamut, could be used in this recipe.

Instead of adding the rye berries to the stir-fry, you can simply spoon the stir-fried vegetables over them.

Makes 4 servings

1 tablespoon canola oil

3 cloves garlic, minced

1 teaspoon minced fresh ginger

1 cup chopped green onion

1 red bell pepper, seeded and cut
into thin strips

1 yellow or green bell pepper,
seeded and cut into thin strips

4 cups sliced bok choy (leaves and
stalks)

1 cup cooked rye berries

¾ cup chopped tomato

½ teaspoon salt

¼ teaspoon freshly ground black
pepper

2 tablespoons reduced-sodium soy
sauce

¼ cup low-sodium chicken stock
mixed with 1 tablespoon
cornstarch

Heat the oil in a deep frying pan or wok. Add the garlic, ginger, and onion, and cook over medium heat, partially covered, until the onion is soft. Stir once or twice as needed. Remove the cover, add the peppers and bok choy, and stir-fry for a few minutes, until tender. Stir in the cooked rye berries, tomato, salt, pepper, soy sauce, and stock-cornstarch mixture. Stir-fry until heated through and the sauce has thickened. Serve hot.

111 calories, 4 g fat, 0.5 g saturated fat, no cholesterol,
3 g dietary fiber, 576 mg sodium

Lower East Side Pumpernickel

Dark, rich, and bittersweet, pumpernickel harkens back to the days when Schwarzbrot *(black bread) was the basic food of European peasants. In America, it's a staple of Jewish and German delis in New York City and elsewhere.*

To shape the dough into a round loaf, make a ball of dough and pull down on the sides, tucking the dough under the bottom. If you make this bread into a round loaf, it will be a rather shallow, "peasant"-looking bread.

Makes 1 large loaf or 2 smaller loaves; about 16 servings

½ cup warm water (110° to 115°)

2 tablespoons packed dark brown sugar

2 packages (4½ teaspoons) active dry yeast

2½ cups bread flour, plus more as needed

4 cups rye flour, preferably dark

1 teaspoon salt

2 cups warm skim milk (110° to 115°)

2 eggs, or ½ cup egg substitute

2 tablespoons dark molasses

3 tablespoons dill pickle juice

½ teaspoon instant coffee

1 tablespoon unsweetened cocoa

½ cup dark raisins

1 egg white, lightly beaten with 1 teaspoon water

Poppy or dill seeds

Pour the water into a bowl and mix in the sugar. Add the yeast and let proof in a warm place until foamy, about 5 minutes.

Meanwhile, mix together the flours and salt. Set aside.

Mix the milk with the eggs, molasses, pickle juice, coffee, and cocoa. Add 1 cup of the flour mixture and stir. Mix in the remaining flour mixture to make a soft dough. Knead in the raisins.

Knead a few minutes on a floured pastry cloth, using the cloth to lift and fold the dough and working in small amounts of additional flour as necessary.

Put the dough in a bowl, cover with a damp kitchen towel or plastic wrap, and set it in a warm place to rise for 1½ hours or until doubled. Punch down the dough.

Shape the dough into 1 or 2 round loaves and set on a sprayed or greased pastry sheet. Or place in a sprayed 9-by-5-inch loaf pan. Cover lightly and let rise in a warm place for 1 hour, until light.

Preheat the oven to 375°. Brush the bread with some of the egg white mixed with water and sprinkle with poppy or dill seeds.

Bake for 35 to 40 minutes or until the bread is crusty and sounds hollow when tapped. Let the bread cool on a wire rack.

---

220 calories, 2 g fat, 0.5 g saturated fat,
27 mg cholesterol, 5 g dietary fiber, 186 mg sodium

Cocktail Rye Loaf

This dense bread, popular in the German-influenced communities of the heartland, is usually sliced very thin and served with an appetizer or with sliced onion and a pungent cheese such as Limburger. It is also sold commercially in small loaves that slice into two-inch squares.

This is a good party bread; bake it on a day that you will be at home and at least one day before you are planning to serve it.

Makes 1 loaf; about 16 servings

¼ cup sugar	1 teaspoon salt
3 cups boiling water	2 teaspoons caraway seeds
4 cups stone-ground rye flour	1½ tablespoons canola oil
1 cup fine bulgur	¾ teaspoon active dry yeast

To caramelize the sugar, cook it in a small nonstick pan over high heat until the sugar has melted, stirring constantly. Continue cooking, without stirring, until the sugar turns a golden brown. This will take about 5 to 8 minutes; do not let the sugar burn. Slowly and carefully pour in the boiling water; the hot sugar will spatter. Continue cooking until the sugar is liquid again. Set aside and allow to cool.

In a large bowl, combine the rye flour, bulgur, salt, caraway seeds, canola oil, and yeast. Mix in the cooled sugar-water combination. Cover with a sheet of plastic wrap and press it against the mixture. Let stand overnight.

Preheat the oven to 325°. Spray or grease an 8-by-4-inch loaf pan and pat the dough evenly into the pan. Smooth the top of the bread with the back of a spoon.

Bake the bread in the center of the oven over a pan of boiling water that is set on the lowest rack. Bake for 2 hours. Let cool in the oven. The bread will be firm to the touch. Let cool completely out of the pan on a wire rack. Cover the bread in aluminum foil and chill overnight before serving. Slice very thin.

---

132 calories, 0.5 g fat, no saturated fat, no cholesterol,
5 g dietary fiber, 135 mg sodium

Mock Sourdough (Light Rye)

A little rye flour is the "magic" ingredient bakers use to give a deeper color and flavor to their white loaves. Rye's earthy flavor and ability to ferment easily gives bread a slightly sour tang. A slow rise—but not as slow as the several days it takes to make sourdough—also helps develop the flavor in this bread.

Makes 1 large loaf; about 14 servings

4 to 4½ cups bread flour
1½ teaspoons active dry yeast
1¾ cups warm water (110° to 115°)
¾ cup rye flour

2 teaspoons salt
Egg substitute or beaten egg white, mixed with a pinch of sugar

Combine 2½ cups of the bread flour, the yeast, 1¼ cups of the warm water, and 2 tablespoons of the rye flour in a mixing bowl to make a soft, sticky dough. Cover loosely and let rise in a warm place for 1 to 1½ hours, until light and spongy.

Stir down the risen sponge. Stir in the remaining ½ cup water, the remaining rye flour, and the salt. Stir in enough bread flour, about 1½ to 2 cups, to make a soft, fairly sticky dough. Knead with an electric mixer fitted with the dough hook (the dough will be sticky), or by hand, using a floured pastry cloth to help knead the dough.

Cover loosely and let rise again until doubled, about 1 to 1½ hours. Punch the dough down and form into an oblong loaf. Cover loosely with plastic wrap and let rise until light, about 1 hour.

Preheat the oven to 375°.

With a single-edged razor blade or a very sharp knife, cut 2 or 3 slashes in the top of the loaf. Brush with the egg mixture. Bake for 35 to 45 minutes, until the bread is golden brown and sounds hollow when tapped. Let cool on a wire rack.

---

166 calories, 0.5 g fat, no saturated fat, no cholesterol,
2 g dietary fiber, 305 mg sodium

Rye Burger Rolls with Caraway Seeds

If you're tired of tasteless hamburger buns, try these rich, earthy ones. They can be baked ahead of time, wrapped, and frozen. For more texture, you can add ½ cup of cooked rye berries to the dough.

Rye-wheat flour, sold in supermarkets, is a blend of white and rye flour.

Makes 8 rolls

2 cups bread flour
2 teaspoons packed dark brown
  sugar
1 tablespoon caraway or dill
  seeds, plus more as needed
1 teaspoon salt
1 package (2¼ teaspoons) active
  dry yeast

1 cup skim or 1-percent milk
2 tablespoons canola oil
¼ cup egg substitute, or 1 egg
1 cup rye-wheat flour
1 egg white, lightly beaten with
  1 teaspoon water

Using the large bowl of an electric mixer or mixing bowl, stir ¾ cup of the bread flour with the sugar, 1 tablespoon of the caraway seeds, salt, and yeast. Set aside.

Heat the milk and oil in a saucepan to 110° or just slightly warmer than when you proof yeast separately. Blend the warm milk mixture and the egg substitute into the dry ingredients. The dough will be very moist. Mix in the rye-wheat flour and the remaining 1¼ cups bread flour. The dough will be very soft and sticky. Sprinkle a pastry cloth with flour and knead the bread lightly until pliable, about 1 to 2 minutes. Using the sides of the cloth as a guide for kneading, lift up the sides and then press the dough down in a kneading style. The dough will still be soft.

Spray or grease a nonstick baking sheet. Divide the dough into 8 pieces. Roll each piece individually in your hands, shaping it into a 2- to 3-inch round. Cover lightly with plastic wrap or a warm cloth. Let the dough rise in a warm place for about 45 minutes.

Preheat the oven to 400°. Brush the rolls with the egg white mixture. Sprinkle the rolls with additional caraway seeds. Bake in the center of the oven for 20 to 25 minutes or until done. The rolls will be a light golden color and firm to the touch. Let the rolls cool on a wire rack. Slice horizontally and serve. Good warm or at room temperature.

*216 calories, 4 g fat, 0.5 g saturated fat, 1 mg cholesterol,
2 g dietary fiber, 297 mg sodium*

Rye Garlic Bagels

The bagel, a round, chewy breakfast bread, was brought to the East Coast by Central European settlers. It has since spread across the country, in flavors ranging from blueberry to dried tomato—although, frankly, many of the so-called "bagels" we've tasted aren't worthy of the name. To make these bagels chewier, substitute 2 tablespoons of gluten for 2 tablespoons of the bread flour.

These bagels are good served with reduced-fat cream cheese flavored with chives, or plain cream cheese with a slice of smoked salmon.

Makes 18 to 20 bagels

1 cup warm skim or 1-percent
   milk (110° to 115°)
¼ cup unsalted butter or
   margarine, at room temperature
   and cut into small pieces
1½ tablespoons sugar
1 teaspoon salt
1 package (2¼ teaspoons) active
   dry yeast
1 egg white, lightly beaten

1½ cups bread flour, plus more as
   needed
1½ cups rye-wheat flour
1 tablespoon canola oil
6 large cloves garlic, minced
1 tablespoon poppy seeds
1 tablespoon sesame seeds
1 egg white, lightly beaten with
   1 teaspoon water

Pour the warm milk into a large mixing bowl. Stir in the butter, sugar, salt, and yeast. Let stand a few minutes to proof the yeast.

Stir in the egg white, then the bread flour and rye-wheat flour, 1 cup at a time. Knead the dough in a mixer or by hand until a smooth, soft dough is formed, adding a tablespoon of flour at a time if needed. Shape the dough into a ball and put it in a bowl. Cover with plastic wrap or a warm damp cloth. Let the dough rise in a warm place for 1 hour or until doubled. Punch down the dough and knead on a lightly floured pastry cloth for 2 minutes.

Divide the dough into 18 to 20 pieces. Roll out each piece of dough into a pencil shape and connect the edges to form a coil about ½ inch thick. Continue until all the bagels have been prepared. Set the bagels on a sprayed baking sheet, cover with plastic wrap again, and let rise until light, about 1 to 1½ hours.

While the bagels are rising, prepare the garlic. Heat the oil in a frying pan. Cook the garlic, stirring almost constantly, over medium-low heat, watching so the garlic does not burn. The garlic should be golden. Stir in the poppy seeds and the sesame seeds. Set aside.

Fill a large frying pan with 1½ inches of water. Bring the water to a boil over medium-high heat. When the bagels have risen, remove with a spatula, one at a time, and slide them, about 6 at a time, into the water. Reduce the heat to medium, so the water does not boil but stays just below a simmer. Cook the bagels for 30 seconds on each side, turning them over with 2 forks. Drain.

Set the drained bagels on a sprayed or greased baking sheet. Brush with the egg white mixture. Sprinkle the garlic mixture lightly over the bagels, top and sides, pressing lightly so that it will adhere to the bagels.

Preheat the oven to 400°. Bake the bagels for 25 minutes or until golden. Remove from the baking sheet and let cool completely. Store in a sealed plastic bag. If not using within a day, freeze for later use.

To serve, slice and toast the bagels.

Based on 20 bagels: 107 calories, 3.5 g fat,
1.5 g saturated fat, 6 mg cholesterol, 1 g dietary fiber,
117 mg sodium

Limpa Bread

Scandinavian immigrants introduced this sweet, aromatic bread to the Midwest. It's a good bread to serve at Christmas. If you don't have fennel, you can use 2 teaspoons aniseed.

Makes 2 loaves; about 24 servings

4 to 4½ cups bread flour

2½ cups rye flour

1 teaspoon salt

2 cups warm skim milk (110° to 115°)

¼ cup packed dark brown sugar

¼ cup dark unsulfured molasses

¼ cup unsalted butter or margarine, at room temperature and cut into small pieces

2 packages (4½ teaspoons) active dry yeast

½ cup warm water (110° to 115°)

1 teaspoon granulated sugar

½ cup chopped candied orange peel

½ cup golden raisins

1 tablespoon fennel or caraway seeds, plus more as needed

1 egg white, lightly beaten with 1 teaspoon water

In a large bowl, combine the bread flour, rye flour, and salt. Set aside.

In a separate bowl or a large measuring cup, mix together the milk, brown sugar, molasses, and butter. Set aside.

Meanwhile, proof the yeast in the warm water mixed with the granulated sugar in the large bowl of an electric mixer fitted with the dough hook. When the yeast is foamy, mix in the milk mixture, then the flour mixture, 1 cup at a time, stirring well after each addition. The dough will be very soft and sticky. Remove the dough to a lightly floured pastry cloth and knead, using the pastry cloth to fold the dough over onto itself. Knead only a few minutes. The dough will be very soft and pliable. Set the dough in a large bowl, cover with plastic wrap or a warm damp kitchen towel. Place in a warm, draft-free area to rise until doubled, about 1½ hours.

Punch down the dough. Again place the dough on a floured pastry cloth or board and knead in the orange peel, raisins, and 1 tablespoon of the fennel seeds. Shape the dough into 2 loaves and place each loaf seam side down in a sprayed or greased 9-by-5-inch loaf pan. Brush the loaves with the egg white mixture and

Witches' Rye?

In the spring of 1692, when some adolescent girls in Salem, Massachusetts, and nearby communities began suffering fits, visions, and odd sensations, the village elders knew just what was ailing them: witchcraft. By September, a seven-member court had convicted twenty-seven people of witchcraft and put twenty of them to death. Another one hundred people were in prison awaiting trial. Then suddenly Massachusetts came to its senses, and the trials and accusations came to an end.

To this day, historians wonder why. Why Salem? Why 1692?

In 1976, biologist Linnda R. Caporael proposed an intriguing theory: Maybe the "bewitched" Salem residents had contracted ergotism.

Ergot, a fungus, infects cereals, especially rye. Through the centuries, people in Europe and, later, the New World ate plenty of rye in the form of bread. Rye, after all, thrived in the cold, damp climates that often killed wheat. Unfortunately, those same climates made rye susceptible to ergot, and outbreaks of ergotism, dubbed "Saint Anthony's fire," sickened and killed plenty of folks and their livestock.

Ergotism can produce mental disorientation and hallucinations, convulsions, muscle cramps, neural disturbances that may include the feeling of being bitten or pinched, gastrointestinal disorders, a ravenous appetite, and, sometimes, death. At least one ergot compound is related to LSD. So are more benign drugs used to treat migraine headaches and stop uterine bleeding.

There is evidence for Caporael's theory, as history professor Mary Kilbourne Matossian pointed out in 1989. New Englanders cultivated rye, and records from the time indicate the kind of weather that favors the growth of ergot. The majority of the "bewitched" suffered symptoms typical of ergotism: "fits," visions, sensations of flying, temporary blindness, nausea, joint pain, burning sensations, and feelings of being kicked, bitten, and pinched. Most of the victims who died were under ten years old, and ergotism, like any poisoning, hits children the hardest. Not only people but animals sickened and died. Although the "bewitched" could have been hysterical or faking, Matossian pointed out that fourteen of them died—which would seem to be taking the game a bit too far.

Other researchers have dismissed Caporael's theory, saying the facts of the case really didn't fit her model. Most explanations for what happened in Salem center on psychological or sociological grounds; the girls who started the whole episode had been dabbling in the occult.

Still, we find a certain grim romance in the idea that food poisoning could have played a role in one of America's most shameful episodes.

By the way, if you're starting to worry about the rye flour in your cupboard, relax. Modern-day harvesting and storage of rye help prevent ergot from getting into the food supply. At any rate, ergot is easy to spot if you know what you're looking for: Infected flour turns bread red.

sprinkle with additional fennel seeds. Cover lightly with a kitchen towel or plastic wrap and let rise in warm, draft-free area until doubled in bulk, about 1 hour.

Preheat the oven to 350°. Bake the bread in the center of the oven for 45 to 50 minutes or until the bread is golden brown and crusty and sounds hollow when tapped. Let the loaves cool on a wire rack.

186 calories, 2.5 g fat, 1.5 g saturated fat,
6 mg cholesterol, 2.5 g dietary fiber, 116 mg sodium

The "New" Specialty Grains

Walking down the aisles of the health food store brings to mind that old rhyme about what brides should wear on their stroll down the aisle: Something old (spelt, Kamut), something new (triticale), something borrowed (teff, from Ethiopia), and something blue (blue cornmeal—but that's another chapter).

If there has been one clear trend in the grain business, it's the emphasis on rediscovering "other" wheats. There's Kamut, which hails from ancient Egypt, and spelt, familiar to any Bible scholar. Then there's triticale, a cross between wheat and rye that has been kicking around, off and on, for thirty years.

For agricultural researcher Gilbert Stallknecht, it all comes down to bread. Bread, after all, is the reason wheat grew to such worldwide prominence in the first place. In his trials with spelt, emmer, and other grains, Stallknecht said, he's shooting for giving home bread bakers the chance to walk into a market and select from several varieties of whole grains: "You could make any kind of loaf you want. You'd have tasty loaves of bread and they'd all be different."

Teff, still a rarity in this country, is not wheat. It is used, though, to make bread: the flat, sour, pancakelike Ethiopian bread called injera. Deeply flavored and suitable for far more than flatbread—it makes a great polenta, for one thing—teff invites further discovery.

Kamut

Some say King Tut's tomb is cursed, but everyone would agree Kamut's existence in the United States has been extraordinarily blessed. In the decade or so since its commercial introduction, the "ancient Egyptian wheat" has shown up in a vast array of foods, including cookies, muffins, pastas, pancake mixes, and cereals.

According to legend, after World War II, a U.S. airman claimed he'd taken a handful of grain from a stone box in a tomb in central Egypt. He gave some of the large kernels to a friend, who mailed them to his father, a Montana wheat farmer. The farmer got them to grow and displayed the harvest of his small crop at the county fair, where it was dubbed "King Tut's wheat." Viewed as nothing more than a novelty, the ancient grain soon faded into obscurity.

In 1977—while King Tut's golden artifacts toured museums in the United States—Montana farmer Mack Quinn and his son, Bob, a plant biochemist, tracked down one remaining jar of Tut's namesake wheat. The Quinns spent a decade growing and researching the ancient grain. They learned that wheats of this type originated in the Fertile Crescent, the area between the Tigris-Euphrates valley and the Nile that was the cradle of several notable ancient civilizations.

They gave the grain the trade name of Kamut (ka-moot), an ancient Egyptian word for wheat. In 1990, the U.S. Agriculture Department recognized the grain, officially named QK-77, as a protected variety. Kamut is grown organically in Montana, Alberta, and Saskatchewan.

A hard amber spring wheat, Kamut is a nonhybrid that yields hump-backed kernels two to three times larger than a kernel of standard wheat. Scientists (who, incidentally, find the airman's tomb story a bit fanciful) know Kamut is closely related to durum, the high-protein wheat used to make pasta, but argue about what subspecies it belongs to.

Kamut is widely available in health food stores as a whole grain, as flakes, as flour, and in various processed foods such as breakfast cereals (flaked or puffed), cookies, and crackers. All of it is organically grown. Juice bars also sell Green Kamut (the juiced leaves), which is similar to wheat grass juice.

Because it's a little drier than wheat, whole grain Kamut keeps well. Kamut flour, however, will develop off-flavors and is best frozen or refrigerated.

To cook whole grain Kamut, soak or toast 1 cup grain and combine it in a heavy saucepan with 3 cups water. Bring to a boil, then cook over low heat for about 1½ hours or until tender; drain. Or use a pressure cooker and cook for 35 to 45 minutes after the cooker reaches pressure. Add salt to Kamut after cooking.

Buttery-flavored and chewy, whole grain Kamut's large kernels are especially suited to salads and pilafs and can be tossed into soups. Use Kamut interchangeably with whole wheat berries, or even rice. Kamut is also processed as bulgur and couscous, which are interchangeable with regular wheat bulgur and couscous.

To cook flaked Kamut, combine ½ cup with 1 cup water, bring to a boil, and cook 3 to 5 minutes on the stove top, or in the microwave (starting with cold water).

Like durum, Kamut flour makes excellent pasta. Kamut noodles are sturdy enough to survive freezing and thawing without falling apart. Kamut flour is also excellent in pancakes, muffins, biscuits, and cookies. Be careful when using it in bread. It's closer to durum than to the hard red wheat used for breads and should not simply be substituted for whole wheat flour.

Kamut

Kamut Pancakes with Pork, Onions, and Prunes

Kamut Parmesan Biscuits

Kamut Pancakes with Pork, Onions, and Prunes

Pancakes are good for more than breakfast. Try them for a quick, hearty dinner. Sweet fruits such as prunes go nicely with both pancakes and pork. Although pork has a reputation for being fatty, pork tenderloin is very lean. Three ounces cooked has only 140 calories and 4 grams of fat.

Makes 4 servings

PANCAKES

¾ cup Kamut flour
¼ cup unbleached all-purpose flour
½ teaspoon salt

1½ teaspoons baking powder
2 tablespoons egg substitute, or 1 egg white
1⅓ cups buttermilk

PORK

2 teaspoons olive oil
½ pound pork tenderloin, cut into bite-size pieces
1 medium onion, thinly sliced
½ red bell pepper, seeded and thinly sliced
2 tablespoons unbleached all-purpose flour
1 cup low-sodium chicken stock

2 teaspoons packed dark brown sugar
¼ teaspoon salt
1 teaspoon dried crushed rosemary
¼ teaspoon freshly ground black pepper
8 medium pitted prunes, coarsely chopped

To make the pancake batter: Combine the Kamut flour, all-purpose flour, salt, and baking powder in a mixing bowl. Stir in the egg substitute and buttermilk and mix just enough to completely moisten the dry ingredients. Set aside.

To prepare the pork: Heat the oil in a large frying pan or saucepan. Add the pork and cook over medium-high heat a few minutes, stirring frequently, just until the pork is no longer pink on the outside. Remove to a plate and set aside.

Add the onion and red pepper to the pan and cook until softened, about 5 minutes. Sprinkle the flour over the vegetables and stir well. Stir in the chicken stock, brown sugar, salt, rosemary, black pepper, and prunes. Cook over medium heat, stirring frequently, until the sauce thickens. Stir in the pork and cook just until heated through. Remove from the heat.

To cook the pancakes: Heat a large skillet or griddle that has been sprayed with nonstick cooking spray. Using about ¼ cup batter for each pancake, spoon the batter into the pan to make 4 pancakes, being careful not to crowd the pancakes (depending on the size of the pan, you may need to cook the pancakes in 2 batches). Cook until golden on the bottom, then turn and cook on the other side until golden.

Place a pancake on each plate. Spoon the pork and prunes over the pancakes. Serve immediately.

---

330 calories, 6 g fat, 1.5 g saturated fat,
37 mg cholesterol, 5.5 g dietary fiber, 691 mg sodium

Kamut Parmesan Biscuits

Kamut flour has a slightly yeasty flavor that goes well with cheese. This somewhat heavy dough is wet and sticky; the steam created during baking helps lighten the dough. Still, these are not light and fluffy biscuits, but a bit heavier, like rolls.

Makes 8 biscuits

1 cup Kamut flour
½ cup whole wheat pastry flour,
    plus more as needed
1 tablespoon baking powder
½ teaspoon salt

3 tablespoons cold unsalted butter
    or vegetable shortening
1 cup buttermilk
2 tablespoons freshly grated
    Parmesan cheese

Preheat the oven to 450°. Spray an 8-inch cake pan with nonstick cooking spray.

Mix the flours, baking powder, and salt in a mixing bowl. Cut in the butter with a pastry blender or 2 knives to make a crumbly mixture. Stir in the buttermilk. The dough should be very wet and sticky. Give the dough about a half-dozen vigorous stirs with a wooden spoon. Divide the dough into 8 pieces.

With floured hands, roll the pieces of dough into balls about 2 inches in diameter, dusting with just enough flour to keep them from sticking all over your hands. Place in the prepared cake pan, with the sides nearly touching.

Sprinkle the Parmesan evenly over the biscuits, pressing gently into the dough. Bake the biscuits for 15 to 18 minutes, until golden. Serve warm.

---

145 calories, 5.5 g fat, 3 g saturated fat,
14 mg cholesterol, 3 g dietary fiber, 319 mg sodium

Spelt

It might seem like one of the new kids on the block, but spelt is older than Moses. Archaeologists believe it was being cultivated 9,000 years ago, well before people began growing the more modern bread wheats, and the Old Testament contains numerous references to spelt.

At the turn of the century, American farmers were planting some 600,000 acres of spelt, which was brought to the United States by European immigrants, especially the Pennsylvania Dutch and others of German ancestry. After World War I, it virtually vanished, making way for the higher-yielding, easily threshed hard winter wheats. Only the Amish farmers continued to grow spelt.

After getting requests from both domestic and European customers for an organically grown spelt, Purity Foods, a major Midwestern distributor of health foods, reintroduced it to the commercial market in 1987.

By the mid-1990s there were about 8,000 to 12,000 cultivated acres of spelt, mostly in Ohio, Indiana, and Michigan—although it is being grown as far west as Washington and as far east as New York. Health food stores stock spelt flakes, whole grain spelt, spelt flour, spelt ready-to-eat cereal, and various processed foods, such as crackers and breads, made from it. There's a large market for spelt in Europe, says Don Stinchcomb, president of Purity Foods—especially Germany, France, and Italy, where it's called *farro* and used in polentas and the breads of Tuscany.

Some plant researchers debate whether spelt is actually a true wheat. Home cooks and bakers who don't relish scientific nuances can consider it wheat; it tastes a lot like wheat, and it has gluten, making it suitable for bread baking.

Unlike the bread wheats, spelt doesn't thresh off the plant; it must be hulled. Like hard red winter wheat, it is planted in the fall and harvested in the summer.

Spelt comes in thousands of varieties, like wheat, but four major ones are grown in the United States: Roquin (ro-KAI), cultivated for its exceptional bread-baking qualities; vita 1 and vita 2, the most commonly grown spelts, whose seeds originally came from the World Seed Bank; and Oberkumeratkorn, which is grown primarily in Canada.

Spelt tastes like wheat but tends to be a little milder and, occasionally, to have sweet-musty undertones, a bit like hazelnuts.

Spelt's advocates say it has a unique type of gluten that's easier to digest than the gluten in familiar wheat, meaning some people who are sensitive to wheat might find spelt more digestible. Some research—very preliminary at this stage—has supported that notion. If you are allergic, never experiment with a new food except under a doctor's supervision.

You should have no trouble finding at least one form of spelt in a health food store. Like whole wheat flour, spelt flour will become rancid; use it up quickly or keep it in the freezer. The same goes for spelt flakes.

Spelt does contain gluten, making it suitable for breads. However, its gluten is not as durable as that of wheat. Wheat doughs can take a lot of beating and, in fact, require it. Spelt breads should be mixed for a shorter length of time—no more than 3 to 4 minutes in an electric mixer, slightly longer by hand.

Perhaps because it is richer in complex carbohydrates than wheat, spelt works very well in sponge or *levain* (sourdough) breads. (As dough rises, enzymes convert complex carbohydrates to simple carbohydrates for the yeasts to feed on.) It substitutes nicely for the rye flour in the Mock Sourdough on page 245.

To cook the whole grain, soak 1 cup spelt kernels overnight or toast them, then add to 3 cups boiling water. Reduce the heat to low and cook, mostly covered, for 45 minutes to an hour, until tender. Spelt can be substituted in any recipe that calls for wheat berries.

Cook spelt flakes as you would rolled oats, using ½ cup flakes to 1 cup water. Add the spelt to boiling water and cook for 2 to 3 minutes, or combine the spelt and water in a deep container and cook in the microwave on high (100 percent) for about 3 minutes or until tender. Uncooked spelt flakes are good put on top of breads or toasted in granolas.

Spelt

German-Style Plum Tart With a Spelt Crust

Spelt Parker House Rolls

German-Style Plum Tart with a Spelt Crust

This Germanic dish, often called a kuchen, is basically a flat coffee cake. Be sure to use really good plums. If they're not in season, use ripe but firm peeled pears or apples. This is excellent for breakfast, or even as a luncheon course with cheese.

Makes 16 servings

1 cup skim or 1-percent milk
¼ cup unsalted butter or
   margarine
1 package (2¼ teaspoons) active
   dry yeast
¼ cup warm water (110° to 115°)
2 cups spelt flour or whole wheat
   flour

1½ to 2 cups bread flour
1 teaspoon salt
⅓ cup plus 2 tablespoons sugar
2 pounds (about 10 to 12) ripe
   but firm medium plums
½ teaspoon ground cinnamon

In a saucepan over medium heat, heat the milk and butter together just until the milk is warm. Stir until the butter melts. In a small bowl, dissolve the yeast in the warm water and set aside for 5 minutes or until foamy.

In a large mixing bowl, combine the spelt flour, 1½ cups of the bread flour, the salt, the 2 tablespoons of sugar, and the yeast. Stir in the warm milk-butter mixture. Knead by hand on a floured pastry cloth, or in a heavy-duty mixer fitted with the dough hook, until the dough is smooth and springy. The dough should be soft and somewhat sticky; work in more bread flour, a teaspoon at a time, as needed to keep the dough from sticking to the cloth or the sides of the bowl.

Place the dough in a bowl, cover with a damp kitchen towel or plastic wrap, and set aside in a warm place to rise until doubled in bulk, about 1 to 1½ hours.

Punch down the dough. Pat the dough evenly into a 12-by-18-inch baking pan that has been sprayed with nonstick cooking spray, or pat into rectangles on 2 smaller sprayed baking sheets. The dough should be about ¼ inch thick. Let rise again until light and puffy, about 15 to 30 minutes.

Preheat the oven to 450°.

Cut the plums in half lengthwise and remove the pits. Cut most, but not all, of the way through each plum half. Press plums, skin side up, evenly over the crust, slightly fanning out the cut halves. Mix the cinnamon with the remaining ⅓ cup sugar and sprinkle over the plums.

Bake the tart for 15 to 25 minutes, until the crust is a deep golden color and the plums are tender and giving off juice (don't worry if they look a little scorched). Serve warm or at room temperature.

*191 calories, 3.5 g fat, 2 g saturated fat, 8 mg cholesterol,
4 g dietary fiber, 142 mg sodium*

Spelt Parker House Rolls

An old American favorite, these "pocketbook" rolls get a twist with whole grain flour.

Makes about 16 rolls

1 package (2¼ teaspoons) active
  dry yeast
¼ cup warm water (110° to 115°)
1 cup skim or 1-percent milk
2 tablespoons canola oil
2 tablespoons packed dark brown
  sugar
1 teaspoon salt

1½ cups spelt flour or whole
  wheat flour
1½ cups unbleached all-purpose
  flour
1 egg, lightly beaten
2 tablespoons unsalted butter or
  margarine, melted and cooled

Dissolve the yeast in the warm water; set aside.

In a saucepan over medium heat, heat the milk with the oil, sugar, and salt just until warm, not hot.

In a large mixing bowl, blend the spelt flour with 1 cup of the all-purpose flour. Add the warm milk mixture, yeast mixture, and egg. Beat to make a soft, sticky dough. In an electric mixer fitted with the dough hook, or on a lightly floured pastry cloth, knead the dough until smooth and stretchy, working in just enough all-purpose flour to keep the dough from sticking.

Place the dough in a bowl, cover with a damp kitchen towel or plastic wrap, and set aside in a warm place to rise until doubled in bulk, about 45 minutes to 1 hour.

Punch down the dough. Roll out to a ¼- to ⅓-inch thickness. Cut into rounds with a 3-inch biscuit or cookie cutter. With a wooden spoon handle or the dull side of a knife, press an indentation down the middle of each round. Brush the rounds very lightly with the melted butter, then fold in half along the indentation line (the butter should be on the inside of the roll). Place the rolls on a large baking sheet that has been sprayed with nonstick cooking spray. Brush the tops lightly with additional melted butter.

Cover lightly with plastic wrap and let rise in a warm place until light, about 25 to 45 minutes.

Preheat the oven to 400°. Bake the rolls for 10 to 15 minutes, until golden. Serve slightly warm.

122 calories, 4 g fat, 1 g saturated fat, 18 mg cholesterol,
2 g dietary fiber, 146 mg sodium

Triticale

For centuries, rye and wheat grew together in the same fields—wheat as the crop the farmer was trying to grow and rye as the weed that would survive the most awful weather. By the late nineteenth century, scientists had begun playing around seriously with the idea of creating a fertile cross between wheat and rye. They were looking for a cereal crop that would have the overall protein and bread-making qualities of wheat, with the high lysine content and stamina of rye.

European breeders succeeded in the early twentieth century, but it wasn't until the late 1960s that triticale (trit-i-KAY-lee), which gets its name from a blending of wheat, *Triticum,* and rye, *Secale,* really got started as a commercial crop in Canada and the United States. Some health food purists objected to this engineered grain, but triticale garnered plenty of positive attention as a "superfood" that could do its share to help alleviate world hunger. Triticale's fictional descendant, quadro-triticale, even popped up in that legendary *Star Trek* episode, "The Trouble with Tribbles."

Then the hoopla faded away, and triticale was shoved to the back shelves of the health food store—if you could even find it there. One big problem was that early varieties of triticale didn't perform very well in the field. The plants tended to lodge (fall over in the field), yields were poor, and the kernels were shriveled. When the government dropped its price supports for triticale, just about everybody stopped growing it.

The new varieties of triticale are outstanding and outperform many wheats, says agricultural researcher Gilbert Stallknecht. Researchers are now experimenting with hard white triticale, which, like the hard white wheats, would have good bread-baking qualities with a milder flavor than red triticale or wheat.

Although some health food stores stock triticale berries, flakes, and/or flour, the grain shows up most frequently as an ingredient in multigrain flours and cereal mixes.

Triticale resembles wheat in the field, with larger heads. The kernels resemble wheat or rye berries. Triticale has a flavor that's a bit deeper than that of wheat—if we were mathematicians, we'd call it "wheat squared"—with just a hint of rye's grassiness.

Triticale flour contains gluten, but not as much as wheat, and its gluten is not as strong. It works best mixed with some wheat flour, and in breads that don't require too much kneading or rising. Triticale flour is closer to wheat flour than rye in heaviness, so you don't have to make doughs overly wet.

Cook whole triticale berries as you would wheat or rye berries. Soak 1 cup triticale several hours or overnight in cold water and drain. Add to 3 cups boiling water, cover loosely, and cook over low heat for 45 to 60 minutes, until cooked through but still a bit chewy. Like rye or wheat berries, soaked or cooked triticale berries can be added to breads for a chewier texture.

To cook triticale in a pressure cooker, use 3 cups water to 1 cup rye berries, and cook for 25 to 30 minutes after the cooker comes up to pressure. To microwave the berries, combine 2½ cups cold water with 1 cup triticale in a deep bowl. Microwave on high (100 percent) for 10 minutes, then reduce the heat to medium (50 percent) and microwave for 30 minutes or until cooked through.

To cook triticale flakes, add ½ cup of the grain to 1 cup boiling water and cook for 2 to 3 minutes, or combine the rye flakes and water in a deep container and cook in the microwave on high for about 3 minutes. Use uncooked triticale flakes to decorate breads; brush the top of the loaf with a little egg or egg white so they adhere.

Triticale

Dilled Triticale Batter Bread

Triticale Carrot Muffins with Oat Bran

Dilled Triticale Batter Bread

This bread requires no kneading—a boon to busy bakers. It's inspired by an old American favorite, a casserole bread made with dill and cottage cheese that won the Pillsbury Bake-Off in 1967. This version for the new millennium is made with whole grain flour and yogurt—today's answer to cottage cheese.

Makes 1 loaf; about 12 servings

1 cup plain nonfat yogurt

2 tablespoons canola oil

¼ cup warm water (110° to 115°)

1 cup bread flour

2 tablespoons sugar

1 package (2¼ teaspoons) active
   dry yeast

1 teaspoon salt

¼ cup egg substitute, or 1 egg

2 cups triticale flour (or whole
   wheat flour)

¼ cup finely chopped green onion

2 tablespoons finely snipped fresh
   dill, or 2 teaspoons dill seed

Coarse salt (optional)

In a saucepan over low heat, or in the microwave on medium-high, heat the yogurt, oil, and water until very warm (120°) but not too hot.

In a large mixing bowl, combine the bread flour, sugar, yeast, and salt. Add the warm yogurt mixture and egg substitute. Beat at low speed for 3 minutes.

By hand, stir in enough triticale flour to make a stiff batter. Stir in the onion and dill. Give the batter about 20 vigorous stirs.

Cover the bowl loosely with plastic wrap and set aside in a warm place to rise until doubled in bulk, about 45 minutes to 1 hour.

Preheat the oven to 350°. Spray a 2-quart round casserole dish with nonstick cooking spray. Beat the dough for 1 minute, then turn into the dish. If desired, sprinkle the top lightly with coarse salt. Bake for 45 to 50 minutes or until the bread is a deep golden color and sounds hollow when tapped. Let cool before slicing.

*155 calories, 3 g fat, no saturated fat, 1 mg cholesterol,
3.5 g dietary fiber, 203 mg sodium*

Triticale Carrot Muffins with Oat Bran

Rich in fiber and beta-carotene, these moist, not-too-sweet muffins keep well (see page 16 for storing and reheating muffins).

Makes 12 muffins

1¼ cups triticale flour or whole
   wheat flour
¾ cup oat bran
2 teaspoons baking soda
1 teaspoon baking powder
½ teaspoon salt
2 teaspoons ground cinnamon

¼ teaspoon ground allspice
½ cup honey
¾ cup plain nonfat yogurt
½ cup egg substitute, or 2 eggs
2 tablespoons canola oil
1½ cups finely shredded carrots
½ cup dark raisins

Preheat the oven to 375°. Spray a muffin tin with nonstick cooking spray, or line it with paper liners.

   In a large bowl, combine the flour, oat bran, baking soda, baking powder, salt, cinnamon, and allspice. Add the honey, yogurt, egg substitute, and oil; stir just until mixed. Gently stir in the carrots and raisins. Spoon the batter into the muffin cups, filling about three-quarters full. Bake for about 20 minutes or until the muffins are browned and firm and a tester inserted into the center of the muffin comes out dry. These are best served slightly warm.

163 calories, 3 g fat, 0.5 g saturated fat, 1 mg cholesterol,
4 g dietary fiber, 289 mg sodium

Teff

To biologist Wayne Carlson, teff is a cultural artifact, the living equivalent of an arrowhead or carved mask.

   He first discovered the tiny grain when he was working in Ethiopia in the 1970s. Teff, or t'ef, to more closely approximate its Amharic pronunciation, is a food staple in Ethiopia and nowhere else in the world. The Ethiopians use it mostly to make a large, sour, crepelike flatbread called injera. When Carlson returned home to the

States, he discovered to his surprise that he missed teff. He figured the Ethiopian immigrants in the States would miss it even more. So he decided to try growing it in Idaho.

Carlson described this cultural transfer in the jargon of his trade: "This is a biological symbiosis; the people and the plant are mutually supporting. I was trying to transfer that cultural component from Ethiopian culture into our culture. The Ethiopians are the original hosts for this symbiotic organism. Their being here means they can be hosts for it here."

Teff did encounter a different culture in Idaho. For one thing, Carlson had to adapt the plant to mechanical threshing: "We don't have oxen and scythes here." And he had to put up with jokes and raised eyebrows from his neighbors, who thought his choice of crop a bit odd.

Most of the customers for teff are, not surprisingly, the 100,000-plus Ethiopian immigrants in the United States. A small but growing number of other people have discovered its deep, distinctive flavor.

T'ef means "lost" in Amharic and relies on the Ethiopians' love of double meanings and innuendos, said Carlson. On one level, the word refers to the fact that when other crops fail or are lost, teff will survive. On a second level, it refers to the size of the grain—it takes 150 seeds to equal the size of 1 wheat berry. If you drop teff, it's lost for good.

Unfortunately, teff seems to have become lost in yet another sense. While we were writing this book, Arrowhead Mills quit distributing it, and the grain disappeared from the shelves of many health food stores.

Teff, *Eragrostis tef*, is a bright green, shiny grass that tends to lodge (fall over) when it matures. The tiny seeds are ivory and dark brown. Teff has a pleasantly robust flavor like wheat, tea, and hay rolled into one.

Teff is available in groceries that stock Ethiopian ingredients, in some health food stores and by mail order (see page 297).

Teff flour ferments easily and makes an excellent sourdough starter for pancakes, muffins, and waffles.

Whole grain teff is usually cooked as a porridge. Because it's sticky, the grains adhere together well and it makes an excellent polenta, or mush. Just pour the porridge into a square or loaf pan and let it sit; it will firm up nicely.

To cook whole grain teff, do not rinse it first; it's too tiny. Stir 1 cup of the grain into 3 cups of boiling water. The seeds are tiny and will float until they begin to absorb water. Cook over low heat, stirring occasionally, until the teff has absorbed the liquid and is tender, about 15 to 20 minutes.

To microwave teff, add 3 cups boiling water to 1 cup teff. Microwave on high (100 percent) for 5 minutes, then reduce the heat to medium (50 percent) and microwave for another 8 to 10 minutes or until the teff has absorbed the liquid.

Teff's deep flavor begs for spicy fare. We pair it with plenty of garlic, onion, chiles, or herbs. It's good with chicken and all sorts of vegetables.

Teff

Autumn Ratatouille on Teff

Spiced Lentils in Sourdough Teff Crepes

Autumn Ratatouille on Teff

This dish, which plays the gold and red of squash ratatouille against the deep brown of teff, is as vibrant as the season it's named for and makes a good dinner party entrée. Make the teff ahead of time so that it has time to firm up.

Makes 6 servings

1½ cups teff
4½ cups water

¼ teaspoon salt

RATATOUILLE

1 medium kabocha or butternut
   squash (2 to 2½ pounds)
2½ tablespoons olive oil
1 tablespoon minced garlic
1 cup chopped red onion
1 large red bell pepper, seeded and
   diced
1 cup diced fresh or canned
   tomato

2 tablespoons minced fresh
   parsley
2 teaspoons minced fresh sage or
   basil
Balsamic or sherry vinegar
½ teaspoon salt
Freshly ground black pepper

Prepare the teff: Place the teff, water, and salt in a 2-quart saucepan. Bring to a boil over medium heat. Reduce the heat to low, cover the pan, and cook, whisking occasionally, for about 30 minutes or until the teff is the consistency of thick porridge. Pour into a 9-inch square baking dish or cake pan that has been sprayed with nonstick cooking spray. Let cool completely. If desired, cover and refrigerate for up to 3 days.

To make the ratatouille: To peel the squash, pierce it with a knife in 2 or 3 places, then place it in the microwave (put the butternut on its side). Microwave on high for 2 minutes, then turn and microwave another 2 or 3 minutes, until the skin begins to soften. Let stand 10 minutes, then cut into large chunks, remove the seeds, and cut the flesh from the peel. Cut the squash into ¾- to 1-inch dice.

Heat the oil in a deep frying pan, preferably nonstick. Add the garlic and onion and sauté for 1 minute, then add the red pepper. Cook over medium heat, stirring frequently, until the pepper begins to soften. Stir in the tomato and squash. Cook, stirring often, until the squash is very tender, about 15 to 20 minutes. Stir in the parsley, sage, vinegar, salt, and black pepper, and cook for another minute to heat through. Remove from the heat.

Fry the teff: Cut the cooled teff into 6 rectangles and remove from the baking dish. Heat a large frying pan sprayed with nonstick cooking spray. Add the teff and cook over medium heat until golden on the bottom, then turn and cook on the other side until golden. Place a piece of teff on each of 6 plates. Spoon the warm ratatouille over the teff. Serve immediately.

*302 calories, 7 g fat, 1 g saturated fat, no cholesterol,
12.5 g dietary fiber, 286 mg sodium*

Spiced Lentils in Sourdough Teff Crepes

Authentic injera, the Ethiopian flatbread, is no picnic to make. The batter is fermented for several days, then poured over a woklike utensil to be cooked into a thin pancake. It's also pretty sour for many Americans' tastes. We've come up with a crepe that is inspired by injera but takes less work to make and is more to mainstream tastes.

Stack the leftover crepes between sheets of waxed paper, wrap tightly in foil, and freeze. Reheat in a 300° oven and roll around chili or sautéed vegetables.

Makes 4 servings (12 crepes), with leftover crepes

CREPES

⅔ cup teff flour
⅓ cup unbleached all-purpose
  flour
Pinch of active dry yeast

1 cup warm water (110° to 115°)
½ cup egg substitute, or 2 eggs
¼ teaspoon salt

FILLING

1½ cups red or green lentils,
  picked over and rinsed

3 cups water or unsalted stock

1 tablespoon unsalted butter or
  canola oil

3 cloves garlic, minced

1½ cups chopped onion

1 tablespoon minced fresh ginger

1 to 2 jalapeño or serrano
  peppers

½ teaspoon ground coriander

½ teaspoon salt

½ cup low-sodium chicken or
  vegetable stock

1 medium lemon

To make the crepes: In a glass bowl, combine the teff flour, all-purpose flour, yeast, and water. Cover loosely with plastic wrap and let stand at room temperature for several hours or overnight, or until the batter is bubbly and smells tangy. Stir in the egg substitute and salt.

Heat a 6- or 7-inch crepe pan that has been sprayed with nonstick cooking spray. Pour about 2½ tablespoons of the batter into the pan, twirling the pan so the batter thinly coats the bottom. Cook just until the crepe no longer looks wet, about 10 to 20 seconds. Carefully flip the crepe and cook the other side a few seconds, until set. Continue until the batter is used up. Crepes should be thin; if too thick, add a little more butter. You will have about 12 crepes, enough for this recipe with some left over. Stack the crepes between sheets of waxed paper.

To make the filling: Bring the lentils and water to a boil. Turn the heat to low and cook, partly covered, for about 10 to 15 minutes for red lentils or 30 to 35 minutes for green lentils, or until tender but not mushy. Drain.

Heat the butter in a skillet that has been sprayed with nonstick cooking spray. Add the garlic, onion, ginger, chile peppers, coriander, and salt. Cook, stirring, until the onion is softened, about 5 minutes. Gently stir in the lentils and stock; cook just until heated through. Cut the lemon in half. Squeeze the juice from one half over the lentils and stir. Cut the remaining half into 4 wedges or slices to use as a garnish.

Roll the warm crepes around the warm lentils, using 2 crepes per serving. Garnish with the lemon wedges.

408 calories, 4.5 g fat, 2 g saturated fat, 8 mg cholesterol,
13 g dietary fiber, 405 mg sodium

Cereals on the Horizon

The success of such products as Kamut and spelt, as well as the need to expand the range of food grains available to a rapidly growing world population, inspires plant scientists and farmers constantly to search for nutritious cereals that will thrive under a wide range of conditions. There are, indeed, some grains poised on the horizon. Maybe one of them is the next Kamut or amaranth.

"We're still using the varieties Moses used in the Old Testament," said Gilbert Stallknecht, of Montana State University's Agricultural Research Station in Huntley, Montana, referring to spelt, emmer, and einkorn. Although some experimentation is going on with spelts, modern researchers have done very little breeding with these ancient crops. Emmer and einkorn, ancient wheats that Stallknecht is experimenting with, are not available retail yet, and may not be for a few years. Stallknecht has made bread with emmer wheats and found it tasty. "It's a heavy bread like rye, but I think it tastes better."

The Rodale Institute Research Center in Kutztown, Pennsylvania, has been extensively studying intermediate wheat grass. That's worth noting, since it was Rodale that almost singlehandedly introduced amaranth to U.S. consumers. Intermediate wheat grass is one of those grains that has been under our noses all along—but not as a food. It is used as a cover crop to fill in unsightly places such as highway verges and old mine sites. It yields a grain that is nutty-flavored, mild, and sweet. Despite its name, it is not wheat and is not related to the wheat grass found in the produce department of health food stores, which is simply sprouted wheat. To eliminate such confusion, Rodale markets small bunches of the grain in its store as Wild Triga (TREE-gah).

Intermediate wheat grass has one characteristic that could easily win the hearts of farmers everywhere: Unlike any of the other cereal grains, it's a perennial.

Multigrain Recipes

This chapter makes a home for those recipes that use ready-mixed multigrain flours or cereals, or that are made of several grains, with none really dominating.

Multigrain flour, multiblend flour, seven-grain cereal, eight-grain flour, Ezekiel flour—by whatever name they're labeled, these mixes usually blend grain and legume flours. One multigrain flour we used contained wheat, triticale, oat, corn, soy, barley, and buckwheat. Another had wheat, triticale, rye, mullet, oat, buckwheat, barley, and soy. Still a third mixed flours of wheat, barley, pinto bean, green lentil, millet, and spelt.

Any multigrain flour should work fine in the following recipes.

When buying a multigrain flour, check to make sure it lists wheat as the first ingredient. Otherwise, you cannot use it in baking without adding wheat flour.

Multigrain flours and mixes store only as well as their ingredients. Keep them in a cool, dry place or in the freezer.

Multigrain Recipes

Oatmeal Multigrain Bread

Multigrain Breadsticks

Multigrain Bubble Bread

Steamed Boston Brown Bread

Multigrain Persimmon Pancakes with Honeyed Pears

Savory Granola

Oatmeal Multigrain Bread

This is a dense, rich bread with an almost cakelike texture and flavor

Makes 2 loaves; about 24 servings

1½ cups seven-grain cereal
¾ cup quick-cooking (not instant) oats
¾ cup rye flour
2 packages (4½ teaspoons) active dry yeast
2¾ cups warm 1-percent milk (110° to 115°)

½ cup packed dark brown sugar
3 tablespoons unsalted butter or margarine, melted and cooled
2 teaspoons salt
4 to 5 cups bread flour
1 egg white, lightly beaten
Crushed granola or uncooked oats

Combine the cereal, oats, rye flour, and yeast in a large mixing bowl. Stir in the warm milk, sugar, and butter. Mix with an electric mixer fitted with the dough hook, or stir by hand with a wooden spoon.

Stir in the salt and enough additional flour to make a very wet, sticky dough. To knead this wet dough, sprinkle a pastry cloth with flour and use the cloth to help fold the dough over itself. Knead until smooth. Put the dough in a bowl, cover with a damp kitchen towel or plastic wrap, and set in a warm place to rise for 1 to 1½ hours or until doubled. Punch down the dough.

Preheat the oven to 375°.

The dough will still be fairly sticky; turn out onto a floured board and use floured hands to shape it. Shape it into 2 regular loaves and place the loaves in 9-by-5-inch loaf pans sprayed with nonstick cooking spray, or shape the dough into 2 round loaves and place the loaves on a sprayed baking sheet. Brush the loaves with the egg white and sprinkle with crushed granola. Bake for 25 to 35 minutes or until the loaves are golden and crusty and sound hollow when tapped.

Let the bread cool on a wire rack.

---

*228 calories, 3 g fat, 1 g saturated fat, 5 mg cholesterol,
2.5 g dietary fiber, 202 mg sodium*

Multigrain Breadsticks

The flour we used in these breadsticks contained eight different grains, but multigrain flours vary a great deal. Any of them is good to use in this recipe, as long as it contains wheat flour.

Breadsticks—basically just long rolls—are fun to make, and they freeze well. Before baking you can roll them in a mixture of sesame seeds and poppy seeds, or just one kind of seed.

Makes 16 breadsticks

1 teaspoon sugar

1¼ cups warm water (110° to
    115°)

1 package (2¼ teaspoons) active
    dry yeast

1½ cups bread flour

2½ tablespoons canola oil

1¼ cups multigrain flour

¾ cup whole wheat flour

¾ teaspoon salt

White cornmeal

1 egg white, lightly beaten with
    1 teaspoon water

1 tablespoon sesame seeds

1 tablespoon poppy seeds

1 tablespoon dried chopped garlic

First make a sponge: In a bowl, dissolve the sugar in the warm water. Stir in the yeast until dissolved. Let stand in a draft-free area about 5 minutes or until the yeast begins to bubble. Mix in 1 cup of the bread flour. Let the mixture stand for 1 hour, until light and spongy.

Stir in the oil, the remaining bread flour, the multigrain flour, the whole wheat flour, and the salt. The dough will be soft and sticky. Place the dough in a bowl and cover with plastic wrap or a damp kitchen towel. Let rise in a warm place until doubled in bulk, about 1 hour.

Punch down the dough. Divide the dough into 16 pieces. Roll out each piece into a pencil shape about 8 inches long. Set the breadsticks on a nonstick baking sheet sprinkled with white cornmeal. Cover and let rise about 25 to 35 minutes. Brush with the egg white mixture. Mix together the sesame seeds, poppy seeds, and garlic and put on a flat plate. Roll the breadsticks in the seed mixture.

Preheat the oven to 400°. Bake the breadsticks in the center of the oven for 18 to 20 minutes or until they are firm and sound hollow when tapped. Let cool on a wire rack.

*115 calories, 3 g fat, 0.5 g saturated fat, no cholesterol,
2.5 g dietary fiber, 105 mg sodium*

Multigrain Bubble Bread

Some folks call this coffee cake Monkey Bread, presumably because of its wrinkled "face." It is inspired by the 1950 Betty Crocker cookbook, where it went by the name Hungarian coffee cake.

Whatever you call it, this attractive sweet bread makes a good centerpiece for a Sunday brunch, or a nice host/hostess gift for holidays. It's the ultimate self-serve coffee cake; guests just pull off pieces to eat.

It looks best when baked in a fluted tube pan.

Makes 12 generous servings

1 cup skim milk
½ cup honey
1 teaspoon salt
2 teaspoons grated orange zest
**2 packages (4½ teaspoons) active
   dry yeast**

1 egg, lightly beaten
¼ cup canola oil
2 cups multigrain flour
2½ to 3 cups bread flour

FILLING

⅔ cup sugar
1¼ teaspoons ground cinnamon
1 teaspoon grated orange zest
⅓ cup coarsely ground nuts

**3 tablespoons unsalted butter or
   margarine**
2 tablespoons fresh orange juice

In a small saucepan, heat the milk and honey until warm (110° to 115°). Pour the milk mixture into a large mixing bowl and stir in the salt, orange zest, yeast, egg, and oil. Stir in the multigrain flour, then add enough bread flour to make a soft, fairly sticky dough.

Knead the dough in a heavy-duty electric mixer—it will resemble a very thick batter—until smooth and springy. Or knead by hand on a floured pastry cloth, folding the dough over itself several times.

Place the dough in a bowl, cover with a damp kitchen towel or plastic wrap, and set aside in a warm place to rise until doubled in bulk, about 1½ hours.

Meanwhile, make the filling: Combine the sugar, cinnamon, orange zest, and nuts in a small bowl. In another small bowl, melt the butter and mix with the orange juice.

Oil or spray a 12-cup (9-inch) fluted tube pan or a 9- or 10-inch angel food cake pan.

Punch down the dough. Roll into a long rope and cut into 24 pieces. Roll each piece into a ball. (The dough balls do not have to be uniform in size.) Roll each piece of dough in the orange juice mixture, then roll evenly in the sugar mixture.

Layer the dough balls, staggering the layers slightly, in the pan. Cover loosely with a damp kitchen towel or plastic wrap and let rise in a warm place for about 45 minutes, or until light.

Preheat the oven to 350°.

Bake the bread in the center of the oven for 35 to 45 minutes or until it is golden and feels firm. Let cool for 5 minutes, then invert the bread onto a serving plate. (If it separates into pieces, just rearrange the pieces into a bread.)

Serve slightly warm.

---

371 calories, 11.5 g fat, 2.5 g saturated fat,
26 mg cholesterol, 3.5 g dietary fiber, 197 mg sodium

Steamed Boston Brown Bread

This classic bread, originally brought over from England, is traditionally steamed. (Baking was a chancy affair in the days of cooking over fireplaces.) Moist, sweet, and rich, it tastes best served warm. It is a traditional Saturday night accompaniment to Boston baked beans.

Makes 2 or 3 small loaves; about 24 servings

1 cup plus 2 tablespoons whole
  wheat flour
1 cup rye flour
1 cup yellow cornmeal
¾ teaspoon salt

1 teaspoon baking soda
¼ cup water
¾ cup dark unsulfured molasses
2 cups buttermilk
1 cup dark raisins

In a large mixing bowl, combine 1 cup of the whole wheat flour and the rye flour, cornmeal, and salt. Set aside.

In a second mixing bowl, stir the baking soda into the water. Add the molasses and buttermilk. Stir into the flour mixture. Mix the raisins with the 2 tablespoons whole wheat flour and stir into the batter.

Spray or grease two 2-cup molds with tight-fitting covers, or three 16-ounce cans (with paper labels and one end removed).

Spoon the batter into the molds, cover the molds, and tape or tie down the covers so that the rising bread won't force them off. If using cans, cover the tops tightly with aluminum foil.

Put the molds on a wire rack set in a pot, kettle, or steamer, allowing the water to come three-quarters of the way up the sides of the molds. Cover tightly and steam for 2½ to 3 hours or until a tester inserted into the bread comes out clean. Add hot water as necessary to maintain the water level.

Unmold the bread, let cool slightly, and serve.

Note: If you use cans to steam the bread, an easy way to unmold each loaf is to open the bottom of the can with a can opener, then loosen the bread by running a knife between it and the can. Gently push the bread out of the can.

---

108 calories, 0.5 g fat, no saturated fat, 1 mg cholesterol,
2 g dietary fiber, 129 mg sodium

Thus Saith the Lord

In some flour and baking catalogs, you'll find reference to Ezekiel mix or flour, a blend of several grain and legume flours.

The recipe for this intriguingly named flour comes from a biblical reference, specifically Ezekiel 4:9. God is issuing instructions on how Ezekiel is to symbolically enact the coming siege of Israel for the benefit of the misbehaving Israelites. The instructions include a recipe: "Take thou also unto thee wheat, and barley, and beans, and lentils, and millet, and vetches [spelt], and put them in one vessel, and make thee bread thereof. . . ."

The modern version of the flour includes white and whole wheat flours, barley, spelt, soy, pinto beans, lentils, and millet. In addition to being biblically correct, it's very nutritious. And it makes wonderful bread.

Multigrain Persimmon Pancakes with Honeyed Pears

Persimmons, the cheerful orange fruits that arrive in your supermarket in late fall and early winter, come mostly from California. Their sweet, squashlike flavor and pulpy texture make them ideal for using in cakes and baked goods. They are not ripe until they are soft to the point of being squishy. Scoop out the pulp with a spoon, discarding the bit of stringy pith in the center. Puree it in a blender or food processor—or just mash thoroughly with a fork.

Sweet yet sophisticated, these spiced pancakes are ideal for special occasions, such as a winter holiday brunch.

Makes about 18 pancakes; 6 servings

PEAR TOPPING

1½ tablespoons unsalted butter or
  margarine
2 teaspoons finely chopped fresh
  ginger
4 large or 5 medium pears,
  peeled, cored, and sliced

1 tablespoon fresh lemon juice
1 teaspoon vanilla
⅔ cup honey
1 tablespoon rum, brandy, or
  Cognac (optional)

PANCAKES

1 cup multigrain flour
1 cup unbleached all-purpose
  flour
1 tablespoon sugar
1 teaspoon baking powder
1 teaspoon baking soda
¼ teaspoon salt
1 teaspoon ground cinnamon

½ teaspoon ground ginger
¼ teaspoon ground allspice
½ cup egg substitute, or 2 eggs,
  lightly beaten
1 cup persimmon puree (from 2
  medium persimmons)
1½ cups buttermilk
1 tablespoon canola oil

To make the pear topping: Heat the butter in a shallow, nonaluminum saucepan. Add the ginger, pears, and lemon juice and cook over medium heat, occasionally stirring gently, for 1 to 2 minutes. Stir in the vanilla, honey, and rum; cook over high heat until the pears begin to soften and the liquid is somewhat syrupy. Remove from the heat and set aside. (The pears may be prepared up to a day ahead of time; reheat before serving.)

To make the pancakes: Heat a griddle or heavy frying pan that has been sprayed with nonstick cooking spray.

In a medium mixing bowl, whisk together the flours, sugar, baking powder, soda, salt, cinnamon, ginger, and allspice. (If the baking soda is lumpy, rub it between your fingers before adding.)

Make a well in the center of the dry ingredients and add the egg substitute, persimmon puree, buttermilk, and oil to make a thick batter. Mix just until the dry ingredients are incorporated.

Spoon the batter onto the griddle, using about ¼ cup for each pancake and being careful not to crowd the pancakes. Cook until the edges are set and starting to dry, then turn and cook until golden, about 3 to 4 minutes total. Keep the pancakes warm in a 150° oven while you fry the remaining batter.

Arrange the pancakes on plates, allowing 3 per serving. Spoon the warm pear sauce over them and serve immediately.

*470 calories, 7 g fat, 2.5 g saturated fat,
10 mg cholesterol, 8 g dietary fiber, 504 mg sodium*

Savory Granola

This mix is designed for those who prefer savory snacks to sweet. It's good trail food for hikers, bikers, climbers, or picnickers. It can also be served as a side dish; put 1 cup granola in a pan with 1 cup low-sodium stock or water, and cook over low heat until the granola absorbs the liquid.

If you have raw wheat germ on hand, just add it to the oats and other flakes so it toasts.

Makes about 6 cups

2 cups old-fashioned oats
**1 cup uncooked spelt, Kamut,
 wheat, or triticale flakes**
¼ cup canola oil
1 tablespoon honey or rice syrup
**1 tablespoon Worcestershire or
 soy sauce**
**1 tablespoon Cajun-style
 seasoning mix**

¼ teaspoon salt (optional)
¾ cup toasted wheat germ
**½ cup coarsely chopped pecans or
 walnuts**
½ cup roasted unsalted soybeans
**1 cup puffed brown rice, kasha,
 or millet**

Preheat the oven to 350°.

Spread the oats and other flakes out on a very large, ungreased baking sheet or in a roasting pan. Toast in the center of the oven, stirring once or twice, for 8 to 10 minutes or until the grains begin to smell "toasty."

While the grains are toasting, heat the oil, honey, Worcestershire sauce, Cajun seasoning, and salt, if using, in a small saucepan, stirring frequently, until hot.

Add the wheat germ, nuts, soybeans, and puffed cereal to the toasted grains. Pour the oil mixture over and stir and toss to thoroughly coat the grains with the mixture. Continue baking another 8 to 10 minutes, stirring once, until the granola is golden and dry.

Let cool completely, then transfer to airtight jars or tins. This keeps well and can be frozen.

Per serving (⅓ cup): 146 calories, 7.5 g fat,
1 g unsaturated fat, no cholesterol, 2.5 g dietary fiber,
132 mg sodium

Some Personal Favorites

All of the recipes in this cookbook are wonderful, of course. But what follows is an assortment of our hand-picked favorites. These are dishes that we make over and over again, because they taste great, because they look great, or because . . . well, just because.

You'll notice that most of them are sweet. That's no accident, since we both love desserts far more than we should. And several are good party or holiday recipes. That's also no accident. We love to cook, and nothing pleases us more than playing to an appreciative audience.

Some Personal Favorites

Whole Wheat Apricot Noodle Pudding with Raspberry Sauce

Quick-Lunch Quesadillas

Snowpeople Pizzas

Stay-in-the-Refrigerator Bran Muffins

Classic Oatmeal Raisin Cookies

Lower-Fat Oatmeal Apricot Cookies

Virginia's Christmas Granola

Whole Wheat Apricot Noodle Pudding with Raspberry Sauce

This pudding makes a fine party recipe, as it actually tastes best if baked the day before serving. Let cool and refrigerate. Remove from the refrigerator and cut the cold pudding into 12 rectangles, but do not lift out the pieces. Reheat for 15 minutes in a preheated 350° oven, then lift out the pieces with a spatula.

This is good with or without the raspberry sauce. You can substitute raisins for the apricots, if desired.

Makes 12 servings

½ pound medium-width yolk-free egg noodles, cooked according to package directions

½ pound medium-width whole wheat noodles, cooked according to package directions

15 ounces part-skim ricotta cheese

½ cup nonfat sour cream

4 egg whites, beaten to stiff, glossy peaks

1½ cups egg substitute, or 6 eggs, lightly beaten

1 cup sugar

3 cups dried apricots, soaked in hot water 15 minutes, drained, and cut into quarters

2 cups 2-percent milk

RASPBERRY SAUCE

4 cups fresh raspberries, rinsed and picked over, or 3 packages (10 ounces each) frozen unsweetened raspberries, defrosted

½ cup sugar

2 tablespoons cornstarch

¼ cup water

2 to 4 tablespoons raspberry liqueur (optional)

Preheat the oven to 350°. Spray or grease a 9-by-13-inch glass ovenproof casserole dish.

Mix the noodles together in a large mixing bowl. Mix in the ricotta cheese, sour cream, beaten egg whites, egg substitute, sugar, and apricots.

Spoon the noodle mixture into the prepared pan. Pour the milk over the pudding. Set the pan in the center of the oven. Bake for 1 hour and 15 minutes or until the top is crusty and golden brown and a tester inserted into the center of the pudding comes out clean.

While the pudding is baking, prepare the sauce: Put the berries in a saucepan. Stir in the sugar mixed with the cornstarch, and the water. Simmer for 8 to 10 minutes, until thickened. Remove from the heat and add the raspberry liqueur, if using. If desired, strain the sauce to remove the seeds. Let the sauce cool, pour into a bowl, cover, and refrigerate until ready to serve.

When the pudding is baked (or reheated), cut into 3-inch squares and set on a platter. Serve with the raspberry sauce.

---

437 calories, 5 g fat, 2.5 g saturated fat,
14 mg cholesterol, 8 g dietary fiber, 146 mg sodium

Quick-Lunch Quesadillas

After spending hours riveted to a computer screen, Virginia hardly feels like making an elaborate lunch. Still, peanut butter and jelly wears thin after a while. Her solution is to open some jars and cans and toss some filled tortillas in the skillet for a soul-satisfying lunch. For lack of a better name, she calls this instant lunch "quesadillas." It's not award-winning fare, but it's surprisingly satisfying. It's also low in fat and high in fiber.

Makes 4 servings

4 whole wheat tortillas,
  preferably fat free
½ cup fat-free refried beans
¼ cup salsa, homemade or
  bottled

½ cup (about 2 ounces) grated
  reduced-fat Monterey Jack or
  mild Cheddar cheese
2 teaspoons olive oil

Spread each tortilla with 2 tablespoons of the refried beans. Spoon 1 tablespoon of the salsa over the beans. Sprinkle with 2 tablespoons of the cheese.

Heat about ½ teaspoon of the olive oil in a 10-inch skillet. Add 1 tortilla and cook over medium heat until golden on the bottom, then fold the tortilla over to make a half-moon shape. Cook for a few seconds longer, then remove to a plate. Cut in half.

Repeat with the remaining tortillas. Serve warm.

---

163 calories, 5 g fat, 2 g saturated fat, 10 mg cholesterol,
3.5 g dietary fiber, 458 mg sodium

Snowpeople Pizzas

Barbara's whimsical white pizzas are a hit with her brother, Gary Maniff, of Randolph, Massachusetts, who loves to make them during the winter season. Sometimes he hosts pizza parties at which he supplies the crusts and lets guests choose from various toppings to decorate their own pizzas.

Makes 6 individual pizzas

WHITE CORNMEAL CRUST

½ teaspoon honey

1 package (2¼ teaspoons) active
   dry yeast

1 cup warm water (110° to 115°)

2 cups unbleached all-purpose
   flour, plus more as needed

¼ cup white cornmeal, plus more
   as needed

1 teaspoon dried basil

½ teaspoon salt

2 tablespoons olive oil

TOPPINGS

1½ cups part-skim ricotta cheese

½ teaspoon dried, crumbled
   rosemary

Reconstituted dried tomatoes, (see
   page 16) chopped

Sliced black olives

Marinated artichoke hearts,
   drained and separated

1 small red or green bell pepper,
   thinly sliced

To make the crusts: Dissolve the honey and the yeast in the warm water until it begins to bubble.

Meanwhile, mix the flour and cornmeal with the basil, salt, and oil in a food processor or in the large bowl of an electric mixer fitted with the dough hook. To mix the dough by hand, use a bowl and a wooden spoon.

Add the yeast mixture and process until a smooth, soft, almost sticky dough is formed, about 5 to 10 seconds. If using an electric mixer, mix about 3 minutes. If mixing the dough by hand, mix about 3 to 5 minutes.

Turn the dough out onto a lightly floured surface or pastry cloth and knead a few minutes, until smooth and elastic. If the dough is too sticky, add more flour, a tablespoon at a time, until it reaches the desired consistency. Put the dough in a bowl and cover lightly with oiled plastic wrap or a damp kitchen towel.

Let the dough rise until doubled in bulk, about 45 minutes to 1 hour. Punch down the dough and let stand 5 minutes. Knead for a few minutes, until smooth.

Roll out the dough. Cut into six 3-inch circles and six 5-inch circles. Press the smaller and larger circles together to make 6 snowpeople shapes, wetting the adjoining edges so they adhere better. Use the extra scraps of dough to make scarves and hats for the snowpeople. Sprinkle nonstick baking sheets with a small amount of additional cornmeal. Set the snowpeople on the pans using a large spatula. The crusts can be wrapped and frozen at this point, or baked immediately.

To bake the crusts, pierce in several places with the tines of a fork. Let the dough rise 10 minutes. Preheat the oven to 425°. Bake the crusts on the lowest rack in the oven for about 5 minutes or until firm to the touch. Let cool. If desired, wrap and freeze.

(If you have baking tiles, line the lowest rack of the oven with them and bake the crusts directly on the tiles; this will make the crusts crisper.)

To finish the pizzas, preheat the oven to 425°. Sprinkle a small amount of additional cornmeal on nonstick baking sheets, and set the cooled crusts on them. (Again, if using baking tiles, omit the pans and use a pizza peel or a large spatula to transfer the pizzas to the tiles.)

Mix the ricotta cheese with the rosemary. Spread the cheese over the circles of dough. Use tomatoes and olives for eyes, mouths, or buttons as you desire. Use separated artichoke hearts, peppers, and olives or other garnishes on the hats and scarves.

Bake the snowpeople on the bottom rack of the oven for about 15 minutes or until the toppings are hot. Serve immediately.

323 calories, 11 g fat, 4 g saturated fat,
19 mg cholesterol, 2.5 g dietary fiber, 390 mg sodium

Stay-in-the-Refrigerator Bran Muffins

This batter will stay refrigerated for up to ten days, allowing you to impress last-minute guests by producing freshly baked muffins in a snap. It's also perfect for the small family, since you can bake only a few muffins at a time. For variety, add grated lemon or orange zest, currants, or bits of dried cherries.

Makes 24 muffins

3 cups 100% Bran or All-Bran cereal

1 cup boiling water

1¼ cups unbleached all-purpose flour

1¼ cups whole wheat flour

2½ teaspoons baking soda

¾ teaspoon salt

½ teaspoon ground cinnamon

½ cup chopped dried apricots

½ cup egg substitute, or 2 eggs, lightly beaten

1½ cups buttermilk

⅓ cup canola oil

½ cup dark unsulfured molasses

½ cup honey

Put the cereal and boiling water in a large bowl, mix, and let stand for 8 to 10 minutes. Stir.

In a separate bowl, mix the flours, baking soda, salt, cinnamon, and apricots. Stir in the egg substitute and softened cereal. Add the buttermilk, oil, molasses, and honey. Mix just enough to combine the ingredients; do not overbeat.

Pour the batter into a container, cover tightly, and refrigerate until ready to bake. The batter will keep in the refrigerator for up to 10 days.

When ready to bake, preheat the oven to 425°. Line a muffin tin with paper liners. Stir the batter. Fill the muffin cups three-quarters full. Bake in the center of the oven for 20 minutes or until the muffins are slightly springy to the touch and a tester inserted in the center of a muffin comes out clean.

Let the muffins cool on a wire rack. They are best served warm.

154 calories, 3.5 g fat, 0.5 g saturated fat,
1 mg cholesterol, 5 g dietary fiber, 302 mg sodium

Classic Oatmeal Raisin Cookies

These cookies are not low in fat. But they are such a standard part of the American repertoire that we wanted to offer both this recipe and a lower-fat version (see page 294). These have the classic oat-cookie profile: They're crisp on the outside and chewy on the inside, and they combine the nutty flavor of oats with butterscotch undertones. A little five-spice, with its intriguing whisper of anise and cinnamon, gives them a "Christmasy" flavor. You can also substitute dried cranberries, cherries, or currants for the raisins.

Makes about 2 dozen large (3-inch) cookies

1 cup unsalted butter, at room
   temperature
¾ cup packed light brown sugar
⅔ cup granulated sugar
2 eggs
2 teaspoons vanilla
1½ cups unbleached all-purpose
   flour

1 teaspoon baking soda
½ teaspoon salt
¼ teaspoon Chinese five-spice
   powder or ground cinnamon
3 cups old-fashioned oats
1 cup dark raisins

Preheat the oven to 350°. Lightly oil or spray cookie sheets with nonstick cooking spray.

In a mixing bowl, cream the butter until fluffy, then add the brown sugar and granulated sugar, and beat until light. Beat in the eggs, then the vanilla. In a second mixing bowl, combine the flour, baking soda, salt, and five-spice together, then add to the egg mixture. Beat just until the flour is completely incorporated. Add the oats and raisins.

Drop the dough onto the cookie sheets, using about 2 tablespoons dough per cookie. An ice-cream scoop is ideal for measuring. Be sure to leave at least 2 inches between the cookies.

Bake for 12 to 15 minutes or until golden. Let cool on the cookie sheets for 2 to 3 minutes, then remove to wire racks to cool completely. The cookies are best eaten the same day they're made, but they freeze well or can be stored in a cookie jar.

*198 calories, 9 g fat, 5 g saturated fat, 39 mg cholesterol,
1.5 g dietary fiber, 88 mg sodium*

Lower-Fat Oatmeal Apricot Cookies

Ground apricots substitute for part of the fat in these cookies and, together with raisins, help sweeten them. Egg substitute replaces regular eggs. A small amount of butter is used for flavor.

If you prefer, you can substitute ¾ cup dried cranberries for the chopped apricots and add 1 teaspoon grated orange zest to the dough.

Makes 30 cookies

3 cups quick-cooking (not instant) oats
1 cup packed dark brown sugar
1 cup golden raisins
¾ cup chopped dried apricots
½ cup unbleached all-purpose flour
½ cup whole wheat pastry flour
1 teaspoon baking powder
1 teaspoon baking soda
¾ teaspoon salt

¾ teaspoon ground cinnamon
½ cup egg substitute, or 2 eggs, lightly beaten
¼ cup unsalted butter or margarine, at room temperature and cut into small pieces
⅓ cup chopped dried apricots, pureed in a blender or food processor with ⅓ cup boiling water

Preheat the oven to 350°. Spray baking sheets with nonstick cooking spray.

In a large mixing bowl, combine the oats, brown sugar, raisins, and apricots.

Stir in the flours, baking powder, baking soda, salt, and cinnamon. Blend in the egg substitute, butter, and apricot puree.

Using a tablespoon, drop scant tablespoons of dough onto the prepared baking sheet about 2 inches apart. Press down with the back of a fork.

Bake in the center of the oven for 10 minutes or until the cookies are firm, golden brown on the bottom, and light brown on top. Let the cookies cool on wire racks. Store the cooled cookies in an airtight container.

106 calories, 2 g fat, 1 g saturated fat, 4 mg cholesterol,
2 g dietary fiber, 75 mg sodium

Virginia's Christmas Granola

Virginia likes to give this granola to friends and colleagues at Christmas. You can vary it to taste, of course, but the dried cherries, which are expensive, tend to make it holiday-special. If you're not giving it away, cut the recipe in half.

Be sure to thoroughly toast the grains and nuts; that's what helps set this recipe apart from the many so-so granolas on the market. It's really good with pecans or filberts (hazelnuts), but you can use any nut you like or even omit the nuts.

Makes about 12 cups

8 cups old-fashioned oats
1½ cups wheat germ
1 cup chopped nuts
1 cup toasted corn kernels or
    nuggets
1 cup pure maple syrup,
    preferably dark amber

½ cup canola oil
½ teaspoon salt
½ teaspoon maple extract, or
    1 teaspoon vanilla extract
Pinch of ground cinnamon
½ cup dried blueberries
1 cup dried tart cherries

Preheat the oven to 350°.

Spread the oats out on a very large baking sheet or in a roasting pan. Toast in the center of the oven, stirring once or twice, for 10 minutes, or until the oats begin to have a toasty smell.

Stir in the wheat germ, nuts, and corn. Toast, stirring once or twice, for another 10 minutes.

While the grains are toasting, heat the maple syrup, oil, salt, extract, and cinnamon in a small saucepan over medium heat, stirring frequently, until hot.

Add the blueberries and cherries to the toasted grains. Pour the syrup mixture over and stir thoroughly to coat the grains with the mixture. Continue baking another 15 to 20 minutes, stirring once or twice, until the granola is golden and no longer sticky.

Let cool completely, then transfer to airtight jars or tins. The granola keeps very well and can be frozen.

Per serving (¼ cup): 138 calories, 5.5 g fat,
0.5 g saturated fat, no cholesterol, 2 g dietary fiber,
34 mg sodium

Mail Order Sources

Various Flours and Grains

BROWNVILLE MILLS
P.O. Box 145
Brownville, NE 68321
(800) 305-7990

Large selection of grains, flours, seeds, and baking mixes, many organically grown, including triticale grain, flour, and flakes; barley grits; Ezekiel flour; blue cornmeal; and millet flour. Also, hand and electric grain and flour mills.

KING ARTHUR FLOUR
P.O. Box 876
Norwich, VT 05055
(800) 827-6836

Unbleached all-purpose, cake, and pastry flours; professional-quality bread flours, whole-grain flours and whole grains, whole white wheat flour, and Oatrim, an oat-derived fat substitute.

MOUNTAIN ARK TRADING COMPANY
799 Old Leicester Highway
Asheville, NC 28806
(800) 643-8909

Distributor of a wide variety of products, including whole grains (such as teff and quinoa), flour and seitan. Many organically grown. Retail and bulk prices.

STOCKTON ROLLER MILL
P.O. Box 26
St. Charles, MN 55972
(507) 932-4308

Organically grown grains for sprouting or eating, including amaranth, barley, buckwheat, corn, Kamut, oats, millet, triticale, and wild rice. Also, flours and pancake and muffin mixes.

WALNUT ACRES ORGANIC FARMS
Penns Creek, PA 17862
(800) 433-3998

Wide variety of organic products, including grains and flours, pastas, baking mixes, twenty-grain cereal, whole grain bagels and English muffins, and amaranth graham crackers. Products also available in health food stores and some supermarkets.

Corn

ADAMS MILLING COMPANY
Route 6, Box 148A
Napier Field Station
Dolthan, AL 36303
(334) 983-4233

Authentic "whole heart" grits, stone-ground cornmeal, and corn dog mix. Free price list.

FALLS MILL AND COUNTRY STORE
134 Falls Mill Road
Belvidere, TN 37306
(615) 469-7161

Stone-ground grits, white and yellow cornmeals (whole and bolted). Also, cracked and whole wheat, buckwheat, rye, and rice flours.

LOS CHILEROS DE NUEVO MEXICO
P.O. Box 6215
Sante Fe, NM 87502
(505) 471-6967

Chicos (dried corn), blue corn popcorn, roasted blue cornmeal cereal, hominy. Also, panocha (sprouted wheat flour). Price list.

NATIVE SEEDS/SEARCH
2509 North Campbell Avenue, No. 325
Tucson, AZ 85719
(520) 327-9123

Hopi and Pueblo blue cornmeal, white and blue posole, toasted blue corn masa harina. Also, corn seeds for planting. Catalog $1.

YODER POPCORN COMPANY
345 South 200 E
Flora, IN 46929
(800) 892-2170

Unpopped and popped popcorn and related popcorn products, including poppers, from the Amish/Mennonite country of eastern Indiana. Specialty product is Tiny Tender, a small, nearly hull-less popcorn. Gift packs.

Rice

LUNDBERG FAMILY FARMS
P.O. Box 369
Richvale, CA 95974
(916) 882-4551

Brown and exotic rices and rice mixes, including arborio in white and brown, American basmati, wehani, and japonica. Products also widely available in health food stores, specialty stores, and some supermarkets.

RICESELECT
P.O. Box 1305
Alvin, TX 77512
(800) 232-RICE

Products available in health food stores, specialty shops, and supermarkets. Wholesale only, but does sell one retail gift pack of four rices (Basmati, Kasmati, Texmati, and Jasmati) and four seasoned rice mixes.

SOUTHERN BROWN RICE
P.O. Box 185
Weiner, AR 72479
(501) 684-2354

Organically grown rices and products, including brown basmati, brown rice cream, brown rice flour, and rice bran. Gift baskets.

Other Grains

BLACK DUCK COMPANY
10932 Glenn Wilding Place
Bloomington, MN 55431
(612) 884-3472

Minnesota cultivated wild rice and Canadian lake rice at reasonable prices. Also, wild rice soup mixes.

KAMUT ASSOCIATION OF NORTH AMERICA
(Montana Flour and Grains)
P.O. Box 691
Fort Benton, MT 59442
(800) 644-6450

Kamut and Kamut products. Wholesale, but will sell mail order as well.

MANITOK FOOD AND GIFT
P.O. Box 97
Callaway, MN 56521
(800) 726-1863

Hand-harvested wild rice. A not-for-profit cooperative owned and operated by the White Earth Band of Minnesota Ojibwa. Ask for catalog.

NU-WORLD AMARANTH
P.O. Box 2202
Naperville, IL 60567
(708) 369-6819

Amaranth and amaranth products, including flour, toasted flour, and barbecue sauce.

PURITY FOODS
2871 West Jolly Road
Okemos, MI 48864
(517) 351-9231

Spelt and spelt products. Primarily wholesale, but will sell spelt to customers who don't have ready access to stores selling spelt products.

THE TEFF COMPANY
P.O. Box A
Caldwell, ID 83606
(208) 455-0375

Whole grain teff and teff flour. Company can direct you to a mail-order distributor or send the grain directly in large quantities.

WHITE MOUNTAIN FARM
8890 Lane 4 North
Mosca, CO 81146
(800) 364-3019

White and black quinoa.

Bibliography

Associated Press. "Study Says Wheat to Become Top Grain." *Longmont, Colorado, Daily Times-Call*, November 5, 1995.

Bayless, Rick, and Deann Groen Bayless. *Authentic Mexican Cooking*. New York: Morrow, 1987.

Bennani-Smires, Latifa. *Moroccan Cooking*. Casablanca: Al Madariss, 1975.

Bumgarner, Marlene Anne. *The Book of Whole Grains*. New York: St. Martin's Press, 1976.

Cole, John N. *Amaranth: From the Past for the Future*. Emmaus, Penn.: Rodale Press, 1979.

Ebeling, Walter. *The Fruited Plain: The Story of American Agriculture*. Berkeley: University of California Press, 1979.

Fussell, Betty. *Crazy for Corn*. New York: HarperPerennial, 1995.

———. *The Story of Corn*. New York: Knopf, 1992.

Geffen, Alice M., and Carole Berglie. *Food Festival: A Guidebook to America's Best Regional Food Celebrations*. Woodstock, Vermont: The Countryman Press, 1994.

General Mills. "Sky-High Baking." Minneapolis: 1994.

Goldbeck, Nikki, and David Goldbeck. *The Goldbecks' Guide to Good Food.* New York: New American Library, 1987.

Griggs, Barbara. *The Food Factor: An Account of the Nutrition Revolution.* London: Penguin Books, 1988.

Jones, Evan. *American Food: The Gastronomic Story.* Woodstock, N.Y.: The Overlook Press, 1990.

Kirlin, Katherine S., and Thomas M. Kirlin. *Smithsonian Folklife Cookbook.* Washington, D.C.: Smithsonian Institution Press, 1991.

Logsdon, Gene. *Small-Scale Grain Raising.* Emmaus, Penn.: Rodale Press, 1977.

London, Sheryl, and Mel London. *The Versatile Grain and the Elegant Bean.* New York: Simon & Schuster, 1992.

Matossian, Mary Kilbourne. *Poisons of the Past: Molds, Epidemics, and History.* New Haven, Conn.: Yale University Press, 1989.

Miller, Joni. "American Spaghetti Tops Tasting," *Cook's Illustrated*, May/June 1994: 21–23.

Neal, Bill, and David Perry. *Good Old Grits Cookbook.* New York: Workman Publishing, 1991.

Owen, Sri. *The Rice Book.* New York: St. Martin's Press, 1993.

Peikin, Steven R. *Gastrointestinal Health.* New York: HarperCollins, 1991.

Powers, Marie. "Wild Rice: Lake-Country Treasure." *Cuisine*, October 1980: 45–47.

Root, Waverley, and Richard de Rochemont. *Eating in America.* New York: Morrow, 1976.

Sass, Lorna J. *Great Vegetarian Cooking Under Pressure.* New York: Morrow, 1994.

———. *Recipes from an Ecological Kitchen.* New York: Morrow, 1992.

Schneider, Elizabeth. "Whole Grains Explained." *Food Arts*, July/August 1994: 90–94; October 1994: 84–86; and March 1995: 26–30.

Simmons, Marie. *Rice: The Amazing Grain.* New York: Henry Holt, 1991.

Walden, Howard T., 2d. *Native Inheritance: The Story of Corn in America.* New York: Harper & Row, 1966.

Weaver, William Woys. *Pennsylvania Dutch Country Cooking.* New York: Abbeville Press, 1993.

Wigmore, Ann. *The Sprouting Book.* Wayne, N.J.: Avery Publishing Group, 1986.

Wood, Rebecca. *Quinoa, the Supergrain.* Tokyo: Japan Publications, 1988.

Index